The Politics of Coalition in Korea

This book examines how inter- and intra-party coalition-building affects governability in South Korea. Focusing on the Kim Dae-jung administration (1998–2003) as a case study in the failure of a government to turn electoral success into stable governability, or ability to implement reform policies, the book's research draws on two bodies of literature which, though focusing on the same dependent variable (cabinet or government stability), have rarely been used in tandem: coalition research on parliamentary systems and studies of divided government in presidential systems.

Youngmi Kim argues that a weak institutionalization of the ruling party and the party system accounts for political instability and inefficient governability in Korea and, in doing so, her study makes a number of key contributions to the field. Theoretically it proposes a framework that integrates a rationalist approach with one that acknowledges the role of political culture. It further enhances the understanding of factors affecting governability after coalition-building across regime types and aims to build on recent demands for broader cross-regime analysis of minority/divided government and of the determinants of governability. This has important comparative implications as coalition-building within (semi-)presidential systems has occurred in other post-authoritarian contexts. The book finally provides a new data set that fills a gap in a field where Western cases constitute the main focus of research.

The Politics of Coalition in Korea will be of interest to students and scholars of Korean studies, Korean politics, Asian studies and Asian politics.

Youngmi Kim is an Assistant Professor in the Department of Public Policy, and International Relations and European Studies at Central European University, Hungary.

Routledge Advances in Korean Studies

1 **The Politics of Economic Reform in South Korea**
A fragile miracle
Tat Yan Kong

2 **Market and Society in Korea**
Interest, institution and the textile industry
Dennis McNamara

3 **Social and Economic Policies in Korea**
Ideas, networks and linkages
Dong-Myeon Shin

4 **North Korea in the World Economy**
Edited by E. Kwan Choi, Yesook Merrill and E. Han Kim

5 **Legal Reform in Korea**
Edited by Tom Ginsburg

6 **Women, Television and Everyday Life**
Journeys of hope
Youna Kim

7 **Transformations in Twentieth-Century Korea**
Edited by Chang Yun-Shik and Steven Hugh Lee

8 **The Development of Modern South Korea**
State formation, capitalist development and national identity
Kyong Ju Kim

9 **Industrial Relations in Korea**
Diversity and dynamism of Korean enterprise unions from a comparative perspective
Jooyeon Jeong

10 **The Global Korean Motor Industry**
   The Hyundai Motor Company's global strategy
   Russell D. Lansbury, Chung-Sok Suh and Seung-Ho Kwon

11 **Korean Workers and Neoliberal Globalisation**
   Kevin Gray

12 **Korea in the New Asia**
   East Asian integration and the China factor
   Francoise Nicolas

13 **Foreign Direct Investment in Post-Crisis Korea**
   European investors and 'mismatched globalization'
   Judith Cherry

14 **Korea Confronts Globalization**
   Edited by Chang Yun-Shik, Hyun-ho Seok and Donald L. Baker

15 **Korea's Developmental Alliance**
   State, capital and the politics of rapid development
   David Hundt

16 **Capitalist Development in Korea**
   Labour, capital and the myth of the developmental state
   Dae-oup Chang

17 **Political Protest and Labour Movements in Korea**
   Solidarity among Korean white-collar workers
   Doowon Suh

18 **Retirement, Work and Pensions in Ageing Korea**
   Edited by Jae-jin Yang and Thomas R. Klassen

19 **South Korea Under Compressed Modernity**
   Familial political economy in transition
   Kyung-Sup Chang

20 **New Millennium South Korea**
   Neoliberal capitalism and transnational movements
   Edited by Jesook Song

21 **Human Rights Discourse in North Korea**
   Post-colonial, Marxist and Confucian perspectives
   Jiyoung Song

22 **Digital Development in Korea**
Building an information society
Myung Oh and James F. Larson

23 **The Politics of Coalition in Korea**
Between institutions and culture
Youngmi Kim

The Politics of Coalition in Korea

Between institutions and culture

Youngmi Kim

LONDON AND NEW YORK

First published 2011
by Routledge
2 Park Square, Milton Park, Abingdon, Oxon OX14 4RN

Simultaneously published in the USA and Canada
by Routledge
711 Third Avenue, New York, NY 10017

Routledge is an imprint of the Taylor & Francis Group, an informa business

© 2011 Youngmi Kim

The right of Youngmi Kim to be identified as author of this work has been asserted by her in accordance with the Copyright, Designs and Patent Act 1988.

All rights reserved. No part of this book may be reprinted or reproduced or utilized in any form or by any electronic, mechanical, or other means, now known or hereafter invented, including photocopying and recording, or in any information storage or retrieval system, without permission in writing from the publishers.

Trademark notice: Product or corporate names may be trademarks or registered trademarks, and are used only for identification and explanation without intent to infringe.

British Library Cataloguing in Publication Data
A catalogue record for this book is available from the British Library

Library of Congress Cataloging in Publication Data
Kim, Youngmi.
　The politics of coalition in Korea : between institutions and culture / Youngmi Kim.
　p. cm. – (Routledge advances in korean studies)
　Includes bibliographical references and index.
　1. Coalition governments–Korea (South) 2. Coalitions–Korea (South) 3. Korea (South)–Politics and government. I. Title.
　JQ1729.A795K56 2011
　320.9515–dc22
　　　　　　　　　　　　　2010041744

ISBN 978-0-415-56215-7 (hbk)
ISBN 978-0-203-82113-8 (ebk)

Typeset in Times by
Wearset Ltd, Boldon, Tyne and Wear

To My Father, Kim Si-bong

Contents

List of figures and tables	xi
Acknowledgements	xiii
Note on the text	xv

1 Introduction 1
  Introduction 1
  Coalition politics in South Korea in historical perspective 2
  From electoral success to ungovernability 3
  Explaining coalitions 5
  The institutionalization of parties and party systems 9
  Methods and limitations 14
  The structure of the book 15

2 Historical background and the formation of the Korean party system 18
  Introduction 18
  The five Republics from 1948 to 1987 18
  The Korean party system during the period of democratic consolidation (1988–1997) 29
  Summary 48

3 Internal factors: party politics and organization 51
  Introduction 51
  Explaining intra- and inter-party conflicts: what happened and why? 52
  The impact of governability: party organization 70
  Summary 91

4 Regionalism and the reform of the electoral law 94
  Introduction 94

Regionalism 95
*The reform of the electoral law: the process of compromise and
   negotiation and the rational choice of the political actors 108*
Summary 120

5 **Ideological cleavages and the debate over the National
   Security Law**   122
Introduction 122
Ideological differences among voters and parties 123
The National Security Law's influence on party ideology 140
The ruling party's attempt to abolish the so-called 'evil law' 142
Summary 150

6 **When majority does not rule: the Roh Moo-hyun and the
   Lee Myung-bak administrations**   153
Introduction 153
The Roh Moo-hyun administration 154
Roh Moo-hyun's call for a 'grand coalition' 159
*The conservatives come back into power: the Lee Myung-bak
   administration 161*
Summary 167

7 **Conclusions**   169
Introduction 169
Summary of the main arguments 170
Broader implications and conclusion 176

Notes	178
Bibliography	188
Index	199

Figures and tables

Figures

1.1 Two dimensions to measure governability	11
2.1 Party seat numbers after coalition-building in February 1998	47
2.2 Party seat numbers after political reorganization: '*Jeonggye-Gaepyeon*' ('political system reorganization') in May 1999	47
3.1 Fission and fusion of parties and party leaders (1997–2003)	60
3.2 Parties between state and civil society	75
3.3 Coalition-building (1960–2003)	81
4.1 Coalition-building since democratization	96
4.2 Regional distributions of votes in the Thirteenth Presidential Election	99
4.3 Regional distributions of votes in the Fourteenth Presidential Election	103
4.4 Regional distributions of votes in the Fifteenth Presidential Election	104
5.1 Opinion on aid to North Korea	125
5.2 Opinion on the National Security Law	126
5.3 Respondents' ideological stance	127
5.4 Party position on the policy space: 1990–2000	147
6.1 Party seat numbers from the 2004 general election to the 2010 local elections.	161
6.2 Support for presidential performance in 2006 and 2010	164
6.3 Seat numbers in the National Assembly	166
6.4 Coalition-building	168

Tables

1.1 History of coalition	4
2.1 Regional cleavage in Korea	33
2.2 Electoral votes from the presidential elections	35
3.1 Numbers of party members in Korea and other countries	73

3.2 The stance of parties in Korea between the state and civil society during the Kim Dae-jung administration 74
3.3 Central party income (unit: million *won*) (%) 78
4.1 Electoral votes from the presidential elections 102
4.2 Votes gained in the Sixteenth General Elections on 13 April 2000 105
4.3 Votes gained in the Fifteenth General Elections on 11 April 1996 106
5.1 Province and aid to North Korea: cross-tabulation 128
5.2 Measures of association between province and aid to North Korea 129
5.3 Province and National Security Law: cross-tabulation 130
5.4 Measures of association between province and National Security Law 131
5.5 Rejection versus acceptance of anti-communist ideology 133
5.6 Respondents' opinion on reunification 136
5.7 Cross-tabulation of opinion on the National Security Law and reunification 137
5.8 Measures of association between the National Security Law and reunification 138
6.1 Seat numbers (by party) in the National Assembly from 2004 to 2010 155

Acknowledgements

This book stems from the support of several institutions and people. The book is derived, originally, from my PhD research; I am profoundly grateful to my former supervisor, Professor Glenn D. Hook, at the School of East Asian Studies, University of Sheffield, for his advice, insights, encouragement and patience throughout my doctoral career. I consider myself very lucky and privileged in meeting and working with him during my PhD. I was fortunate to find in Professor Charlie Jeffery a supportive and patient mentor, and in the University of Edinburgh a wonderful institution.

Many in Korea have also made a great contribution to this project before and during my fieldwork there, in particular Professor Kim Byung-kook at Korea University and the East Asia Institute (EAI). I am especially grateful to him for generously allowing me to use the raw data from the EAI Social and Political Surveys for my research.

The University of Sheffield and the Korea Foundation provided financial support; without their help it would not have been possible to complete my dissertation, and from there to move on to an academic career at the University of Edinburgh, University College Dublin and Central European University (CEU) in Budapest. The ESRC Post-Doctoral Fellowship, the Leverhulme Trust Early Career Research Fellowship allowed me to further develop my research in coalition-party politics more broadly in East Asia. My new institutional home, CEU, made it possible for me to focus on finalizing this book. I am also grateful to the British Academy, the Korea Foundation, the Japan Foundation, the Economic and Social Research Council and the University of Edinburgh which all supported the organization of a workshop and a conference in 2007. Part of the research on governability across regime types owes a lot to that workshop and all those who contributed, and especially professors Fiona Yap, Junko Kato, Robert Elgie, Jose Antonio Cheibub and Carol Mershon; part of Chapter 4 was published in the *Japanese Journal of Political Science* (vol. 9, no. 3, 2008). Chapter 6 examines most recent developments in the latest two administrations up until 2010. Part of it was published as a book chapter in the *Korea Yearbook* 2008 and as a journal article published by the Korea Economic Institute in Washington, DC as part of their Korea Academic Paper Series.

I also thank Professor Cas Mudde at Antwerp University (Belgium), previously at Edinburgh University, who encouraged me to work on the case of coalition governments in South Korea. I thank Professor Peter M. Sales at the University of Wollongong in Australia who supported and encouraged me to be studious in the very early stages of my academic career. I was also lucky to meet Professor Kim Hyung-a at the Australian National University. She has constantly encouraged me while discussing my research and common interest in Korean politics. I thank her sincerely for her encouragement and enthusiasm.

I wish to thank all my colleagues and friends in Sheffield, Edinburgh, Dublin and now in Budapest who in several ways have helped me throughout this project. I want to say thank you to Kuniko Ishiguro, Allan Craigie, Craig Wilkie, Dasha Grajfoner and Eve Hepburn. I also thank Cho Kyoung-mi, Baek Mi-youn, Lee Jae-hyung and Choi Hee-seop in Korea. I am very grateful to the artist and singer Cho Young-nam and Chi Eun-ju who helped me in gaining access to key political figures in Korea.

Finally, I wish to thank my mother Lee Jung-rim and brother Kim Young-jun in Korea for their encouragement and patience especially during my doctoral career. With the sweet memory of my father in my heart, he has made me strong, diligent and motivated. My special thanks go to my family-in-law in Italy, for their encouragement and special care. I also thank my best soul mate, Matteo Fumagalli. A tireless and enthusiastic supporter, Matteo has made me think more and harder about my research, allowing me to explain myself in a more logical way. Matteo's 'bothering' questions accompanied every single step of this long, challenging, but rewarding journey.

Overall during my research I learned not only about coalition politics but also that life is harsh and beautiful at the same time. I learned to be stronger and more disciplined. I thank you all sincerely.

Note on the text

In this book I follow the new Romanization system established by the Korean Government (Ministry of Culture and Tourism) on 7 July 2000 for the correct pronunciation of Korean words. This is available at: www.mct.go.kr/open_content/administrative/news/notice_view.jsp (accessed on 8 January 2006).

In the case of Korean names, this study follows the East Asian pattern of having the family name followed by the given name. Korean names in general are hyphenated between the two letters of their first name, for example, 'Kim Dae-jung', but in the bibliography some names are shown without a hyphen, like 'Youngmi Kim'.

1 Introduction

Introduction

This book examines how the dynamics of inter- and intra-party coalition-building have affected governability in South Korea. Coalition-building has been a major political strategy to win office and subsequently to pass laws in the National Assembly after democratization. However, rapid fission and fusion of parties and 'annexation' or defection of legislators before or after elections have surprisingly received scant attention in the literature.

Focusing on the Kim Dae-jung administration (1998–2003) as a case study of the failure of turning electoral success (winning presidential elections) into stable governability[1] due to having a large opposition in the legislature, the study sheds light on the politics of coalition formation and break-up. The case of Kim Dae-jung's administration (a minority coalition government) is particularly appropriate as it represents a vantage point from which to observe how post-democratization governments in Korea struggled to implement reform policies; Kim Dae-jung's coalition government struggled with political crises, stalemates and deadlocks in the legislature. Proposals for new laws seeking to introduce reform policies that would consolidate not only electoral but also social and economic democracy were opposed by the opposition party and sometimes even by the coalition partner itself. As a result of conflicts in the legislature, many reform policies could not be passed.

Are political instability and government inefficacy derived from minority or divided government, or coalition-building? Why were legislators more actively engaged in the fission and fusion of parties after democratization? Why did most of the ruling parties after democratization seek to enlarge the size of the ruling parties in the legislature? What are the factors constraining mechanisms of compromise and negotiation instead of fission and fusion of parties or legislators?

Under presidential or semi-presidential systems where the government does not risk losing office until the fixed-term ends – as no barriers such as a votes of no confidence exists – it does not seem rational to build coalitions to achieve majority status. If that is the case, why did the ruling parties continuously seek to attract defectors from the opposition parties to achieve majority status in the legislature? Is the size of government a necessary or crucial factor to run office smoothly?

2 *Introduction*

In order to answer the questions above, my research draws on two bodies of literature which, though focusing on the same dependent variable (cabinet or government stability), have rarely been used in tandem. Coalition research on parliamentary systems focuses on the formation, size and termination of government (Bogdanor 1983; De Winter *et al.* 2002; Kim 2008a; Laver and Schofield 1990; Strøm and Müller 2001). Research on presidential systems has concentrated on political deadlock as a result of minority or divided government (Cheibub and Chernykh 2008; Colomer and Negretto 2005; Elgie 2001; Elgie and McMenamin 2008; Kim 2008a, c; Linz 1990; Mainwaring and Shugart 1997; Negretto 2004; Yap and Kim 2008).

It is this book's main contention that the low level of institutionalization and the political culture embedded in Korean society (including among political actors and voters) are the crucial determinants of the country's ungovernability. This chapter sets the context to the study by providing some background to the study of coalition politics in South Korea.

Coalition politics in South Korea in historical perspective

Since the start of democratization in 1987,[2] two political leaders won political elections through a strategy based on coalition-building in South Korea: Kim Young-sam (1993–1997) and Kim Dae-jung (1998–2003). Roh Moo-hyun (2003–2008), formerly presidential candidate of the New Millennium Democratic Party (MDP), has also greatly benefited from entering a coalition with Chung Mong-joon, the leader of the People's Power 21 (PP 21) Party in order to win the 2002 presidential election, even though Chung Mong-joon withdrew his support for Roh Moo-hyun eight hours before the presidential elections on 18 December 2002 (*Donga Ilbo* 20 December 2002). Because coalition-building seems to have become a constant in Korean politics, it is necessary to examine the factors prompting parties to enter a coalition, and whether coalition-building is a main factor of instability within the government and a factor negatively affecting governability, here understood as the government's ability to implement state reform policies (Coppedge 2001).

In fact, coalition-building had played a role even in the transitional period from authoritarian rule to democracy, as the military regime was forced by the opposition into a process of bargaining and compromise. The ruling Democratic Justice Party merged with two opposition parties in 1990: the Unification Democratic Party led by Kim Young-sam and the New Democratic Republican Party led by Kim Jong-pil. The three parties merged and later renamed themselves as the Democratic Liberal Party and agreed to nominate Kim Young-sam as presidential candidate for the then-approaching elections. The politics of coalition-building turned out to be successful in winning office and led to the electoral success of Kim Young-sam, who became the first non-military president after a long period of authoritarian military rule. A second moment where coalition-building seemed to be decisive in Korea's political life was before the 1997 presidential elections, when the ruling party faced internal divisions and the political environment was in turmoil following the outbreak of the 'Asian crisis' and the simultaneous condemnation of its perceived inefficiency by the public. The opposition National Congress for New Politics party leader, Kim Dae-jung, formed an alliance with the United Liberal Democrats party leader, Kim Jong-pil, in order to fight the election. After a long history as an opposition leader, Kim Dae-jung finally became president as a result of winning this election.

Since 1987, coalition-building has played a crucial role in determining electoral success in presidential elections. A serious drawback, however, as will be discussed in the following chapters, is represented by the fact that electoral success is no guarantee of effective governability or political stability either. As a matter of fact, governability has been constantly undermined by permanent factionalism internal to the coalition and to the parties themselves.

Apart from the continuous fission and fusion of political parties, the behaviour of voters also contributed to the creation of minority governments and large oppositions. Where voters have various preferences of policies and/or parties, it seems fairly common and ordinary to find that voters do not converge on support for a single majority party but spread their preferences across the political spectrum. This is all but ordinary in a democratic country. The problem with Korea was that, facing big opposition parties, winning office did not guarantee the administration's governability.

The first time the opposition party won office through democratic elections, the Kim Dae-jung administration set out with an extensive agenda. Yet the ruling party found it difficult to implement its policies from the early outset of the legislature. The administration could not follow up its first coalition agreement, which consisted of appointing its coalition partner as a prime minister, because it faced a large opposition in the legislature. Facing a political deadlock in the National Assembly, the ruling coalition parties immediately started to enlarge the size of the ruling parties by attracting defectors from the opposition parties. Enlarging the government's size at all costs did not seem to bring any solution to the political deadlock, however. Quite the contrary: the conflicts in the legislature grew deeper, not only with the opposition parties but also with the coalition partner(s), as well as with factions within the ruling party.

From electoral success to ungovernability

This study examines one of the fundamental puzzles in the study of political parties and governments: how parties win office, but fail to develop efficient governability. In Korea, the ruling parties struggle with a minority status[3] and hence face difficulty in passing laws, and therefore seek to attract defectors from competing parties. This was particularly so in the case of the Kim Dae-jung administration, which struggled to implement reform policies in the legislature and faced large opposition parties and ultimately deadlock in the legislature. However, attaining majority status in the legislature did not secure governability, as the ruling parties continued to suffer from internal conflicts among politicians with different policy preferences and regional support bases. In fact, Strøm and

4 *Introduction*

Müller note that minority governments need not necessarily be unstable, as they show in large comparative studies of coalition governments in Western Europe (Kim 2008 a, c; Pech 2001; Strøm 1990; Strøm and Müller 2001).

This phenomenon of 'stable, but unstable governments' (with a party ruling over a long period of time, despite high factionalism and political instability) is not exclusive to Korea, but also occurs in other recently democratized countries such as Taiwan, Uruguay, Ukraine and Mexico. Even more-established democracies, namely Japan and Italy, are cases in point where coalition politics and intra-party factionalism have dominated the political scene for decades (Giannetti and Laver 2001; Kato and Kannon 2008; Kim 2008a, c; Laver and Kato 2001; Mershon 2001, 2008).

Survival and office-seeking are the (intuitive) basic goals of political parties. However, the ultimate goal of a party does not only lie in seeking office, but also in maintaining the same power that was achieved by winning elections. Political parties in Korea provide a clear example of organizations that are successful in doing the former objective, but fail in achieving the latter one. In other words, ruling parties in Korea have succeeded in office-seeking but have failed in maintaining a stable form of governability. Most of these governments were sustained by a coalition of two or more parties, and the present Lee Myung-bak administration is the first government after democratization to have won office without building a coalition (see Table 1.1).

Through an in-depth study of intra-party political dynamics, this book examines what has happened in the legislature by looking at three significant case studies (see pp. 51–152) during the Kim Dae-jung administration, how the political actors reacted to political crises or deadlocks and why coalitions did not or could not work. The main research question I seek to answer is the following: what are the factors influencing governability by a minority coalition government in a semi-presidential system?

Table 1.1 History of coalition

Coalitions	Parties
Party merger (1990)	DJP+UDP+NDRP=DLP
Coalition (1997)	NCNP+ULD
Parties alliance (2002)	MDP+PP21* Alliance broke down eight hours before Presidential Election

Source: author.

Notes
DJP   the Democratic Justice Party led by the then-president Roh Tae-woo
UDP   the Unification Democratic Party led by Kim Young-sam
NDRP   the New Democratic Republican Party led by Kim Jong-pil
DLP   the Democratic Liberal Party after the three parties' merger
NCNP   the National Congress for New Politics led by Kim Dae-jung
ULD   the United Liberal Democrats led by Kim Jong-pil
MDP   the New Millennium Democratic Party led by Kim Dae-jung, later by Roh Moo-hyun
PP 21   the People's Power 21 led by Chung Mong-joon

In order to do so, the study examines a series of related questions:

1 Why have coalition governments been unstable in South Korea?
2 How does the fission and fusion of political actors affect government performance?
3 Is factionalism a permanent feature of Korean party politics?
4 How do cultural factors affect political behaviour?
5 What does rationality mean for Korean political actors?
6 How do institutions or regime types impact on governability?

The case of the Kim Dae-jung administration represents an example of coalition minority or divided government in a semi-presidential system in the process of consolidating democracy. The study of coalitions in South Korea, especially the Kim Dae-jung administration, adds a new, non-Western set of data to the expanding field of coalition studies, as well as to the debates on regime types and democratic governability. By discussing the behaviour of Korean political actors, it will also take into account Korean political culture (particularly Confucianism) to make sense of the choices of party leaders, members and voters. In so doing, the study seeks to integrate rational choice theory and cultural variables thereby contributing to a refinement of existing coalition theories.

Explaining coalitions

It is possible to identify two main approaches to the study of coalition-building and governability: coalition research in parliamentary systems and regime studies in presidential systems. Coalition studies are mainly concerned with the formation of the government, the size of the government or government duration, and deal with confidence votes focusing especially on large-N data sets in European countries and mainly in parliamentary systems (Bogdanor 1983; De Winter *et al.* 2002; Kim 2008 a, c; Laver and Schofield 1990; Strøm and Müller 2001). Coalition studies are also largely based on thin, parsimonious analysis. With regard to issues of governability and democratic consolidation, on the other hand, scholars have concentrated on the relationship between regime types (asking which type is superior in terms of governability, whether it is a parliamentary, presidential or semi-presidential system) and political deadlock as a result of minority or divided government (Cheibub 2002; Cheibub *et al.* 2004; Elgie 2001; Figueiredo and Limongi 2000; Kim 2008a; Linz 1990; Mainwaring and Shugart 1997; Negretto 2003; Yap and Kim 2008).

   Although studies of coalition governments have typically been framed within a positivist paradigm adopting a quantitative methodology, which includes large-N comparison of cases mostly selected from Western European countries, large-N comparison data are of limited use when trying to come to terms with the following questions: why do coalition governments fail in terms of governability? How do the governments run the administration after winning office? Why do political actors split and merge with other parties? To answer such questions, more attention needs to be paid to single or small-N comparative studies with in-depth qualitative methodology (Bäck 2003; De Winter *et al.* 2002; Kim 2008a; Laver 1989; Lees 2000; Mershon 2001).

In the case of scholars of regime-type studies, a frequently made argument is that presidential systems institutionally create divided or minority governments and they fatally lead to a 'crisis of governability' (Linz and Valenzuela 1994), or political deadlock and political instability. Presidential regimes were widely assumed to be less cooperative due to the tension in executive and legislative relations in the 1980s with many cases in Latin America, where presidential regimes were often blamed for poor political performance and the failure of democratic governance. Here, governance is understood as *the process of governing* 'rooted in trust and regulated by rules of the game negotiated and agreed by network participants' (Rodes 2000, cited in Kersbergen and Waarden 2004: 148). Mainwaring and Shugart argue that 'there is no universally best form of government' (1997: 3). Instead they point to 'lower level of development and non democratic political culture' as reasons for the poor performance of presidential systems (ibid.: 53). As Sartori (1994, cited in Mainwaring and Shugart 1997: 53) contends, undisciplined parties are problematic not only in a presidential system, but they could be even worse in a parliamentary system. Cheibub (2002) also maintains that highly disciplined parties would mitigate tensions in the legislature and avoid political crises such as deadlock by forming legislative coalitions. As noted here, the two divisions of studies on coalition governments and presidentialism seem to present a case selection bias: coalition governments in the West European countries and presidential systems in Latin American countries.

Another point that is assumed to be crucial for cabinet stability is the size of government. The size of government is a key variable commonly used to explain governability or the duration of the government. The small size of government such as a minority government or divided government is widely believed to be related to the poor performance of a government as it faces big opposition in the legislature. However, the terms 'minority government' and 'divided government' were also used in explaining different cases as minority was employed for the parliamentary system and divided government often utilized in the presidential system. Robert Elgie (2001: 6–10) shows that minority governments in parliamentary systems are equivalent to divided governments in presidential regimes. Quoting Mayhew (1991, cited in Elgie 2001: 8), Elgie notes that divided government is related to 'inter-branch confrontation' such as deadlock in the legislature. Elgie (2001: 11) defines divided government as 'the situation where: the executive fails to enjoy majority support in at least one working house of the legislature'. As mentioned, although both minority government and divided government imply facing a large opposition in the legislature and not reaching majority status, it seems that scholarly debates remain in their 'waterproof compartments', splitting along the study of regime types (parliamentary vs presidential). Nevertheless, it appears to us that they eventually try to answer the very same question: why is a small size of government (minority or divided government) unstable or why do minority or divided governments face political crises and fail in terms of governability or government efficacy?

The term 'stability' can also cause confusion. Different terms such as 'cabinet stability', 'political stability', 'government efficacy' or 'governability' are used in studies of coalition governments and divided governments. When a different institution is studied, even the term used can be different, or the same term can be used in different ways. In parliamentary systems, cabinet stability is related to government termination. The termination of a government can occur through election, resignation, losing confidence votes and so on (Huber and Martinez-Gallardo 2004: 32). However, in presidential systems, governments mostly survive until the term ends. Mainwaring and Shugart (1997: 13) note that when presidents lose control in the legislature, facing a large opposition, they often fall into a lame-duck period towards the end of the president's tenure. Unlike a prime minister in the parliamentary system, a president cannot dissolve the legislature and call new elections. As a presidential regime does not have such mechanisms to resolve conflicts in the legislature, when presidents find themselves in a lame-duck period or facing political deadlock the government often suffers from political instability or government inefficacy. The government is not able to implement reform policies due to lack of support in the legislature. Therefore, unlike cabinet stability in a parliamentary system, governability or political or regime (in)stability were more common terms used in the study of presidential systems.

Coppedge argues that

> governability could embrace every political phenomenon related to stability, order, and legitimacy; the rule of law, law abidingness, efficient bureaucracy, a strong merit system, low crime rates, constitutional succession, low strike rates, long lasting cabinets, strong corporatist institutions, and many other aspects of institutionalization.
> (2001: 7; see also Coppedge 1995; Huntington 1968)

Thinking about how party systems contribute to governability, Coppedge's article focuses particularly on the impact of the party system on the ability of governments to make policies decisively. He argues that inefficient or unstable governability can be characterized by 'stalemate, impeachment, vetoes, cabinet instability, and any other manifestation of executive-legislative conflict' that may boost any political crisis and regime breakdown (Coppedge 2001: 7). In this book I will use governability or government efficacy as the main dependent variable and this will be examined in terms of the ability of the government to pass and to implement policies decisively.

The study of coalition politics in Korea

The study of coalitions and coalition governments is new in Korean scholarship.[4] This is due to a number of reasons. First, this can be partly ascribed to widespread negative perceptions of coalition-building by many scholars such as Son (1999) and Park (2003), who view coalition-building and the search for broader political alliances as key factors in bringing about factionalism and conflicts among parties. Coalitions are not perceived as effective or efficient political actors, but rather are seen as coming out of opportunistic or electoral marketing by pure office-seekers. A second reason stems from the fact that South Korea does not seem to belong anywhere in the mainstream of existing coalition studies, mostly focused on Western cases and parliamentary systems. South Korea's system is semi-presidential and its location in North-East Asia has somehow isolated it from clusters of regional studies examining and comparing Latin American and/or European countries. Despite an extensive literature on the size of government and formation of coalition government (Axelrod 1972; Laver and Kato 2001; Laver and Schofield 1990; Martin and Stevenson 2001; Riker 1962; Schofield 1983), scholars working on coalitions seem to pay little attention to non-Western cases and non-parliamentary systems. Although a large-N research strategy has been traditionally applied to the study of coalitions, Korea has never fully been taken into account. Scholars working on Korea have mainly focused on democratic consolidation and political deadlock. Fourth, while coalition governments produce majority status to win confidence votes in the legislature (Axelrod 1972; Laver and Schofield 1990; Leiserson 1968; Riker 1962) or some parties prefer to stay as minority governments instead of building coalitions (Strøm 1990), in Korea after winning office the coalition ruling parties did not overcome their minority or divided status, and continued to face a large opposition. Finally, the very issue of government stability or durability does not fit into what is to be explained in coalition studies focusing on parliamentary systems. Under the presidential system, the government does not terminate until the set end of the term of office. Questions of divided government and presidential systems were typically discussed to explain democratic governability with reference to Latin America (Cheibub 2002; Mainwaring and Scully 1995; Mainwaring and Shugart 1997). More recently, scholars have begun asking whether it is regime type (parliamentary or presidential) that affects political stability (Cheibub 2002; Cheibub and Chernykh 2008; Cheibub et al. 2004; Croissant 2003; Elgie 2001; Elgie and McMenamin 2008; Kim 2008b, c; Linz 1990; Linz and Valenzuela 1994; Mainwaring and Shugart 1997). Here, however, the areas of intra-party politics and mechanisms of negotiation and compromise have, overall, remained unexplored (Kim 2008a, b, c). In sum, because of its peculiarity (semi-presidential system, divided government, East Asian case), South Korea has remained in the background of both coalition research and regime studies, and these are the gaps that this study seeks to bridge. An in-depth analysis of intra-party politics, and especially of the process of institutionalization of party organization and party system, can both shed light on key aspects of Korean politics and generate useful propositions for understanding the often unstable politics of newly democratized countries.

The institutionalization of parties and party systems

Early 'classical' coalition studies are mainly drawn from minimal or minimum winning coalition theories assuming that parties would form majority coalitions to win office (Axelrod 1972; Laver and Schofield 1990; Leiserson 1968; Riker 1962). More recently, coalition studies have turned their attention to minority governments and also coalition minority governments; however, in-depth explanations of intra-party politics are missing here and most cases are based on large-*N* data focused on West European countries. This approach fails to explain how political actors behave after winning office, and how this affects government performance. When it comes to non-Western settings, existing coalition theories can cause further puzzles in terms of why coalition minority governments are unstable. Is it because of the size of the governments? Is it because of regime type, as many scholars assumed in the 1980s with regard to cases in Latin America? Minority government or divided government and governability or government efficacy have been the main issues in the recent scholarship, and the comparative studies between presidential regimes and parliamentary systems is a rising issue in the debate on democratic governability and political deadlock, especially in the presidential system. In both streams of studies on coalition-building and presidential regimes, scholars seem to have a selection bias tending towards West European data sets for coalition studies in a parliamentary system and Latin American cases for divided government and presidential regime. Can cabinet stability (in parliamentary systems) or regime stability (in presidential systems) be studied across countries and beyond regime types?

As recent scholarship (Cheibub 2002; Cheibub *et al.* 2004; Elgie 2001; Figueredo and Limongi 2000; Randall and Svåsand 2002) argues, there might be a fundamental element of political stability beyond regime type and the size of government. Mainwaring (1997: 106) points out that the creation of a strong but democratically accountable executive is not a problem unique to the presidential system. Considering intra-party politics in Brazil between 1985 and 1994, he argues that undisciplined parties, party fragmentation and federalism undermined the president's executive power to pursue state reform and economic stabilization, failing in achieving majority support in Congress. Figueredo and Limongi (2000: 152) maintain that

> explanations on parliamentary behaviour and of policy outcomes overemphasize the importance of the separation of powers and the characteristics of electoral and party legislation. They overlook the role of other institutional characteristics, especially the president's legislative powers and the internal organization of the legislative work.

They conclude that determinant factors of governability lie in the characteristics of the decision-making process. Governability is more affected by the legislative powers of the president and the legislative organization than regime types or characteristics of the party system (ibid.: 168). Tsebelis (2002) also focuses on

10 Introduction

the part played by veto players rather than regime types. Tsebelis (ibid.: 19) defines veto players as 'individual or collective actors whose agreement is necessary for a change of the status quo'. Questioning how political institutions affect policies or the characteristics of a political system such as government stability, Tsebelis argues that

> [m]ost of the literature on political institutions uses a single criterion to identify the main characteristics of a polity. For example, political regimes are divided into presidential and parliamentary, legislatures into unicameral and bicameral, electoral systems into plurality and proportional, parties into strong and weak, the party system into two-party and multiparty. The relationships among all these categories are underdeveloped.
>
> (ibid.: 1)

Instead of focusing on regime types or party systems, Tsebelis (ibid.: 3–5) argues that a number of veto players influence policy stability thereby leading to government instability.

An institutional approach to political stability across regime types seems to provide somewhat generalizable theories (Cheibub et al. 2004; Randall and Svåsand 2002; Tsebelis 2002). However, some are still based on the large data sets either in European or Latin American countries, and some are based on parsimonious explanations with thin description. What is missing in the studies of coalition-building and governability in different regime types is an in-depth analysis of intra-party politics. Why political actors are behaving in certain ways in given circumstances and based on what rational goals remains largely unexplored in the literature. How coalitions break down or how governments struggle to cope with the opposition remain similarly under-explored or overwhelmed by the mainstream of theoretically driven studies. Empirical data are collected through quantitative methods that can at times appear rather obscure. By looking at political actors' behaviour and their culture and the way political party is organized, the puzzle over divided or minority coalition government and governability can be resolved and, simultaneously, a deeper understanding of intra-party politics promoted.

In order to gain a deeper understanding of the causes behind the instability of the Kim Dae-jung administration, this book analyses intra- and inter-party politics from 1998 to 2003. The cases of the recent Roh Moo-hyun (2003–2008) and Lee Myung-bak (2008-present) administrations show that the size of ruling parties is not a sufficient condition to secure governability when parties fail to link with citizens and suffer from conflict of interest within the party and with the opposition parties. Drawing from the work of Panebianco, Randall and Svåsand, and Mainwaring, I hypothesize that minority government and coalition stability will be dependent on two main factors: the level of institutionalization within the party and the party system.

1 Internal party dynamics: the Kim Dae-jung administration experienced a high level of internal factionalism as well as conflicts with coalition part-

ners. The government started in office as a coalition government, so I categorized the conflicts with factions and the coalition partner in terms of the internal dynamics of the party. Factionalism, leadership and the cohesiveness of the parties' organization will be discussed in this context.

2   Party system: the coalition government not only struggled with internal factions but also the opposition parties forced political deadlocks in the legislature. When ruling parties face major oppositions, a failure to compromise and negotiate will obviously generate political crises in the legislature, especially if the ruling parties seek to introduce reform policies. Regional and ideological cleavages and the failure of the party organization's role to link with citizens will be discussed when attempts were made to pass new bills to mitigate existing social cleavages through institutional mechanisms.

The hypotheses that this book aims to test are as follows:

1   A higher degree of factionalism negatively affects governability.
2   Stronger leadership is likely to make government more stable.
3   The degree of cohesiveness of party organizations affects governability.
4   Stronger regional cleavages negatively affect governability.
5   A deep ideological cleavage is likely to undermine governability in terms of implementing new laws.
6   If the party organization fails to link with citizens, the government is likely to be less stable.

By testing these hypotheses, I aim to show how the level of institutionalization and political culture matter. The final chapter of this book, focusing on the two

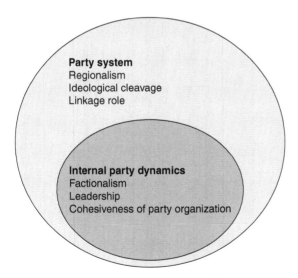

Figure 1.1 Two dimensions to measure governability (source: author).

recent governments, shows that the level of institutionalization has improved as a result of the introduction of new rules and electoral laws. Introducing primaries entailed that selecting presidential candidates would no longer be only the preserve of party elites. New electoral laws (Mixed Member Proportional System)[5] allowed small parties such as the Democratic Labour Party to survive in the National Assembly. The process of institutionalization has also influenced local political culture to some extent, although parties and political elites are still deeply rooted in their regional, school and family ties, leaving much space for more incisive, if likely to be controversial, reforms in the future.

Panebianco (1988: 53) defines institutionalization as 'the process by which an organization incorporates its founders' values and aims'. The goals or ideological aims of the party organization form its shape, and the goals of party organization are expressed through institutionalization. According to Panebianco, parties can be categorized by degree of institutionalization and this can be measured by the organization's degree of autonomy towards its environment and its degree of 'systemness'. If a party has little autonomy and is dependent on the external environment, it can hardly meet its goals; on the other hand, if a party has autonomy vis-à-vis the external environment, it has more control over its organizational goals. 'Systemness' refers to the 'internal structural coherence of the organization' (ibid.: 56). A higher degree of systemness refers to the control of subgroups and therefore control of uncertainty. Systemness also has a positive correlation with autonomy. If the party organization has higher autonomy vis-à-vis the environment and higher systemness, the party organization is strongly institutionalized. Therefore, if the party is highly institutionalized it can control the uncertainty of the environment and also has strong control in its own hands rather than in the hands of subgroups. In other words, if a party is highly institutionalized, it has a high level of autonomy towards the environment and coherent organization, so it maintains control in achieving its goals. Panebianco also notes party organization activities can be distinguished by competency, environmental relations, management, internal communication, formal rules, organizational financing and recruitment. In this chapter, I test party organization and levels of institutionalization according to the degree of coherence of the party, leadership and environmental relations such as the role of linkage with citizen or social cleavages.

Randall and Svåsand (2002: 12) have defined the concept of institutionalization as 'the process by which the party becomes established in terms both of integrated patterns of behaviour and of attitudes or culture'. Therefore institutionalization can be analytically broken down into internal and external aspects. Internal aspects comprise developments within the party and external aspects are about the relationship with the society or other institutions, probably within the party system itself. The internal and external aspects also have a structural and attitudinal components. For Randall and Svåsand, party institutionalization can be characterized along four dimensions: systemness, value infusion, decisional autonomy and reification. For them, systemness refers to strong organization, and value infusion can be seen as party cohesion. Autonomy is about the level of independence of the party and reification refers to establishment in the public imagination. Randall and Svåsand (ibid.: 14) note that these four elements represent the core elements in the process of party institutionalization.

Alongside examining the level of party institutionalization, however, it is also important to see parties in the context of the party system. To study why the ruling coalition parties failed in their reform agenda and faced political crises in the legislature, I examine not only the ruling party and its coalition partner(s) but also its relationship with the opposition as well. Thus this book looks at two levels of institutionalization, within the party and also within the party system. Randall and Svåsand (2002) note that less attention has been given to the institutionalization of the party system. Party institutionalization has been focused on explaining the weak performance of democratic governance or democratic consolidation (Diamond 1989; Mainwaring and Scully 1995). However, the level of institutionalization of the party system also seems crucial to the party system as a whole. Randall and Svåsand (2002: 5) argue:

> there is much less agreement on which particular qualities individual parties should have, or what kind of party system is most conducive to democratic governance. In this context, different criteria have been cited – for instance concerning the ideal number of parties, the degree of ideological polarization, the relative merits of two-party, three-party or dominant party system and the relationship between parties and underlying social and cultural cleavages.

Randall and Svåsand further argue that individual party institutionalization is not always compatible with the institutionalization of the party system. They also see the institutionalization of the party system in terms of internal and external aspects. Internal aspects can be seen in the relationships within individual parties and external relationships with other institutions such as the state. This can be regarded as the degree of autonomy from the state. Randall and Svåsand (ibid.: 8) see 'the more parties, collectively and their activities are supported by public measures such as public subsidies, access to media and legal protection for their existence for instance in the constitution or in ordinary laws, the more the party system can be said to be institutionalized'.

However, Randall and Svåsand maintain that the institutionalized party does not necessarily contribute to the institutionalization of the party system. Two significant issues emerge here: the evenness of party institutionalization and its identification with an exclusive ethnic or cultural grouping (ibid.: 8–9). By 'evenness', Randall and Svåsand mean the extent to which the level of political party institutionalization is relatively uniform across the party system. If one particular party is privileged under an authoritarian regime with, for example, special access to the media or funding, the remaining parties cannot redress these benefits. In this case, one institutionalized party does not contribute to the level of institutionalization of the overall party system. Another issue is the party's identification with certain groups. If a party has absolute support from certain

14 *Introduction*

groups, there would be no fair competition but a monopoly of support. This actually happened in South Korea as voters in certain regions identified themselves with charismatic leaders creating strong regional cleavages.

Mainwaring (1998: 69) also conceptualized party-system institutionalization across four dimensions: stability in patterns of inter-party competition, party roots in society, legitimacy of parties and elections, and party organization. He argues that a more institutionalized party-system enjoys stability and does not suffer from high fluctuations of votes. Parties are strongly rooted in society and each enjoys firm legitimacy from other parties and the voters while individual parties are ruled by individual party leaders. In other words, it is parties that produce their leaders and not the opposite, leaders' creating parties, which has instead happened in many instances in South Korea.

Thus this research builds on the insights of Panebianco, Mainwaring, and Randall and Svåsand's work on the level of institutionalization. The level of institutionalization will be assessed by taking into consideration two dimensions: external and internal aspects of the parties. In other words, I will examine the institutionalization of parties and the institutionalization of the party system. For the internal aspect, I look at the party organization itself – factionalism, leadership and cohesion of the organization, such as funding and recruitment. For the external aspect, I examine the organization's role in linking with the citizens, regional and ideological cleavages. In this book I therefore examine if a minority coalition government exhibits weak institutionalization of both party and party system, and infer that if this is the case it would affect its ability to implement reform policies.

Methods and limitations

This study makes use of both qualitative and quantitative methods. It combines four techniques of data collection: content analysis of media outlets, archival research, analysis of existing survey data and elite interviews. Content analysis of Korean media and party platforms identified leaders' strategies of coalition formation and the motivations behind legislators' defection. The analysis of party politics and political actors' strategies and behaviour was based on daily newspapers and current affairs magazines covering especially the period 1998–2010, though archival searches were conducted to include the period 1990 onwards. As the Korean Integrated News Database System (KINDS) website[6] contains most of the newspapers and weekly and monthly magazines published in South Korea, research was also conducted by the use of key words and dates. Newspapers that were not included on the KINDS website had their own websites available; therefore, a large amount of information was available online. Electoral results and party platforms were collected from public records mostly available online, and survey data on voters' regional and ideological preferences were collected from the various research centres such as the East Asia Institute and Korea Society Opinion Institute, as well as newspaper public opinion polls. As a consequence, most of the information gathered owes a lot to the technological development of the Internet. This was complemented with data collected during a period of fieldwork conducted during the spring of 2004, summer 2005, spring 2006 and winter 2009. In total, 25 in-depth semi-structured interviews were undertaken with members of the Korean political elite, and survey data were used to explore popular attitudes differentiated by regional and ideological preferences. The latter (raw data in SPSS files) were made available by the Seoul-based East Asia Institute and covered the year 2002 (Survey Data on Political and Social Opinions in South Korea 2002).

An unavoidable question arising from the decision to focus on a single case (country) study concerns the generalizability of the findings related to the case itself. This book makes no claim to generalizability. However, the case of the Kim Dae-jung administration is significant because of its 'typicality' in that it presents typical problems that have emerged in recently democratized countries (Korea, a number of Latin American states and elsewhere). In the last chapter, I use the two subsequent administrations as control cases. If my argument holds in the case of the Kim Dae-jung administration (1998–2003), then I should find out that an increased level of institutionalization shows more democratic procedures in candidate selection for the presidential and general elections. The pro-Roh Mo-hyun Uri party briefly enjoyed a majority status in the legislature until the party fell prey to internal factionalism and disintegrated. The Lee Myung-bak administration (2008–present) can rely on a surplus majority in the parliament, since the Grand National Party gained a majority of seats in the 2008 general election. At the same time, a surplus majority was made possible by attracting non-party-affiliated legislators and merging with minority parties. Once again, coalition politics played a crucial role in Korea. Moreover, despite some progress in the institutionalization of the system, some problems have represented themselves, such as intra-party factionalism party splits, and fierce opposition hindering the functioning of the legislature.

Other key questions discussed in this book (in reference to minority coalition government, its dynamics, formation and instability) are relevant in parliamentary systems. Coalition-building is a common phenomenon in parliamentary as well as presidential or semi-presidential systems. Parties build coalitions to win office or to pass bills in the legislature in the presidential systems of many countries, especially where recently democratized. Studies of government efficacy or governability were also mainly focused on the regime type or the characteristics of the presidential system, especially in terms of the division of power between the legislature and the executive.

The structure of the book

This book consists of seven chapters. The introduction has briefly provided the background to the main issues under analysis and discussed the relevance and choice of the Korean case, in itself and within the literature. I also outlined the framework to be used and the hypotheses that build on the framework and discussed the methods used to collect and analyse the data.

Chapter 2 revisits the formation of Korea's party system during the authoritarian period and post-democratization era. A review of the authoritarian period highlights the constant characteristics and cleavages in the political system particularly since democratization, namely the presence of a strong anti-communist ideology, personalism and leadership struggles, and regionalism. A key characteristic of the Korean political system is the relative insignificance of ideological cleavage. Facing the North Korean threat and the legacy of decades of authoritarian governments' anti-communism pushed most of the parties and the voters' ideologies to the right, against communism. The irony is that ideological division in South Korea does not lie in the conventional distinctions such as right and left or conservative and progressive. Where most parties are converged to the right, as in the Korean case, the only clear division is anti-communism or policies towards North Korean politics. Therefore blurred ideological division has been a main characteristic of party politics; however, an apparent change has occurred with the advent of the Kim Dae-jung administration.

Chapter 3 discusses the dynamics of intra-party politics by examining factionalism, the party funding system, leadership and the party's capacity to link with the citizens. By looking at the conflicts with the opposition party in the legislature, I explain how the coalition's ruling parties faced deadlocks in the legislature. However, there were conflicts not only with the opposition but also with coalition partners within the government. An analysis of issues of party organization, funding, leadership and factionalism will show how the weak institutionalization of Korean political parties lies at the core of a continuous process of fission and fusion and ultimately political instability.

In Chapter 4 I move on to the party system level and explain how the government failed to introduce one of its key reform projects that would mitigate strong regionalism in South Korea by introducing new electoral laws. The controversies over electoral laws will emphasize how governability does not seem to derive from the size of the government but rather from the internal cohesiveness of the organization. In this chapter, I test two hypotheses on strong regionalism and how the degree of cohesiveness of the party organization affects governability. A key finding here concerns the salience of regional cleavages. The chapter illustrates how regionalism has been shaped after democratization and how regional support for the parties affected the legislators' behaviour while negotiating and compromising on the reform of the electoral laws. In providing electoral data showing strong regionalism in the general elections and the presidential elections, I argue that, when a party is strongly tied to a regional constituency, it fails to gain nationwide support, thereby weakening governability, as the battle over implementing reform policies clearly shows.

Chapter 5 provides evidence of ideological conflicts within the coalition parties and the opposition parties by discussing how the Kim Dae-jung administration tried to abolish or at least to amend the National Security Law, until then used to shield authoritarian governments from opposition political actors. The government's Sunshine Policy (or engagement policy) towards North Korea began with wide support, with even the opposition agreeing to provide some substantial aid towards North Korea. A key point raised here is that ideological division in the country is also related to regional division. Voters for the ruling party supported the Sunshine Policy and also the abolition of the National Security Law mainly in the Honam region; on the other hand, supporters for the coalition partner's party and opposition party were against the policies. Therefore, ideological preference turned out to be a regional 'South–South' conflict, rather than a conflict opposing the two Koreas (North and South).

Chapter 6 tests the argument put forward in the previous chapters by looking at the two administrations that followed Kim Dae-jung's: the Roh Moo-hyun and Lee Myung-bak administrations. In both cases, the president's term was accompanied by a majority party in the legislature (though very briefly in the former case). If the argument about the importance of size in the legislature holds, these are the cases where we would find evidence. By contrast, and in line of the argument I put forward in the rest of the book, what we have is a structural proneness to intra- and inter-parties and party system.

Chapter 7 summarizes my argument, namely that there are internal and external factors undermining a coalition minority government's capacity to carry out reforms. This is mainly due to the low level of institutionalization of political parties and the party system. A socially and historically embedded Confucian culture among the political actors and voters also contributes to instability.

2 Historical background and the formation of the Korean party system

Introduction

This chapter provides essential background information on contemporary Korean political history, highlighting the constant characteristics and cleavages of the political system, before and after democratization. The scope of the chapter is to identify the structural preconditions that paved the way for both Kim Dae-jung's electoral success and difficulties in implementing political reforms. Some of these difficulties are rooted in Korea's post-war history, including, as will be shown in the following pages, factionalism and personalism, blurred ideological differences among various political actors, and the presence of large business conglomerates (*Jaebeols*). What I will demonstrate in this chapter is how these factors emerged in Korean politics and how they affected the development (or, better, the underdevelopment) of the country's political system. Along with a brief discussion of the six Republics – from 1948 to 1992 – the chapter covers in more detail three administrations: Roh Tae-woo (1988–1992), Kim Young-sam (1993–1997), and the emergence of coalition-building before the Kim Dae-jung (1998–2003) tenure. The chapter is structured as follows. The first section provides a general historical background which covers the period from 1948 (when the Republic of Korea was established) until the start of democratization in 1987 (end of the 'Fifth Republic'). Section two delineates the Korean party system during the period of democratic consolidation (1988–1997) and discusses the formation of political coalitions during the Sixth Republic and prior to the start of the Kim Dae-jung administration. Finally, the conclusion identifies the main characteristics of the Korean political system.

The five Republics from 1948 to 1987

In the early twentieth century, the ruling *Joseon* Dynasty was absorbed by the Japanese Empire and the country remained under colonial rule for 35 years, from 1910 to 1945. After Japan's surrender to the USSR in the North and to the US in the South, the USSR and the US divided the peninsula in two along the thirty-eighth parallel (*3.8 Seon* (line)) and Korea was ruled by the US–Soviet 'joint commissions' from 1946 to 1947. Since then, two separate states and political

The formation of the Korean party system 19

systems have emerged on the peninsula, one in the North backed by the Soviet Union and China, and one in the South supported by the United States. South Korea became a fundamental geo-strategic bulwark for the West's struggle against communism during the Cold War. The 1950–1953 Korean War and the stand-off that followed crucially marked the development of the (South) Korean political system.

The First Republic 1948–1960

Rhee Syng-man, one of the members of the 'Shanghai Provisional Government' succeeded in lobbying the United States Congress for the independence of the South. Through a successful alliance with state bureaucrats and business leaders (and the support of the US administration), Rhee became the first president of the Republic of Korea in 1948. Under Rhee, the First Republic lasted until 1960. Before the First General Election, the main political actors were the Independent Central Committee led by Rhee Syng-man, the Korea Democratic Party led by Kim Seong-su and Song Jin-woo, the nationalist Shanghai provisional government faction led by Kim-gu (nationalist), the centre–left People's Party led by Yeo Un-hyeong, and the Joseon Communist Party led by Park Heon-yeong. Park Heon-yeong left South Korea and went to the North in order to pursue the unification of Korea. Many among the nationalist or moderate leftist elites such as Kim Gu and Kim Gyu-sik were excluded or forced to retire from active politics. With the strong backing of the United States, Rhee Syng-man consolidated his power by marginalizing most of his political opponents, especially those on the left of the political spectrum.

During the Cold War, the US supported figures like Rhee who held to a conservative, strongly right-wing ideology and fundamentally anti-communist views. Under the National Security Law,[1] Rhee's government arrested 13 members of the National Assembly in late 1949 (Choi 2002; Cumings 1997: 216). They were members of the National Assembly whose opinion was close to North Korea's 'North and the South unification discourse'. This marks the beginning of the government's practice of taking advantage of National Security Law to repress political opponents. The role of the National Security Law will be discussed in Chapter 5 (and partially in Chapter 6) where I will examine how the law was used to oppress political opponents and those who hold leftist views, and how they essentially made anti-communism the only legitimate ideology in the country. By then, many elites who lost most of their property in North Korea over the 1946 land reform[2] had moved down to South Korea and became fierce anti-communist activists. Using anti-communism as a propaganda tool to legitimate its power and policies, the government also actively sought to marginalize political opponents through the National Security Law. Under the National Security Law, it was virtually impossible for leftists or even moderates to survive in the political system. This ultimately led political ideology to converge on the right. As Rhee had clamped down on most of the leftist parties, the ruling party faced another conservative opposition party, the Korea Democratic Party.

Rhee's administration mainly relied on the economic support of the US from 1948 to 1960 in return for political support in the fight against communism. Reliance on US economic aid had its downsides for the Korean economy. Domestic industries focused on import substitution reproducing the support material imported from the US such as sugar, flour and textiles. There were many small factories producing military substitutes during the war which, after the war, were no longer in demand. The closure of heavy industrial factories generated high unemployment. Farmers also suffered from the import of cheaper agricultural products. Poverty and widespread corruption defined this stage of post-war Korean history. Nationwide civil society movements emerged and mobilized against the regime and the corruption of the government. The so-called '4.19 movement', the student uprising that took place on 19 April 1960, brought President Rhee's rule to an end. The proximate causes of '4.19' lay in the resentment of the population towards the assassination by the police of a student who had taken part in a mass protest against the government, who were accused of manipulating electoral results in order to preserve power (Cumings 1997: 339–346). The casualties amounted to over 6,000 demonstrators,[3] mostly students, at the hands of the police. Cumings (ibid.: 346) notes: '[S]till, there was no left wing and no labor union worthy of the name in South Korea; it maintained a remarkably narrow political spectrum.'

The Second Republic 1960–1961

When the Liberal Party's[4] rule ended, the opposition Democratic Party[5] took office and introduced a bicameral parliamentary regime. This became known as the Second Republic, led by the president, Yun Bo-seon, and the prime minister, Jang Myeon. It was the first democratic regime with a bicameral parliamentary system in South Korea, though it was short-lived, as it lasted only from April 1960 until May 1961. South Korea achieved a formally democratic regime for the first time after exiling Rhee to Hawaii, but the relationship between the ruling elites and society remained tense and confrontational.

The executive power was very weak and the population was suffering from mass poverty, and more students were demanding reunification with North Korea, something which was vehemently and understandably rejected by the right-wing parties. The Democratic Party was founded in 1955 from a faction of the Korea Democratic Party, the ruling party under the US military administration from 1945 to 1948 before the first republic was founded, and newer groupings consisting of the defectors from the Rhee government. The Korea Democratic Party tended to represent the interests of landlords with a conservative ideology, and it became the opposition New Democratic Party later under the Park administration. Anti-communist ideology and the elites' efforts at self-preservation in power were the glue keeping the ruling party's factions together.

Following the demise of Rhee's administration, proposals to turn Korea into a presidential system began to be aired and discussed. However, the general elections under the new regime gave the Democratic Party a landslide victory. In the

29 July 1960 general election, the Democratic Party gained 175 seats in the lower house and 31 seats in the upper house out of 233 total seats, gaining 75 per cent of the total votes. The leftist Social People's Party gained four seats and one seat in each house only and the Liberal Democratic Party two seats and four seats respectively (Choi 1996: 47; Kim 2000: 340). Choi Jang-jip (1996: 47) argues that the result of the general elections gave birth to a new regime that was strikingly similar to the previous one. The new regime did not show any new political cleavage, and the conservative authoritarian elites inherited the power structure from the Liberal Democratic Party. Given that new political actors were not allowed to emerge – especially with a different ideological orientation – it appears evident that the Democratic Party would win most of the seats in the legislature if the only competitor, the Liberal Democratic Party, fought on the same ideological spectrum. Lipset and Rokkan (1967: 11, cited in Choi 1996: 49) note that when ideology is strong, small differences among the parties appear more evident and there is less room for compromise.

Another noteworthy issue is that it was widely discussed in the mainstream of presidential regime studies in the 1990s that a parliamentary system would work better than a presidential system in Korea. In fact, two major coalitions in 1990 and 1997 in South Korea were built on the agreement of changing the regime type from the presidential to the parliamentary system. However, when a society suffers from economic and political crises, neither system works properly, as Faundez (1997, cited in Mainwaring and Shugart 1997: 20) illustrates with regard to the Chilean case: 'parliamentarism might well have failed to endure in Chile through the difficult conditions of the 1930s.' This argument is bolstered by the case of parliamentarism in South Korea from 1960 to 1961. This seems to suggest that, rather than regime type, some other mechanism within the party and the party system might be the key to ensuring governability.

The Third Republic 1961–1972

When the Democratic Party took office, plans were made to decrease the size and influence of the military, and this led army officers to become more involved in the country's political life. A military coup led by General Park Chung-hee finally opened the way to the Third Republic in 1961. Cumings (1997: 353) notes that the real mastermind behind the coup was Kim Jong-pil, a graduate of the Military Academy in 1949 and a nephew of Park Chung-hee (by marriage). Kim Jong-pil played a crucial role in founding the KCIA (the Korean Central Intelligence Agency) and the Democratic Republican Party that supported Park Chung-hee as president. The military occupied the president's office and all political activities were banned under martial law.

It was not until 1 January 1963 that 'the nation re-foundation committee' lifted the ban on all political activities. The original plan of the military coup was to hand over power from the military to the civilian government after amending the constitutional law, turning Korea from a bicameral parliamentary system into a mono-cameral presidential system in early 1963. Kim Jong-pil planned to remain in power and urged Park Chung-hee to continue to rule the country. Kim Jong-pil founded the Democratic Republican Party on 2 February 1963 and Park Chung-hee became a presidential candidate in the presidential elections. By that time, Yun Bo-seon, the second president after Rhee Syng-man during the first parliamentary regime from 1960 to 1961, had founded the opposition Civil Rule Party against the rule of the military on 18 January 1963. The Civil Rule Party emerged out of a coalition among the small opposition parties and factions: the Democratic Party, Liberal Democratic Party and New Democratic Party. However, fission and fusion among the opposition parties and factions continued before the presidential elections. Some factions under Park Sun-cheon and Hong Ik-pyo, who were the main political actors in the ruling Democratic Party under the Second Republic, defected from the opposition coalition party and founded the Democratic Party on 18 July. Some factions from the Democratic Party, New Justice Party and other small parties also built a coalition and founded the People's Party. The continuous fission and fusion of opposition parties and factions and their infighting over the presidential candidate accelerated the ruling party's decision to consolidate its organization and provided the party with the chance to win the presidential elections.

Park Chung-hee fought against Yun Bo-seon, who was the opposition party leader, and won 1.5 per cent more of the vote than Yun: Park gained 46.6 per cent and Yun gained 45.1 per cent of the vote. Park Chung-hee became the president in the Fifth Presidential Election on 15 October 1963. President Park's administration was defined by his commitment to economic development which would lead the country towards industrialization. This provided him with necessary political legitimacy and eventually led to the so-called 'miracle on the Han River',[6] economic success achieved under an authoritarian government.

While the military government pursued its power and continued to develop a state-led economic plan, the opposition parties and factions continued to merge and split. The Democratic Party and the Civil Rule Party merged and founded the People's Party on 3 May 1965, and Park Sun-cheon was elected as chairman of the party. Considering that the Civil Rule Party was much larger than the Democratic Party (the Civil Rule Party had 47 seats and the Democratic Party had 15 seats), internal conflict was inevitable. Park Sun-cheon won the party's internal election after successful negotiations with other small factions. However, dissatisfaction with Park Sun-cheon's leadership remained widespread within the party. In fact, two leaders – Yun Bo-seon from the Civil Rule Party and Park Sun-cheon – built yet another coalition to oppose the ruling party's policy on the normalization of relations between Korea and Japan.

The issue over the normalization of relations between Korea and Japan, however, constituted a blow to the legitimacy of Park's administration as it brought nationwide student protests onto the streets. The effort to normalize relations with Japan was the initiative of the US government. In 1961, before the military coup took place in South Korea, John F. Kennedy became US president and started to encourage Japan and Korea to normalize relations in order to boost the regional economy and security in Northeast Asia (Cumings 1997: 319). In

October 1961, Kim Jong-pil visited Japan for consultation on this issue and Park Chung-hee was invited by Prime Minister Ikeda Hayato the following month. In 1964 Kennedy sent personal letters to Park and Ikeda to urge normalization between the two countries. Kim Jong-pil visited Japan again to negotiate on Japanese 'reparations' over the 36 years of colonization and Japan offered grants and loans on condition of them not being calling 'reparations'.[7] The 'normalization of relations between Japan and Korea'[8] was finally accomplished in 1965 when Korea received a grant of US$300 million and loans of US$200 million.[9] However, Park's policy towards Japan undermined his legitimacy as the public did not follow him on the path of diplomatic recognition of Japan. Street protests mounted. Students joined the demonstrations against the normalization policy with Japan and the opposition parties built a coalition to fight against the authoritarian ruling party.

The opposition party suffered from internal conflict between Park Sun-cheon's faction and Yun Bo-seon's faction and other small factions. Some radical factions within the People's Party defected and founded the New Korea Party in March 1966. At the time the parties clashed over whether or not to send troops to Vietnam. To consolidate party cohesion and prepare for the Seventh General Election in June 1967, the New Korea Party started to negotiate with the People's Party and merged the two parties again, founding the New Democratic Party in February 1967. In contrast to the previous coalition, Yun Bo-seon was appointed as a presidential candidate and Park Sun-cheon was councillor of the party and the chairman of the party was Yu Jin-o from the Peoples' Party. Fission and fusion of the parties and factions originated from intra-elite struggles and conflict over power and positions. Without presenting any clear programme on how to run the country in the event of electoral success, the main issue at the time was to win the following general or presidential elections.

Along with the progress in economic development, demands for democratic reforms also increased. Compared to the rapid economic development, the political changes lagged far behind the people's desire for democracy. Despite economic progress, the authoritarian regime was not seen as legitimate. Within the authoritarian ruling structure, both former presidents Rhee and Park attempted to maintain a sort of life-long presidency, the former by manipulating electoral results and 'amending' constitutional laws, and the latter by declaring an emergency 'Yusin System'[10] in October 1972 after three terms of presidency.

Two events threatened the stability of Park's administration. First was US president Richard Nixon's decision (known as the 'Nixon doctrine') to withdraw American troops from Korea. The second reason lay in Park Chung-hee's marginal success in the Seventh Presidential Election in 1971 over Kim Dae-jung, the presidential candidate from the New Democratic Party. Park Chung-hee gained 53.2 per cent of the votes and Kim Dae-jung gained 45.3 per cent. Kim Dae-jung's support came from the non-elite segments of the population (not from the army either, but the masses who voted for Park), including the full support of Jeolla province. It is over the competition between Park Chung-hee, from the Gyeongsang province (or Yeongnam[11] region), and Kim Dae-jung, from the Jeolla province (or Honam region), that regionalism began to emerge as a significant electoral cleavage.[12] While Park Chung-hee achieved 34.8 per cent of the votes in the Honam region, Kim Dae-jung gained 63.3 per cent of votes in Honam. On the other hand, Park Chung-hee received 71.2 per cent in Yeongnam and Kim Dae-jung gained 27.9 per cent (Lee 1998: 32). Regionalism deepened further after democratization in 1987, especially during the Kim Dae-jung administration, as I will show later in Chapter 4. Despite a promising start to his political career, Kim Dae-jung had his fortunes overturned. He was kidnapped in 1973 when in exile in Japan and then detained under house arrest until 1979. Sentenced to death in 1980 following the Gwangju democratization movement, he was then exiled to the United States.

The Fourth Republic 1972–1979

President Park Chung-hee imposed martial law on 17 October 1972. The National Assembly was dismissed and the media were subject to strict censorship and all the universities were closed. This became known as the Yusin system, and this marked the start of Park Chung-hee's Fourth Republic. The rationale of the so-called Yusin constitution was to justify authoritarian rule for the purpose of economic development, political stability and military security until Korea had reached the same level of economic and political development as other advanced countries. The rhetoric of the Yusin Constitution lasted until 1979 when President Park was assassinated by Kim Jae-gyu, the chief of the Korea Central Intelligence Agency (hereafter KCIA). That year saw the largest demonstration among workers and students since 1970, which was mainly due to 'the second Oil shock' after the Iranian revolution, as the accompanying decrease in exports seriously damaged the domestic economy. By then, the Park Chung-hee administration had achieved economic development. However, the development was rather based on cheap labour. By then, labour unions were illegal and oppressed by the government. The labour movement was rather considered as having communist connections (Cumings 1997: 374). Apart from the early economic achievement, the country faced economic difficulties over 'oil shock' in the Middle East. Many factories were closed and hundreds of workers were laid off. The biggest wig trading company, YH, was also one of the companies that experienced hardship over exports and closed the factory, dismissing all factory workers. In August 1979, 187 female workers of the YH company who had been laid off went on strike and finally hid themselves at the opposition New Democratic Party's headquarters. In response, thousands of anti-riot police entered the building and brutally beat up the protestors, legislators, journalists, staff of the headquarters, including female workers. Eventually one of the union leaders, Kim Kyeong-suk, was killed by the anti-riot police. This became known as the 'YH incident' and triggered nationwide demonstrations, especially in Busan and Masan in Gyeongsang province in October. When the factory strikers had asked for help from the opposition party leader, Kim Young-sam, he had allowed them to hide from the riot police in the New Democratic Party headquarters. This gave

Kim Young-sam a chance to gain more popular support. Before the YH incident occurred, many workers, especially women workers, actively learned about their labour rights. The Urban Industrial Mission (UIM),[13] led by a Methodist missionary, played a major role in inspiring the labour movement and also led to peaceful demonstrations against the Yusin system in 1973 (Cumings 1997: 371). In the previous year, a female minister who worked at a factory for two decades and had encouraged the female workers to found a women's labour union was arrested as she was said to have connections with communists (ibid.: 372). This is another case where the government used the National Security Law and the Anti-Communist Law[14] as a way to get rid of political opponents. This is also another reason why labour unions could not actively work or even found a political party, and were effectively blocked from political activities. If there were any, most of the activists were arrested as 'Leftists' and accused of connections with the North under the National Security Law. Cumings (ibid.: 370) argues, however, that the mass labour movements were not led by opposition party leader Kim Dae-jung but 'labor protest and unionization thus arose largely outside the established political system'. Although Kim Young-sam helped the female workers to hide at the headquarters of the New Democratic Party, the union movement was not mobilized by the political opposition leaders. This also well illustrates why and how the elites could easily exclude the unions from their negotiations among the political leaders after democratization was achieved in 1987. As Choi Jang-jip (2002) argues, nationwide demonstrations by millions of workers, students and civilians urged the authoritarian government to open up towards democracy; however, democratization itself was achieved by the elites, the top, not by the ordinary people, the bottom.

After the YH incident, the media, which were under strict government censorship, alleged that the Urban Industrial Mission (UIM) was connected to North Korea. The Carter administration did not support Park's regime and denounced it as 'brutal and excessive' (ibid.: 374). As mentioned earlier, the YH incident influenced the uprisings in Busan and Masan in October 1979. President Park Chung-hee suggested the firmer repression of the demonstrators and the unions but this led his close aide to murder him over conflicts regarding the solution to the massive urban protests including students and labourers in Busan and Masan (this came to be known as the 'Bu-Ma democratization movement'[15]).

The Fifth Republic 1980–1987

Major General Chun Doo-hwan was in charge of investigating the President Park assassination and this gave him a chance to grab power. With his military academy fellow Roh Tae-woo, Chun took part in a military rebellion or coup on 12 December 1979. The so-called '12.12 *Sate* (event or incident)' started with the arrest of 36 officers including Cheong Sung-hwa, who was the chief of staff in the ROK army headquarters (Cumings 1997: 375). Chun's effort to grab power continued with the elimination of opposition politicians and scholars who fought for the introduction of democratic reforms. The Anti-Communist Law and National Security Law, which had been in place since the First Republic, still played a major role in legitimating the government in its arrest of dissidents on the basis of perceived threats to national security.

Under the short presidency of Choi Kyu-ha the following year, students, scholars and opposition politicians once again started to gather on the streets demanding the introduction of democratic reforms. General Chun tried to complete his military coup on 17 May 1980 by declaring martial law: as happened under the martial law of 1972, universities were closed again, drastically restricting political activities, the legislature was dissolved and the media remained under strict censorship. Massive arrests of political opponents followed.

The following day, hundreds of people in Gwangju went on demonstrations against the introduction of martial law, and Chun sent special troops to repress the demonstrators. The tragic outcome became known as the '5.18 Gwangju massacre' which resulted in about 3,586 total victims, including 207 civilian deaths in Gwangju on 18 May.[16] By then Kim Dae-jung was also arrested and sentenced to death, but later the sentence was changed to a life sentence as the US government advised Chun's administration not to execute him. Kim Jong-pil who was a core member of President Park Chung-hee's government was exiled to the United States. Nearly 15 years later, under Kim Young-sam's government, this tragedy led to two former presidents, Chun Doo-hwan and Roh Tae-woo, being jailed for their role in suppressing the Gwangju rebellion and helping Chun take power. This was done in the name of 'setting history right' based on the popular will of the people.

After the military coup, General Chun Doo-hwan became president in February 1981, thereby signalling the start of the Fifth Republic. Lee Gap-yun (1998: 78) indicates that the Bu-Ma and the 5.16 Gwangju democratization movements were crucial to the emergence of the Fifth Republic. Thousands of casualties from the demonstration left sorrow and anger in the hearts of the citizens of Gwangju and many scholars see this as another factor triggering strong regionalism in Jeolla province (Honam region). Choi Jang-jip argues that:

> regionalism is not a conflict between Honam and Yeongnam citizens. It is rather a problem of citizens in Honam: first they see themselves marginalized from elite recruitment during the various authoritarian governments, second they feel a strong relationship with Kim Dae-jung whom they hoped would bring an end to their political marginalization and third collective experience over the 5.18 Gwangju demonstration and its repression by the government.
>
> (Choi 2002: 106)

Kim Dae-jung was the most well-known leader the Honam region produced under the authoritarian governments and he was also a victim of systematic oppression under authoritarian rule such as the disastrous experience of exile to Japan, kidnap in Japan, being run over by a truck, enduring a death sentence[17] due to the National Security Law and later exile to the US. The citizens from

The formation of the Korean party system 27

Honam identified their struggle against alienation with their leader Kim Dae-jung who had been equally oppressed by the authoritarian governments (Lee 1998: 109).

As Chun was also from the Gyeongsang province, this also signalled the rise of the Gyeongsang province in national politics, often known in popular usage as the 'T-K faction'.[18] Taegu is the capital of North Gyeongsang province and Chun Doo-hwan was originally from Taegu. On the other hand, Park Chung-hee was from the southern part of the South Gyeongsang province. They both are assumed to have privileged the development of the Gyeongsang province which also turned into a political privilege in terms of the distribution of power and economic benefits as well as elite recruitment. This led to an increase in inter-regional tensions, especially with Jeolla province, as the inequality in the distribution of resources and wealth deepened. The tensions between these two regions were reflected at the electoral level, and the national vote split along regional cleavages.

However, whether or not the origins of the regional conflict lie in unequal development between the East and the West is a matter of controversy among scholars. Considering that most economic and political resources are concentrated in Seoul, a centre–periphery relations prism may appear a more suitable way of looking at the power struggle. In fact, Henderson (1968) points out that the concentration of resources in Seoul has a long history from the Joseon Dynasty (by then it was called *Hanyang*), arguing that Seoul is not just a big city but is 'South Korea itself' (it often used to be referred to as the 'Seoul Republic'). Lee (1998) argues that Jeolla province is not the only region which is less developed compared to Seoul, located in Gyeonggi province. Gangwon and Chungcheong provinces were not industrialized in the process of development either. Many people from the Honam region were recruited to executive positions in the administration and public sector after the 1980s; therefore, elite recruitment did not appear as a politically salient issue. Rather, regionalism deepened after the 5.16 Gwangju uprising in 1980 and electoral competitions between the regional leaders (Lee 1998: 59).

Under Chun's administration, one of the characteristics of the party system was that the government created ad hoc opposition parties such as the Democratic Korean Party, the Democratic Society Party (socialist party) and the Korea People's Party. The Chun regime planned to take advantage of the continuous fragmentation among the opposition parties and factions. The government planned to break up the opposition parties into factions and then support them in founding new political parties. The Chun administration released many former opposition politicians from political oppression and many of them were offered positions in the newly created opposition party by members of the KCIA. This shows the elite's attitude towards the parties. The parties created or supported by the government may certainly enjoy power and share interests, but not the power they can pose against the government. While the Chun administration supported the creation of opposition parties, the regime also founded the ruling Democratic Justice Party. It was in 1985 that the 'real' opposition party could finally be founded when Kim Young-sam and Kim Dae-jung returned to active political life. The two opposition leaders built a coalition with other opposition political activists and founded the New Korea Democratic Party in December 1984. In the Twelfth General Election in February 1985, the New Korea Democratic Party gained 67 seats in the legislature and became the second largest party, and the ruling Democratic Justice Party gained 148 seats and remained the majority party. The victory of the opposition party spurred severe criticism of the authoritarian government and demands for democratic change of the political system. The government was also pressed to release the political opponents held in prison and the opposition party expanded the democratization movement against the authoritarian government.

The result of rapid economic development by authoritarian governments increased demand for democracy from civil movements and brought the regime to an end in what many scholars have called 'a crisis of success' (Diamond and Kim 2000; Im 1997; Kim 2001) in Korean politics.[19] As authoritarian governments tend to lack legitimacy in the early stages of their rule, Chun's government sought to boost economic development through a state-led plan. Economic development brought about by the authoritarian government provided citizens with higher education and a relatively wealthy lifestyle. In the economic sector *Jaebeol* developed their business in the import and export industry. Hence, once-state-driven economic development no longer seemed to need state guidance or interference, but demanded deregulation and more freedom of the market. By the time Chun Doo-hwan achieved 'world beating economic growth (at least after 1983)' (Cumings 1997: 380), civil-society-led nationwide demonstrations forced the demise of the Chun presidency and the government, itself unstable and weak.

The Chun government had two choices as to how to deal with this nationwide uproar. Similarly to what had already happened in May 1980 (with the civil movement in Gwangju), Chun could either send troops to suppress the demonstrators or compromise and meet their demands. The US administration refused to send troops against the crowd (Kim 2001: 222). As the United States had (and has) control over troops in South Korea, the Chun administration did not have any other option. Under the Carter presidency, the US remained silent on the Gwangju massacre and this severely damaged Carter's human rights agenda and the administration's image. As Cumings (1997: 378) argues, this contributed to his electoral defeat in the next presidential elections. Therefore the only option the Chun government had was to yield to popular demands. As a gesture of compromise, the presidential candidate from Chun's government, Roh Tae-woo, announced the so-called '6.29 democratization declaration' on 29 June 1987 basically accepting fair and free presidential elections.

This signals the start of the democratization era in Korea. Scholars such as Choi Jang-jip and Yun Sang-chul saw in the emergence of the civil movement in June a revolutionary event, a cross-regional and cross-class popular movement which had finally gained momentum against the state power and dominant ruling class of modern political history in Korea (Jeong 1997: 286).

The Korean party system during the period of democratic consolidation (1988–1997)

The '6.29 declaration' brought key changes to the constitution and introduced direct presidential elections, fair and free electoral competition, respect for basic civil rights, improved media freedom and the release of key opposition politicians, including Kim Dae-jung, previously banned from any political activities. When South Korea experienced the first, direct democratic presidential elections in 1987, most citizens and politicians assumed that South Korea had achieved full-fledged democracy. Diamond and Kim (2000: 70) see this as another instance of Korea's 'crisis of success'. Many people in South Korea seem to hold a procedural conception of democracy: electoral democracy seems to be viewed as an accomplishment in itself, without further questions regarding economic or social democracy, let alone the equality of distribution or quality of life. Many, among scholars, politicians and the public, looked content with free and fair elections and no longer seemed to long for further measures of social and economic inclusion.

In the previous section, I briefly discussed the history of post-war Korean politics. As mentioned earlier, the demise of authoritarian rule led to the emergence of a series of questions as to the nature of the party system that arose on its ashes, most notably the fact that large opposition parties appeared to undermine governability. In this section I discuss how the previous governments struggled to avoid large opposition in the legislature within the under-developed party system.

The under-development of the party system

When democratization occurs as a top-down rather than as a bottom-up process, it tends to reflect the interests of the ruling class. This may in the end hinder democratic consolidation. As O'Donnell (1994) notes, when revolution is carried out from the top (not from the bottom), it can be more frequently carried out without violence. However, there seems to be barriers to completing the entire democratic transition. As a result of the compromise, the ruling elites are able to secure their interests (e.g. self-preservation). As mentioned earlier, Choi Jang-jip (1996: 203–204) points out that the most distinctive characteristics of Korean politics lie in the system of representation, in other words *the under-development of the party system*.

Choi underlines that this is due to the strongly developed state under authoritarian governments. The low development of the party system means that there is a distance between 'civil society' and 'the state or political society'. When political society is independent of civil society, the ruling elites tend to be more concerned with their own interests rather than in representing public interests and being accountable for their political activities. Considering that democracy entails not only an electoral, but also a representative function, South Korea achieved electoral democracy but failed in representing the interests and demands of the society and the people.

The party system in South Korea shows that parties have very weak popular support at the grassroots level, reflecting a crisis of participation by the people. Korean democratization has been achieved 'from above' only among the political elites excluding the labour unions or ordinary civil representatives, even though the people's demonstration on the street was the trigger that moved the authoritarian government towards democracy. Choi explains this as 'passive revolution' as conceptualized by Gramsci (1971) or 'revolution from above' by Barrington Moore (1966, cited in Choi 1996: 204). Unlike the bourgeois revolutions in Western Europe (the UK, France), when the ruling elite does not have strong hegemony, these elites tend to transform opposition politicians to support the ruling party through compromise or exchange of interests sub rosa in the absence of a bourgeoisie or middle-class. This reminds us of Barrington Moore's catchphrase (1966): 'No bourgeois. No democracy!' To secure their hegemony, the ruling elites develop the practice of transformism, a major political characteristic of Italy. Choi (1996: 206) applies this concept[20] to explain Roh's effort to secure power with the aid of opposition parties.

The Sixth Republic and the eve of democratization 1988–1992

Roh Tae-woo succeeded in the presidential elections in December 1987, and practically continued military rule despite claiming to be 'a man of the street' or an 'ordinary man'. Opposition politicians Kim Dae-jung and Kim Young-sam were severely blamed for losing the chance of shifting power from the authoritarian government to the civilian one due to their personal rivalry. When Kim Dae-jung was released and gained the right to re-enter political life after the 6.29 declaration, he was in the same party as Kim Young-sam and announced he would not take part in the electoral competition in order to provide a single candidate from the biggest opposition party (by then the New Democratic Party) to compete with the ruling party.

However, both were garnering high support from their own respective home regions: Kim Dae-jung from Honam and Kim Young-sam from Yeongnam. Though the two Kims cooperated under the authoritarian governments to achieve democracy, rivalry between the two leaders dates back to the late 1960s. When both were members of the opposition, the New Democratic Party, Kim Young-sam did not support Kim Dae-jung positioning himself to become the secretary general of the party in 1968. Competition between the two became even more severe when they competed within the party to be a candidate for the presidential election in 1971. For the first internal election of the party, Kim Young-sam won 421 votes and Kim Dae-jung 382, although there were 82 invalid votes out of 885 total votes cast.

To be a candidate, the person needed to gain over 50 per cent of the total votes. In the second intra-party election, Kim Dae-jung gained 458 votes and Kim Young-sam gained 410 votes. This is because Kim Dae-jung succeeded in compromising with people who previously supported another potential candidate, Lee Cheol-seung. When Lee Cheol-seung decided not to take part in the internal (primary) election to be a candidate for presidential elections, Kim Dae-jung gained more votes from those who were originally supporting Lee Cheol-seung. With these extra votes, Kim Dae-jung won the primary election against Kim Young-sam to be a candidate for the presidential elections within the party.

In the following presidential election, Kim Dae-jung competed with President Park Chung-hee. Kim Dae-jung lost the presidential elections, gaining only 43.6 per cent of the votes and Park Chung-hee gained 51.2 per cent (Kim 1994a: 58). After then, Kim Dae-jung and Kim Young-sam suffered from political repression under authoritarian regimes, and later became charismatic opposition leaders fighting together against anti-democratic regimes. Therefore, the conflict between the two over power was nothing new by then and could also be strategically used by other competing parties. In fact, the ruling party seemed to enjoy seeing the competition between the two.

One of the ruling party's strategies to hinder integration of the opposition party – especially between the two Kims – appeared when the politicians took part in a discussion over changing the constitution after the 6.29 declaration (Kim 2001: 226–227). The ruling and opposition parties had different opinions with regard to constitutional reforms. For example, when they finally agreed to set five years as the term for the presidency, the next issue consisted of introducing the vice-presidency. This meant that, should the opposition New Democratic Party win the election, the two Kims would share the posts of president and vice-president in the first term and then switch roles in the following election. This new institution could have helped the opposition party integrate more than before. Had the two integrated within the party and succeeded in the election with a presidential and vice-presidential institution, the party system in South Korea would have presumably been different, and a new social cleavage rather than regionalism might well have emerged. On the other hand, as a vice-presidential system was not introduced, the two Kims' struggle over becoming the presidential candidate became a foregone conclusion. The conflict between the two Kims was just what the ruling party wanted in order to achieve the continuance of their own power and they were very successful in this strategy.

The largest opposition party (the New Democratic Party) finally imploded when Kim Dae-jung left and founded a new party called the Peace Democratic Party, while Kim Young-sam later founded the Unification Democratic Party in 1987. Integration of the opposition parties proved difficult as the two Kims' apparent ambition to gain power prevented them from compromise and negotiation. By this time, Kim Jong-pil, who also after the 6.29 declaration founded a party called the New Democratic Republican Party, became a presidential candidate. The emergence of four presidential candidates acted as a catalyst for voting behaviour to be drawn along the lines of strong regional cleavages: Roh Tae-woo from North Gyeongsang, Kim Young-sam from South Gyeongsang, Kim Dae-jung from Jeolla and Kim Jong-pil from Chungcheong.

Before the 6.29 declaration, voting behaviour exhibited a democratic versus anti-democratic or authoritarian cleavage, also called *Yeochonyado* (與村若都), overlapping with the urban/rural one. The more educated urban population tended to vote for the opposition party (demanding democracy), whereas the less educated people from the rural areas showed support for the ruling party (Kim 2001: 42). The ruling party tried to influence voting behaviour in the rural areas by supplying financial support during the electoral campaign. After democratization, the social cleavages reflecting the democratic versus anti-democratic division disappeared, as people believed that democratization had been achieved in 1987. In the meantime, voting behaviour was divided along regional lines. Many scholars such as Choi Jang-jip (1997) and Lee Gap-yun (1998) noted that this new phenomenon was derived from the party leaders in the period of democratization. Kim Dae-jung believed that he lost the presidential elections as a result of unfair electoral competition under the authoritarian government in 1970, when he competed with former president Park Chung-hee who had strong support from his hometown regions due to his decades-long political campaigning against the authoritarian government.

Kim Young-sam also showed charismatic leadership as an opposition party leader. Both at times cooperated in demanding democracy against the authoritarian regime, and at times competed at elections, although many believe it would have been easier to defeat the authoritarian government in elections if opposition party leaders had cooperated with each other. Instead, the two opposition leaders decided to go into the presidential elections separately. Lee (1998: 114–117), however, argues that this was not a rational choice in terms of maximizing power for the New Democratic Party itself. Although the personal popularity of each candidate was considerable, it was not large enough to defeat the ruling party. In addition, they did not recognize that a majority of the people preferred stability over sudden change – and also, most Korean voters showed a continuous support for the ideologically conservative right. Political parties aim at magnifying political power in the parliament or eventually winning office. Providing that the two Kims cooperated within the party rather than defecting from it, the opposition New Democratic Party could have won the presidential elections considering Roh Tae-woo gained only one-third of the votes and won office. If cooperation between the two Kims had led to electoral victory and to a power-sharing agreement, they could have succeeded one another in the post. That this did not happen shows how personalized and factionalized the opposition party was.

In fact this factionalism among the opposition party leaders did not do them any good in their competition with the authoritarian ruling party, considering the latter's relatively stronger degree of institutionalization following decades of ruling experience and sufficient financial support from the government and other funding sources such as the *Jaebeols*. In terms of candidate recruitment for parliamentary election, the ruling party could also rely on more highly qualified candidates than the opposition parties. The opposition parties continuously founded and dissolved parties according to the circumstances. Moreover, the parties were mostly shaped not by ideology or grassroots support but by the leaders, as I show in Chapters 3, 4, 5 and 6. It is understandable that under authoritarian rule the opposition parties are less organized and exhibited a lower degree of institutionalization, in terms of party members or electoral candidate recruitment and financial support. As a result of struggles over power among the party leaders, four leaders were competing in presidential elections: Roh Tae-woo from North Gyeongsang province, Kim Young-sam from South Gyeongsang province, Kim Dae-jung from Jeolla and Kim Jong-pil from Chungcheong province.

Overall, Roh Tae-woo won the elections with 33.5 per cent of the total votes, and 61.5 per cent out of 35.5 per cent of the votes he gained were from his native North Gyeongsang province. Kim Dae-jung gained 27.4 per cent, and 86.9 per cent of his vote was from Jeolla. Kim Young-sam gained 27.1 per cent, and 54.1 per cent of the total votes he gained came from South Gyeongsang province. Kim Jong-pil also gained 11.5 per cent at the presidential elections, and he gained 30.9 per cent from Chungcheong out of the total votes he gained (Lee 1998: 90). This was the first clear division of regional votes and these new social cleavages in the presidential and parliamentary elections continued until the very recent elections in 2003. Many believe regionalism has a long history and the cleavage lines in Korea can be described as shown in Table 2.1.

Voting behaviour along regional lines, however, has dramatically increased since democratization. Lee Gap-yun (1998: 83) argues that the two opposition party leaders influenced voters to mobilize based on their regional ties. As the two share a very similar background in terms of political careers, ideology and political platform, the only difference for the voters to notice would lie in the candidates' different regional origins. That is why strong regional cleavages started to develop after democratization as the two played important roles in the post-democratization era. It is often called the 'three Kims era' (from 1990 to 2002), as this included Kim Jong-pil, who also played a pivotal role within the other two's competition after democratization of the party system.

Looking at the presidential elections result in the Thirteenth Presidential Elections in 1987, Roh Tae-woo gained 34.4 per cent of the votes from Gyeonggi province (Seoul lies in the centre of the province) and Kim Young-sam gained 28.7 per cent, Kim Dae-jung gained 28.4 per cent and Kim Jong-pil gained 8.4

Table 2.1 Regional cleavage in Korea

The conservatives	The progressives
Strong vote base in Gyeongsang region	Strong vote base in Jeolla region
Industrial areas	Agricultural areas
Support for Park Chung-hee, Kim Young-sam, Lee Myung-bak: anti-communism/ economic growth centred/low taxation	Strong support for Kim Dae-jung/Roh Moo-hyun: support for abolishing National Security Law/North Korean aid/high taxation/equal distribution
Rich	Poor
Central in power	Peripheral in power

Source: author.

per cent. Therefore this does not reflect much regionalism unless public opinion research in Gyeonggi province is examined. However, the regional support from the party leaders' hometowns shows a clear division. Roh Tae-woo gained 68.1 per cent of votes from North Gyeongsang province, Kim Young-sam gained 53.7 per cent from South Gyeongsang province, Kim Dae-jung 88.4 per cent from Jeolla province and Kim Jong-pil 34.6 per cent from Chungcheong province (see Table 2.2).

Lee (1998: 14) notes that the party system in the 'three Kims era' 'deteriorated' as personalized factions rather than parties grew in importance. During that period, party members joined and left political parties following the party leaders' decisions. This might be ascribed to the Confucian culture embedded in Korean society, as also examined elsewhere in this book (Chapters 3, 4, 5 and 6). Party members followed their leaders when they built coalitions or defected from their parties. Parties are divided into factional groupings by their high schools, universities or regional or family ties, which also produced so-called 'crony capitalism'. Most of the recruitment for the electoral candidates was through the regional or alumni ties, personal or family connections.

Furthermore, candidates were not approved by the ordinary party members through any democratic process (bottom-up) but by the party leaders (top-down). For any candidate willing to take part in the electoral competition, it appeared a rational choice to follow their party leaders. It is obvious the parties under the 'three Kims era' were more personalized and less organized internally. Considering Korean history, democracy was achieved more rapidly and in a relatively bloodless way compared to the longer and more tortuous democratizing process in the West. Scholars like Choi Jang-jip argue that this is due to what they define as 'premature' democracy. Electoral democracy was achieved through popular demands and demonstrations, though the democratization process barely moved beyond that. If factional party politics becomes a goal in itself played out by political elites struggling over power, this raises questions over the truly democratic nature of the whole process, no matter how democratically the elites were elected. Choi Jang-jip (2002: 120) argues that the opposition parties ultimately showed a very low level of organization as the parties became personalized factions representing small numbers of elites and their followers' interests. When the opposition parties took office after democratization in 1992 and 1997, it appeared to be a good moment to consolidate democracy. In fact the government failed to bridge the various gaps and cleavages existing in society.

Coalition politics after democratization – the grand conservative coalition in 1990

Since the start of the democratization process, coalition-building was a constant phenomenon in every presidential election and a fundamental part of political and party life in Korea. When Roh Tae-woo won the presidential election with a mere 36.6 per cent of support – raising a fundamental problem of legitimacy (as he was seen as the continuation of authoritarian rule having played an important

Table 2.2 Electoral votes from the presidential elections

Presidential elections	Presidential candidates	Province Gyeonggi	Chungcheong	Jeolla	Gyeongsang (North)	Gyeongsang (South)	Gangwon	Jeju	Total
Thirteenth (1987)	Roh Tae-woo	34.4	33.1	9.9	68.1	36.6	59.3	49.8	38.6
	Kim Young-sam	28.7	20.1	1.2	26.6	53.7	26.1	26.8	28.0
	Kim Dae-jung	28.4	8.9	88.4	2.5	6.9	8.8	18.6	27.1
	Kim Jong-pil	8.4	34.6	0.5	2.4	2.6	5.4	4.5	8.1
Fourteenth (1992)	Kim Young-sam	36.0	36.2	4.2	61.6	72.1	40.8	15.2	42.0
	Kim Dae-jung	34.8	27.3	91.0	8.7	10.8	15.2	32.9	33.8
	Chung Ju-young	19.8	23.8	2.3	17.0	8.8	33.5	15.4	16.3

Source: adapted from Lee (1998: 32).

role in the military coup in support of Chun Doo-hwan) – his administration appeared weak from the very outset. In the following parliamentary elections Roh's ruling party gained even less support than in the presidential elections. The ruling party still remained the biggest party, gaining 125 seats out of a total of 299 (34.0 per cent of the total votes) on 26 April 1988, in the Thirteenth General Election. Therefore the ruling party was confronted with the largest opposition ever in the modern history of South Korea.

For a minority government facing a large opposition party, implementing policies or running the government is obviously a complicated matter. When Roh Tae-woo appointed the chief judiciary of the Supreme Court, the opposition disagreed with his appointment, so Roh's aim of gaining an important post on his side was disrupted. The opposition hindered effective and stable governability as the government hardly gained any support within the National Assembly. In fact, the way to try to pass on Roh Tae-woo's presidential seat to the following leader and minimize struggles over his mode of governability lay in building a coalition with the other opposition parties.

In the middle of 1988, the ruling party already started to hint at the necessity of reorganizing the party system. Even Kim Jong-pil, one of the leaders of the opposition parties, referred to such a necessity in terms of a 'grand conservative coalition' within a conservative versus progressive ideological spectrum (Kim 1994a: 52). The ruling party sought many possibilities for building a coalition with the other parties. As Kim HeeMin (ibid.: 52–53) observes, the ruling Democratic Justice Party was on the right of the ideological spectrum, whereas the Peace Democratic Party was positioned on the progressive or centre-left of the political spectrum. Kim Young-sam's party (UDP) remained on the right between the PDP and the DJP, but unlike the two Democratic Justice Party and New Democratic Republic Party, the Unification Democratic Party had an anti-authoritarian background.

In the presidential elections, Kim Young-sam gained 28 per cent of the vote while Kim Dae-Jung won 27 per cent. However his party gained even less support from the parliamentary election – 23.8 per cent – than in the presidential elections. Here it is worthwhile to pay attention to the vote distribution. In terms of voting rates, Kim Young-sam's party, the Unification Democratic Party, gained 23.8 per cent and Kim Dae Jung's party, the Peace Democratic Party, gained 19.3 per cent in the Thirteenth General Election in April 1988. This means that the Unification Democratic Party gained more support in terms of number of votes. However, when the seat distribution is split by provinces, the actual weight of each vote varies greatly. One single vote in the rural areas is worth more than a single vote in Seoul or any other large urban centre. This is explained in detail in Chapter 4. Considering that the Peace Democratic Party has a very strong support base in the rural areas of the Jeolla province, the number of seats gained was more than the Unification Democratic Party actually garnered in terms of votes. So, Kim Dae-jung's party eventually won 70 seats in the National Assembly, whereas Kim Young-sam's party gained only 59 seats. Kim HeeMin (1997) saw the 1990 party merger as an example of a minimal winning coalition. According to Riker's (1962) minimal winning coalition theory, if any of the members defected from the coalition, the winning status would be lost. The party coalition did not seem to collapse due to the changing party system but rather more due to internal conflicts of interest. This will be discussed when I look at why and how the coalition collapsed in 1995 in a later section along with the question of whether all of the party leaders were interested in changing the constitution.

On the other hand, the possibility of forming a coalition between the Democratic Justice Party and the Peace Democratic Party to overcome regional conflicts was also considered. However, this did not seem to work, as the rest of the parties were keener on reorganizing the party system. Kim Young-ho (2001: 249) explains the three parties' merger as a result of structural factors. First there appeared to be no ideological difference in the parties' policies. Even though the Peace Democratic Party was often recognized as progressive compared to the other three parties, all political parties stood on the right-wing of the ideological spectrum in South Korea. This was due to the use of anti-communist rhetoric after the Korean War and the Cold War period, where North Korea embodied the 'existential threat' to the South (I will return to this in Chapter 5). By then, most of the people were terrified by any chance of war again on the peninsula as they all suffered from post-war starvation and poverty. In particular, people who had lost all their property from the land reform in North Korea and moved to South Korea held strong anti-communist views and remained very conservative-oriented. The Anti-Communist Law and the National Security Law were another reason accounting for the convergence of ideology to the right. Authoritarian governments took advantage of these laws to marginalize political dissidents and, as a result, many among the progressive or communist social activists saw their liberties restricted.

At the elite level, party mergers would not create any ideological conflict. Korean parties are commonly regarded as catch-all parties. Kim Young-ho (2001) argues that coalitions were built not out of ideological or policy reasons, but for the self-interest of elite groups. Korean parties rely on the loyalty of their supporters and the *personal* relationship between the party elite and voters; thus they have a very flexible voting base. In other words, parties are tools of a narrow elite group and these (parties) are formally short-lived, though they tend to revive under a new name along with the very same leaders. Most parties after democratization were new(ly branded) and did not enjoy a strong and wide base of support, but relied on regional support mobilized by the leaders. This means that the parties would not wish to risk being penalized by the supporters in the following election. Even if the leaders merged their parties into a single party, the elites would still retain their personal supporters through their own charisma and personal connections in their own native regions. In addition, all party leaders were monopolizing power in terms of control of funding, financial aid, candidate appointments and so on. This is why the decision for party merger was swiftly agreed among the three party leaders in a very secretive way.

As already noted, Roh Tae-woo faced mounting challenges to his government from the opposition parties from the very start of his presidency. The ruling party faced the request from the public to admit its involvement in, and responsibility for, the Fifth Republic's military coup and the 5.18 Gwangju uprising. In fact, at the time Roh had taken an active part in the coup and in the brutal repression of the Gwang-ju democratization movement. Roh did not seem to have many alternatives but to give in and join/offer coalitions or mergers with the opposition parties. Roh needed to secure his future after his presidency as he realized he may have to follow his predecessors into exile or worse: Rhee Syngman was exiled to Hawaii, Park Chung-hee was assassinated and Chun Doo-hwan was by then kept in a temple called 'Baekdam-sa' (temple). Therefore handing over ruling power to his successor was a crucial issue to Roh, for very personal reasons.

In order to do so, the ruling party planned to change the regime into a parliamentary system. They believed that a bicameral parliamentary system would secure power for the ruling party regardless of the outcome of the presidential elections. What politicians and scholars seemed to overlook, though, was that in a parliamentary system a minority government also often faces large opposition parties. Effective and stable governability does not only depend on the size of the government, but on many other factors such as leadership, the political culture regarding compromise and negotiation, and the level of institutionalization, as shown in the next chapter. Many among the political elites were clinging to the size of the government after democratization and changed party through frequent fission and fusion. The ruling party essentially found a tool (fission and fusion) that would allow it to obtain the two-thirds of parliamentary seats necessary to change the constitution. In the Twelfth General Election in 1985, the opposition New Democratic Party gained 29.3 per cent of the total votes while the ruling party gained 35.2 per cent. The ruling party was able to subjugate most of the opposition parties except the New Democratic Party during the period of Chun's government. The Chun government indirectly created opposition parties such as the Democratic Korea Party and the Korea People's Party and those opposition parties were very loyal to the ruling party but not the New Democratic Party. When public opinion and the opposition New Democratic Party urged the government to change the indirect presidential electoral system into a direct system, the Chun government suggested changing it into a parliamentary system as a gesture of compromise. Since then, the public seems to favour a presidential system. By then, Kim Dae-jung and Kim Young-sam did not support the introduction of the parliamentary system as they both expected to win in a direct presidential election.

On the other hand, Kim Jong-pil preferred a parliamentary system. It was believed that under a parliamentary system the ruling party would not face a big opposition and this would also relax the regional cleavages. Compared to the presidential elections, the general elections showed a less pronounced regional cleavage as candidates from the same region would compete with each other. This means voters would not cling to the voter's hometown background, but to their interests, beliefs, agenda or assessment of the incumbent's political performance. The president would not have to be elected directly under the parliamentary system as long as his party gained the largest number of seats in

The formation of the Korean party system 39

the parliamentary elections. The main problem people seemed to overlook with parliamentary systems is that they also tend to produce minority governments. In the parliamentary system the largest party wins office. To win office, building coalitions has been a very common strategy in Western Europe. However, some parties have opted for ruling from a minority position rather than building a coalition, so as to avoid potential internal conflicts of interest among the coalition members. In the West European parliamentary system, one main reason why politicians pursue the majority status is to survive confidence votes after winning office. Should the party lose a vote of confidence, the party would be left with no other option but to leave office.

Kim Young-sam agreed to the secret deal concerning the adoption of a parliamentary system. One of the reasons why he seemed to support the agreement lay in his assumption that it would open the way for him to become the ruling party's natural candidate for the following presidential elections. Although coalition-building was widely unpopular due to continuous party merges and splits, it has played a positive role too. In fact, it gradually forced the military regime to political concessions through bargaining and compromise. The ruling Democratic Justice Party merged with two opposition parties: the Unification Democratic Party led by Kim Young-sam and the New Democratic Republican Party led by Kim Jong-pil on 22 January 1990. The three merged parties later renamed themselves as the Democratic Liberal Party and proposed that the new party would pursue structural reform policies to end factional conflicts.

Conflicts of interest within the coalition party and with the opposition

After the merger, the party experienced more problems than perhaps originally envisaged. The coalition party suffered from the presence of large opposition parties and also a series of internal conflicts of interest among the party leaders and members of their respective factions. Compromise and negotiation among the opposition parties and ruling party were abruptly interrupted and the opposition boycotted whatever legislative initiative the ruling party tried to pass. When the ruling party finally passed 26 National Assembly regulations without the opposition Peace Democratic Party's attendance at the assembly on 14 June 1990, all of the opposition party members resigned and started to integrate into the dissident movement fighting against the ruling party outside of the parliamentary system. The National Assembly was run by only the coalition ruling parties for 70 days out of the total 100 days of the National Assembly term. When the opposition party returned to the National Assembly, the meetings were held over only 20 days to quickly complete the outstanding business.

In the meantime, internal conflicts within the coalition party were exposed when the media revealed the secret agreement behind the party merger. The document laying out the agreements contained proposals for changing the presidential system to a parliamentary system, and changing the constitutional law was agreed to be carried out within a year (*Donga Ilbo*, 30 October 1990). When the content of the secret agreement was made public, Kim Young-sam refused to work in his parliamentary office as a representative of the party and requested that President Roh stop the process of revising the constitution in order to establish a bicameral parliamentary system. Soon the three factions which had originated from the previous three parties before the parties' merger started to blame each other over this issue. Kim Jong-pil's New Democratic Republican faction[21] blamed Kim Young-sam for not keeping his word on the agreement and Roh Tae-woo's Democratic Justice faction for Kim Young-sam's irresponsible attitude as a representative of the party. Kim Young-sam accused the Roh government of revealing the secret pact among the three leaders. From the beginning of the party merger, Kim Young-sam did not evince enthusiasm for constitutional revision, for turning Korea into a parliamentary system. Nevertheless, when the three leaders met for discussions, Kim Young-sam showed a more evident interest in becoming the presidential candidate.

This was due to the ruling party's ambiguous approach towards the two Kims with regard to the party merger. On the one hand, Roh allegedly approached Kim Jong-pil and promised he would revise the constitution in favour of a parliamentary system. Kim Jong-pil once said that he did not even know Kim Young-sam would also join the coalition. On the other hand, Roh also approached Kim Young-sam to assure him that Kim would be the next candidate for the ruling party at the following presidential elections (*Donga Ilbo*, 7 November 1990). He may have thought that once his position as a leader had been secured, a parliamentary system would be acceptable. For the Democratic Justice faction, revising the constitution in order to introduce a parliamentary system was the main rationale for continuing its position within the coalition, a similar position to the New Democratic Republican faction.

In the end, Kim Young-sam and his followers within the Unification Democratic faction decided not to support the introduction of a parliamentary system. The opposition parties believed that changing to a parliamentary system was part of an authoritarian conspiracy to preserve their ruling status following the end of the Chun administration. The most crucial fact is that adopting a parliamentary system did not gain wide support, either from the people or from the opposition parties. That is why the agreement was written in a secretive way on 6 May 1990. The two factions – Democratic Justice and New Democratic Republican – may have thought this would accelerate the process of changing the constitution.

Considering that the Democratic Justice faction had the largest share in the coalition party, in the case of intra-party elections to select the representative of the party it would be very unlikely for Kim Young-sam to be selected, as the party representative for his faction was numerically much smaller. Kim Young-sam intended to be appointed as a party representative by President Roh Tae-woo. This was how the Democratic Justice faction obtained Kim Young-sam's signature on the agreement, which a few days later would be leaked to the media. Finally the copy of the agreement with the three leaders' signatures was revealed five months later in October 1990. After the agreement, Kim Young-sam became the party candidate without democratic elections but via appointment by President Roh. This example shows the undemocratic nature of internal party organization, and also points to the lack of legitimacy of the candidate within the party, as he did not stand in an internal party election.

Kim Young-sam's reaction put the coalition's survival in peril, when the three coalition partners' disagreements among the factions (including their leaders) broke out openly in public. The coalition government suffered from serious internal conflicts and attacks from the opposition. Had the coalition broken down within the ten months it would have constituted a severe blow to the ruling party. Kim Young-sam's faction might have cooperated with the opposition parties against the ruling party and this would have made President Roh Tae-woo's life more difficult, as he would have had to run the government facing a large opposition again. The breakdown of the coalition would certainly have negative consequences for Kim Jong-pil and Kim Young-sam as well. Had Kim Young-sam's Unification Democratic faction left the coalition, Kim Jong-pil would not have been able to play any role as a 'veto player'. Therefore, the three leaders would not have many other options but to consolidate their relationship again to remain in the coalition. President Roh finally agreed to delay constitutional revision until the party gained popular approval and Kim Young-sam returned to office as a party representative.

The question arises here as to why Kim Young-sam opposed the constitutional revision. By this time he was a representative of the ruling party already, and President Roh would not be eligible as a candidate for the following presidential elections by law. As long as the ruling party won the election in the parliamentary system, Kim Young-sam would be prime minister without any further presidential elections. This shows the extent to which Kim Young-sam's position had become precarious within the ruling party given the small size of his faction. Kim was suffering from severe internal conflicts of interest among the factions. The members of different factions did not seem to share any common views as they were from different background and held different policy preferences, although they were all located on the right wing of the ideological spectrum. For Kim Young-sam, his position as a representative within the ruling party was not stable and he was also aware of the prospect of losing elections lacking wide support from the public. The opposition parties were also under great pressure as they did not want to revise the constitution in order to introduce a parliamentary system. In fact this event seriously damaged President Roh's power. Kim Young-sam eventually gained more power when he returned to his position as a representative of the coalition party and Roh requested that his Democratic Justice faction assist Kim Young-sam as a party representative.

The emergence of a new party system

In the meantime, Kim Dae-jung returned from protesting against the ruling party and his party returned to the National Assembly compromising with the ruling party in the provincial elections in November 1990. The Local Election Law was finally passed in December 1990 in the midst of the turmoil of struggles between the ruling party and the opposition parties. There had been a four-month hiatus in the National Assembly meetings. Kim Dae-jung also built a coalition in September 1991 with another opposition Democratic Party which was a small faction separated from the Unification Democratic Party when seven members, including Lee Gi-taek, leader of the Democratic Party, and Roh Moo-hyun, did not agree with Kim Young-sam on the party merger. The opposition coalition party was named the Democratic Party.

In the following year, the Fourteenth General Election for the National Assembly members was held in March. The emergence of Chung Ju-young, Chairman of Hyundae, the richest *Jaebeol* in Korea, was a rather unexpected event in the party system. Chung Ju-young created a new party called the Unification People's Party. He was by then labelled Korea's 'Ross Perot', given his considerable personal wealth (Cumings 1997: 328). Later, Chung competed in the presidential elections in December 1992. The ruling coalition party only gained a bare majority with 149 seats out of 299 and the Democratic Party gained 97 seats and the new Unification People's Party gained 31 seats and 21 seats for the non-partisan members who were once rejected as candidates for the general election from the existing parties. This time, most of the non-partisan members were ejected from the ruling party as candidates.

Looking at the numbers of non-partisan members elected shows how undemocratic the appointment of the electoral candidate by the leaders of the parties was. Regardless of the candidates' efficiency and potential career, party leaders were likely to 'stick with' their own personal connections or preferences. The people with school or regional connections would be obviously more favoured by the party leaders when they appointed the candidate for the general elections. Later, the ruling party re-gained majority status by accepting defectors from among non-party members. Among the faction leaders within the coalition parties, who has more power to appoint and how many candidates on their own side were other crucial parts of the conflict. The right of the faction leaders to appoint candidates influences the size of factions after elections.

The ruling party did not gain enough seats to revise the constitution. With the support of President Roh, Kim Young-sam's faction was this time more cohesive before the presidential elections. In the meantime, Roh entered the 'lame-duck' phase. Since democratization, the presidential term was set for a single period of five years only. With the fear of life-long presidencies as in the case of the authoritarian experience, the ruling elites agreed on a single term of five years but this overlooked the prospect that the late period of the presidency would produce a lame-duck president. Unlike the previous appointment by the president, Kim Young-sam became a presidential candidate for the election through a democratic internal election. Even though each faction supported its favourite candidate, Kim Young-sam was able to win the internal election.

Kim Young-sam's administration and the first civilian government

In the Fourteenth Presidential Elections in December 1992, three main political leaders competed in the election: Kim Young-sam from the ruling Democratic

Liberal Party, Kim Dae-jung from the Democratic Party and Chung Ju-young from the United People's Party. In the presidential elections, Kim Young-sam gained 41.1 per cent and Kim Dae-jung gained 33.4 per cent of the vote. Chung Ju-young gained relatively low support at 16.1 percent.

Many scholars argue that Kim Young-sam won the election due to the voters' conservative preference. During the electoral campaign, Kim Dae-jung lost considerable support when electoral competitors began to brand him as a 'leftist'. Potential voters showed more fluctuations towards either Kim Young-sam or Chung Ju-young when North Korean spies were arrested in October before the election. Choi Jang-jip (1996: 277; 2002: 151) argues that the 'Cold War anti-communism hegemony' narrowed down the ideological spectrum among the parties and even among voters. This eventually narrowed the representativeness of the people who are often isolated from the conservative mainstream, leaving them un-represented politically.

The convergence of ideology on the right eventually hindered democracy from being consolidated in South Korea. Political reforms in the end played into the hands of the conservative elites, who never brought any radical changes but always sought to protect the ruling elites and the *Jaebeols*. Choi maintains that the *Jaebeols* and media benefited from support by the authoritarian governments, but they have now grown to such an extent that they escape any form of control. When Kim Young-sam finally became president, he introduced some political reforms without any real support in the National Assembly but based on his own charismatic authority and with the support of the mass media. This clearly fits into O'Donnell's definition of 'delegative democracy' (1994), where populist presidents often violate horizontal accountability between the executives and the legislatures.

Political reform under the Kim Young-sam administration: conflict with the Jaebeol

The politics of coalition-building turned out to be successful and led to Kim Young-sam's electoral success: he became the first non-military president after a long period of authoritarian military rule. Kim Young-sam introduced political reforms in the name of the 'rectification of history' or 'setting history right'. Kim Young-sam first removed the TK (Taegu and Kyoungsang[22]) factions who mainly supported Roh Tae-woo from key positions in the government. He also dismantled the *Hanahoe* faction.[23] With the wide support of the public and mass media he had both former presidents, Chun Doo-hwan and Roh Tae-woo, sentenced to jail terms for their military mutiny, the 5.17 Gwangju oppression and the accumulation of illegal funds during their presidencies. After the arrest of Roh Tae-woo on charges of corruption, 'the Special Act on the May 18 Democratization Movement' was introduced. This was introduced to arrest Chun Doo-hwan and his aides.

Roh Jeong-ho (2003: 188) argues that this represented a step back from consolidating democracy in that the Special Bill was created as 'an instrument of those in power, to be wielded against people who are no longer in power'. Introducing such a 'Special Bill' in response to the overwhelming popular demand undermined the rule of law. In the name of 'setting history right' Kim Young-sam overruled the constitution and continued his reform based on his personal charisma.

In the economic sector, one of the most noteworthy reforms was 'real name registration in banking'. This aimed at disconnecting the vicious circle of rent-seeking or clientelistic relationships between the state and *Jaebeol*, as it sought to hinder money-laundering. Reforming *Jaebeol* structures, however, would risk causing side-effects such as economic recessions given the latters' prime role in the country's economy. Korea was mainly run by *Jaebeols* for decades isolating labour's participation in politics. The demise of authoritarian governments left the gigantic *Jaebeols* and this remained beyond the control of the civil government.

The Kim Young-sam government succeeded in controlling the factions of the authoritarian government in its political reform; however, it failed in reorganizing the relationship between the state and *Jaebeol*. The early reform plan for *Jaebeol* shifted to support the *Jaebeol* when the mass media led public opinion to fear the risk of a downturn in the domestic economy. Choi Jang-jip (1996: 261) argues that a high level of economic development and carrying out significant political reforms are not compatible. To transfer from the procedural democracy to substantive democracy there is a cost in transition to be paid. If the government pursues equal distribution in terms of practical democracy, this will put economic development at risk, as the high cost of labour will make companies less competitive in terms of the cost of labour in the world market. On the other hand, if the government supports companies, it is also clear that equal distribution is ignored. *Jaebeols* run their companies according to the liberal market mechanism and their interests lie in maximizing profit, not in the fair distribution of interest and capital.

Fair and equal distribution of social capital can be regulated by the state. However, when the state cannot impose its will on the *Jaebeols*, few reforms are likely to take place. Choi Jang-jip contends that 'governability can be built on a balanced relationship between capital, labor and the state'.[24] Within the conservative hegemony, reform did not gain any support from the National Assembly. Kim Young-sam led political reform alone, with wide support from the mass media and the public in the early stages, but when the reform went deeper the mass media retreated as the mass media itself forms a part of the conservative hegemony. When Kim Young-sam did not gain any support from the public, the mass media led the public in another direction against the policies and Kim Young-sam could not continue any political reform. The more President Kim carried out further reform, the more conservative ruling elites were incorporated and this eventually included his own son being brought to account over money-laundering. Thus Kim Young-sam lacked support from the top and in the end from the bottom, often led by the media, and finally entered the typical period of lame-duck president late in his term of office.

Demise of the grand conservative coalition

While Kim Young-sam was consolidating his power within the party, his faction was planning to diminish the power of its last coalition partner, Kim Jong-pil's New Democratic Republican faction. When Kim Young-sam became president, Kim Jong-pil took the position as a representative of the ruling party. Kim Jong-pil finally left the coalition on 22 January 1995 over the continuous internal conflict among the factions. Soon thereafter, Kim Jong-pil was re-gathering the formal members of TK factions, and with his own faction he founded the United Liberal Democrats in March 1995. By then, the opposition Democratic Party had also split between factions – led by Kim Dae-jung and Lee Gi-taek. In August of the same year, Kim Dae-jung also left the Democratic Party and founded the National Congress for New Politics Party. In the turmoil of the party system among the parties and factions, Kim Young-sam renamed his ruling party the New Korea Party in February 1996. Kim Byung-kook (2000: 59) argues as follows:

> The consolidation of electoral democracy did not, in other words, become a period of institution building and organizational experimentation in party politics for South Korea. Political parties remained institutionally underdeveloped. They were personal instruments of powerful regional leaders, captive to their personal ambitions and shifting strategies, incapable of generating distinctive ideologies and policy programs and organizationally isolated from interest groups in civil society.

All the parties and factions were reorganizing themselves either by merging or splitting to prepare for the Fifteenth General Election for the National Assembly in April 1996. Regardless of the party name or policies, voters converged on the conservative ideology which sought to preserve stability rather than introducing structural changes. The leaders also knew they would still be able to mobilize voters' support in their hometown regions. In the Fifteenth General Election, the New Korea Party gained 34.5 per cent of the votes, the New Congress for New Politics 25.3 per cent and the United Liberal Democrats gained 16.2 per cent of the total votes. Regionalism still showed as a clear division in the election. When party leaders referred to regionally based concepts such as Honam party, Yeongnam Hegemony or Chungcheongdo *Hatbaji*[25] in the electoral campaign, voters in the region were more encouraged to vote in terms of strong regional ties (Lee 1998: 127).

When Lee Hoe-chang was elected in 1997, that was the first time the ruling party elected its presidential candidate by democratic elections. However, Lee In-je, the losing candidate, did not concede defeat and later he joined the presidential elections running for the People's New Party. Some believe the emergence of Lee In-je diminished support for Lee Hoe-chang; however, the ruling party was largely blamed for the 1997 'Asian crisis' and was suffering from internal conflicts as well. In late 1997, Kim Jong-pil proposed amending the constitution to introduce the parliamentary system and sought to form a coalition again. Kim Young-sam, by then in the lame-duck period, did not have much power to mobilize party members. Thus Kim Jong-pil had another opportunity to build a coalition with Kim Dae-jung's party.

The Kim Dae-jung administration: origins and challenges

Kim Jong-pil played a pivotal role again in building a coalition with Kim Dae-jung before the presidential elections with regional hegemony in both Chungcheong and Jeolla provinces. Kim Dae-jung finally won the presidential elections in December 1997 with 40.3 per cent of the votes and Lee Hoe-chang lost the election, gaining 38.7 per cent of the total votes. Kim Dae-jung's victory can be ascribed to the fragmentation of the ruling party (among Lee Hoe-chang and Lee In-je) and also to the formation of a coalition with Kim Jong-pil's party. The intra-party politics under the Kim Dae-jung administration after the coalition was formed will be discussed in Chapters 3, 4 and 5.

Another moment where coalition-building seemed to be decisive in Korea's political life was before the 1997 presidential elections, when the ruling party faced internal factions and the political environment was under mounting pressure due to the outbreak of the 'Asian crisis' and the simultaneous condemnation by public opinion of a perceived inefficient governability. The opposition party leader, Kim Dae-jung, entered an alliance with the United Liberal Democrats party leader, Kim Jong-pil. After a history as an opposition leader in the 1960s, Kim Dae-jung finally became president. Unlike the previous parties' merger in 1990, this was based on the agreement of building a coalition government. Kim Jong-pil's main purpose was again to revise the constitution in order to introduce a parliamentary system.

Since the start of democratization in 1987, two political leaders won political elections through a strategy based on coalition-building in Korea: Kim Young-sam (1993–1997) and Kim Dae-jung (1998–2003). When Kim Dae-jung became president in 1998, the NCNP party (the president's party) had 77 seats (26.3 per cent) out of a total 293 seats, his coalition partner ULD had 43 seats (14.7 per cent) and the opposition Grand National Party had 161 (54 per cent). In combination, the two ruling parties of the coalition government had 120 seats (41 per cent) out of 293, which is still far below a majority (see Figure 2.1).

In the case of Korea, many defectors from the largest opposition party joined the small minority party for more power as the ruling party would be in a position to distribute benefits such as executive positions or the promise of future appointment as a candidate for a parliamentary seat. Out of a total number of 299 parliamentary members, 73 (24 per cent) have defected from their original parties since April 1996 when the legislature started (*Chosun Ilbo*, 18 October 1999).

The small ruling minority party had to secure its political stability but also carry out political reforms. The president introduced the term '*Jeonggye-Gaepyeon*' (political system reorganization) as a way to legitimize his efforts to

The formation of the Korean party system 47

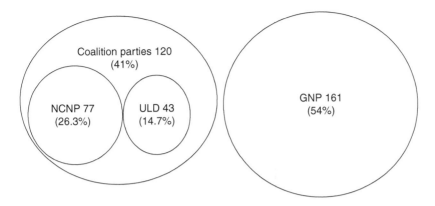

Figure 2.1 Party seat numbers after coalition-building in February 1998 (source: author).

Notes
NCNP   The National Congress for New Politics (later the New Millennium Democratic Party) led by Kim Dae-jung.
ULD   The United Liberal Democrats led by Kim Jong-pil.
GNP   The Grand National Party led by Lee Hoi-chang.

make the ruling party maintain majority seats and to smooth the legislative process without the large opposition party's interruption. What the NCNP did was attract as many defectors as possible from the opposition GNP. Within six months of the president taking office, the NCNP had attracted enough defectors to reach 105 seats and the ULD had 54 seats. The high flux of party members changed the small minority ruling party into a majority coalition government, 159 seats versus 134 seats of the opposition party (see Figure 2.2). This made it even more difficult to reach a compromise with the opposition in the legislature. Park Chan-pyo (2002) argues that '*Jeonggye-Gaepyeon*' was a 'costly fusion'.

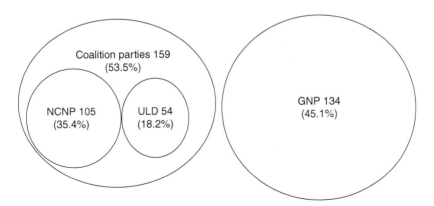

Figure 2.2 Party seat numbers after political reorganization: '*Jeonggye-Gaepyeon*' ('political system reorganization') in May 1999 (source: author).

Scholars such as Larry Diamond, Kim Byung-kook and Choi Jang-jip point out that this manufactured majority government is in fact working against democratic consolidation. If the small ruling party is the result of democracy, the government should find democratic ways of running the government rather than clinging to the magic number of a majority to pass legislative laws without the opposition party's cooperation. How can this high flux of party members and the ruling party's struggles, even violating democratic and moral rules, be explained? As it has been shown, a high flux of mobility among party members threatens political stability in a context where democratic institutions have only been recently introduced. Thus, the puzzle over the unstable coalition governments may be seen as a part of the process of democratic consolidation.

Since 1987, coalition-building has played a crucial role in determining electoral success in presidential elections. A serious drawback, however, as will be discussed in the following chapters, is demonstrated by the fact that electoral success is no guarantee of effective governability or political stability, either. As a matter of fact, governability has been constantly undermined by permanent factionalism internal to the coalition and to the parties themselves.

Apart from the continuous fission and fusion of political parties, the behaviour of voters also contributed to the creation of minority governments and large oppositions. Where voters have various preferences of policies and/or parties, it seems fairly common and ordinary to find that they do not converge on support for a single majority party but spread their preferences across the political spectrum. This is all but ordinary in a democratic country. The problem with Korea was that facing big opposition parties, winning office did not guarantee the administration's governability.

In what was the first time the opposition party won office through democratic elections, the Kim Dae-jung administration set out with an extensive agenda. Yet the ruling party found it difficult to implement its policies from the early outset of the legislature. The administration could not follow up its first coalition agreement, which consisted of appointing its coalition partner as a prime minister, because it faced a large opposition in the legislature. Facing a political deadlock in the National Assembly, the ruling coalition parties immediately started to enlarge the size of the ruling parties by attracting defectors from the opposition parties. Enlarging the government's size at all costs did not seem to bring any solution to the political deadlock, however. Quite the contrary: the conflicts in the legislature grew deeper not only with the opposition parties but also with the coalition partner(s) as well as with factions within the ruling party.

Summary

Since 1987, coalition-building has played a key role in shaping Korean politics. This might well become a permanent characteristic of the Korean political system. A discussion of the post-war Korean political system has shown that three key features have accompanied its formation, both under authoritarian and democratic rule:

- catch-allism and indifference to ideological cleavages;
- personalism;
- and regionalism.

First, blurred ideological division has been one of the main characteristics of party politics in Korea (This will be discussed in greater detail in Chapter 4.) Where all parties tend to gravitate towards the right of the political spectrum, there is little choice in terms of ideological orientation. In light of this, parties have emerged as catch-all political formations. Due to the international situation and the relations with North Korea, the political spectrum has been traditionally dominated by right-wing parties, and it was therefore impossible to tell one party from another from the viewpoint of their ideological programme. In practice, then, most parties converge towards a conservative ideology. Whenever new parties emerged to challenge the dominant party, the latter successfully managed to co-opt the members of these smaller parties. The ideological orientation of the government (which was never in question) aside, problems related to inter-party relations emerged when successful electoral strategies and alliances between major and smaller parties did not actually translate into effective and lasting (stable) ruling coalitions.

Second, party politics in Korea consists of competition between small groups of interest. This fits well into Panebianco's model of oligarchic parties, as the small ruling group tends to exercise a disproportionate influence over a group's collective decision-making (Panebianco 1988: 171), and the findings presented in Chapter 3 will confirm this. Parties are essentially one-man, unstable and volatile.

Third, a related feature is undoubtedly the growing salience of regionalism. Along with charismatic regional elites, voters cast strong regional votes. The former presidents Park Chung-hee, Chun Doo-hwan, Roh Tae-woo and Kim Young-sam were all from Gyeongsang province; Kim Jong-pil, the leader of the United Liberal Democrats, comes from Chungcheong province; and Kim Dae-jung is from Jeolla province. Former presidents paid more attention to developing their home regions, and as a result Jeolla province has been ignored. A look at how development plans have affected the regions differently shows that regional divides are much deeper than ideological contrasts between conservatives and reformists. Here, a major divide opposes the Gyeongsang and Jeolla provinces. This made people from Jeolla province more resentful of state policies and they also suffered from their memory of the Gwangju massacre (see more in Chapter 4).

As shown in this chapter, politics in South Korea is openly confrontational and lacks mechanisms of compromise and negotiation between government and opposition, across and within political parties. To conclude, coalition-building and party mergers have become central elements in the Korean political system and these processes have accelerated since 1987. Most governments so far have been internally divided. Ruling and opposition parties often merged. In the aftermath of the Asian crisis, the alliance with Kim Jong-pil allowed Kim Dae-jung to win the presidential elections. In Chapters 3 to 5, I present and discuss the difficulties that the Kim Dae-jung administration encountered during his efforts to carry out the announced policies to reform the Korean political system, and why these efforts failed. Chapter 6 examines the post-Kim Dae-Jung period by investigating the two subsequent administrations (Roh Moo-hyun and Lee Myung-bak). Doing so provides an interesting vantage point on the two administrations in Korea that have managed to attain majority status but nevertheless fell back on the 'same old problems' of factionalism within the ruling party and poor relations with the opposition. While the level of institutionalization of party gradually increased thanks to some reforms introduced during the Roh administration, structural problems remain in Korean party politics.

3 Internal factors
Party politics and organization

Introduction

Critics of presidential systems typically concentrate on the possibility of such systems producing 'minority presidents', where the majority in the parliament does not reflect the political views of the president. This can then result in political deadlock. This assumption seems to be appropriate when describing the case of the Kim Dae-jung administration. However, recent scholarship (Cheibub 2002; Cheibub and Chernykh 2008; Cheibub and Limongi 2002; Cheibub et al. 2004; Elgie and McMenamin 2008; Kim 2008 b, c; Mainwaring and Shugart 1997) questions the extent to which deadlock is structural in the cases of minority governments or coalitions in presidential systems. In fact, the above-mentioned scholars contend that minority governments do not necessarily face deadlock and coalition governments are not necessarily unstable.

In this chapter I examine the internal dynamics of Korean political parties to understand why the minority coalition government of Kim Dae-jung suffered from political stalemate or deadlocks in the legislature. This chapter focuses on political parties and the party system as a whole in order to understand how conflicts among and within parties affected governability. By doing so, it endeavours to fill a gap in the literature on the importance of party politics in presidential and semi-presidential regimes (Elgie 2004; Mainwaring 1993; Mainwaring and Shugart 1997). My main focus is on the seemingly structural deadlock that the Korean political system experienced during the Kim Dae-jung administration, contra the assumptions held in the literature. By showing why the deadlock was broken and how the government tried to tackle it, the chapter advances two main claims. First, size of government (i.e. number of seats in the parliament) does not matter. Even when majority status was attained, it can be argued that instability nonetheless persisted. Second, attention should rather be paid to issues of party organization. Understanding how the party system and parties are run and function sheds significant light on the whole coalition formation and instability process. While parties and party systems can be studied in many different ways, the main focus in this chapter is on the nature of party organization. I draw from Angelo Panebianco's seminal work on the issue (1988) in order to examine how party politics and the conflicts therein affect the

52 *Internal factors*

cohesion of the coalition and the relationship between government and the opposition party.

The chapter is divided into two main sections. The first examines a series of political deadlocks, starting from the one very early into the Kim Dae-jung administration (involving the approval vote of the prime minister) to the ULD's battle to be recognized as a 'floor negotiation group'[1] and thereby having access to larger state funds, and to include the political conflict over the amendment of the constitution (1999). The main argument put forward is that deadlock is not caused by the size of the ruling party per se, but by the characteristics of the party organization and the party system. This is also noted by Cheibub with regard to presidential systems (2002). The second section builds on this finding and moves on to examine various dimensions of party organization. Following Panebianco's conceptualization of party organization (1988), I consider the following criteria: level of factionalism, leadership, funding system and party–citizens linkage. This chapter aims to elucidate intra-party politics and its influence on governability. This will be done by testing three hypotheses:

1   A higher degree of factionalism negatively affects governability.
2   Strong leadership is likely to make governments more stable.
3   If the party organization fails to link with the citizens, the government is likely to be less stable.

Explaining intra- and inter-party conflicts: what happened and why?

From success to ungovernability

When the opposition[2] finally won office in 1997, the expectations of the public were very high, particularly with regard to the government's reform agenda. The ruling coalition that emerged from the presidential elections instead fell prey to internal factionalism – a factor that derailed the government's reform plans and dashed the public's expectations. Kim Dae-jung's administration showed the highest rate of fission and fusion among the members of the National Assembly and this eventually affected the government's legitimacy and governability.

From the very beginning, the National Assembly Sessions proceeded in a turbulent way. Two conflicts were present in the Kim Dae-jung administration: the first was with the coalition partner ULD over the share of power in the administration; and the second was with the big opposition party, the then New Korea Party and later the Grand National Party (or *Hannara* Party, hereafter GNP), successor to the New Korea Party. Many laws introducing new policies on social and economic reform were opposed by the opposition party and could not be passed in the National Assembly. The proposed policies required a large majority. In the case of amending the constitution, it needed to be approved by two-thirds of the total seats in the legislature. The ruling coalition started with 120 seats (41 per cent) out of the total of 293. When the new government introduced policies restructuring the banking system, for instance, the opposition lawmakers mounted a fierce opposition to the law (*Hankook Ilbo*, 1 January 1998). This did not bode well for governability and in fact signalled the start of a struggle that the ruling coalition parties would subsequently face through the entire period of office.

This section focuses on these conflicts (between the coalition and its partner, as well as the opposition party) and asks how the government sought to overcome this impasse. The fission and fusion of political parties constitutes the strategy adopted to unblock the situation. The government therefore became increasingly involved not only in bringing about reforms in the economic, social and political arenas but also in controlling the conflicts of interest within the coalition parties and with the opposition party.

Deadlocks: why doesn't size matter?

The approval vote for the prime minister

The Kim Dae-jung administration won office by building a coalition with the previous coalition partner of the ruling party, Kim Jong-pil, a leading figure of the Democratic Republic Party under the Park Chung-hee administration, who was determined to change the constitution (as was discussed in Chapter 2). Therefore, Kim Dae-jung began his administration with a key structural problem: the potential conflict of interest between the most conservative party (led by Kim Jong-pil) and one (led by Kim Dae-jung) seeking to develop a 'third way' beyond left and right. The agreement upon which the coalition was established guaranteed that the constitution would be changed by the end of 1999 at the latest. The two party leaders agreed to share power. If they won office, Kim Dae-jung was to be president and Kim Jong-pil prime minister. The prime minister would thus be able to carve out a role in making decisions in domestic affairs (*Chosun Ilbo*, 19 January 1999). The two leaders agreed to have equal rights to appoint ministers of the ministries, thus half of the ministers would be appointed by President Kim Dae-jung and the other half would be appointed by the prime minister-designate, Kim Jong-pil (*Segye Ilbo*, 22 December 1997). The case of the vote of approval for the prime minister illustrates this well. As a part of the coalition agreement, the first action of the president was to appoint Kim Jong-pil as prime minister, a nomination that would then need to be ratified by the members of the National Assembly. This was a necessary move to consolidate the ruling coalition, as Kim Dae-jung's party could count on only 77 law-makers and the coalition partner's 43 law-makers. A majority (50 per cent plus one) of the National Assembly members' attendance for the vote was needed to allow Kim Jong-pil to become prime minister. It also required two-thirds of the votes from those who took up their seats in the chamber when the vote was called.

In theory, this condition was not insurmountable. If the NCNP and the ULD succeeded in negotiation with non-party-affiliated legislators, then the ruling coalition parties would need the support of just 13 out of 163 opposition members belonging to the GNP. Kim Jong-pil could rely on personal connections with many members within the Grand National Party ranks. Many of them were in fact from the Chungcheong province, including some from the same high school, while others were alumni from the same university. Some of them also used to work with Kim Jong-pil in previous parties, the Democratic Republic Party in the Park Chung-hee era and the United Liberal Democrats under the Kim Young-sam administration. There was more than enough margin to achieve compromise and coordination.

Rational choice is one possible explanation of why the Grand National Party vigorously objected to Kim Jong-pil becoming prime minister. If Kim Jong-pil became prime minister, this was thought to damage the GNP in the following local elections in June 1998 and the general election, especially in Chungcheong province, where Kim Jong-pil had loyal electoral support (see Chapter 4). If the GNP were to support Kim Jong-pil to be prime minister, this would appear as if the GNP accepted the legitimacy of the ruling coalition parties. This would also help Kim Jong-pil to gain stronger support from Chungcheong province. The National Congress for the New Politics[3] had strong support in Seoul, Gyeonggi and Jeolla provinces, so if the GNP lost in the following local elections this would give the Grand National Party a chance to become the party of Gyeongsang province only. This would also influence financial support from the *Jaebeols* or other interest groups that provided funding for the Grand National Party. Therefore, the Grand National Party had to fight for its own survival in the legislature. The main objective of the GNP was to break the coalition between the NCNP and the ULD and gain power again. Additionally, relying on the largest number of seats in the legislature it appeared difficult for the opposition party to accept the loss of the presidential elections. Linz's (1990) argument on dual legitimacy between the executive and the legislative is well illustrated in the case of South Korea. A president directly elected through popular vote gains the legitimacy to implement reform policies through what is referred to in the literature as 'delegative democracy'.[4] However, a large opposition party also gains legitimacy from the people; thus it also seeks to pass and implement policies through the legislature. Apart from the survival strategy (obtaining the approval of the assembly), one should also note that the political culture (at both party and public level) still remained influenced by the legacy of authoritarianism. More generally, this political culture was embedded in Confucian beliefs. The top-down procedure of the decision-making process and highly concentrated power were far from unusual for people in Korea. Once the strategy was agreed by the elites, the ordinary legislators of the party had to follow the committee's decision in the National Assembly, as will become clearer in the following pages. The ordinary legislators were even referred to as 'hand-raising robots'[5] that do nothing more than raise their hands for voting in the National Assembly.

At the approval vote for the prime minister, all the legislators of the GNP were 'advised' to attend the vote but to submit empty ballot sheets. In doing so the opposition party would avoid popular blame for not attending an important

National Assembly meeting. At the same time, the empty ballot sheets would force the vote to be annulled. Within 20 minutes of the start of voting on 2 March 1998, the legislators of the United Liberal Democrats became aware that opposition party members were handing in blank ballots. The National Assembly descended into chaos with the ruling party legislators asking to have the ballot declared void and the opposition party legislators instead demanding the voting be completed. The public watched scenes of actual fighting among legislators on a live TV broadcast (*Donga Ilbo*, 3 March 1998).

The vote was cancelled at the last moment and the president appointed Kim Jong-pil as a deputy (or an acting) prime minister on 3 March. It took nearly six months to arrange another vote, which in fact took place on 17 August. Kim Jong-pil became the prime minister, gaining 171 votes of support in the National Assembly. However, this was only after the political reorganization (*Jeonggye-Gaepyeon*) of the ruling parties which attracted high numbers of defectors from the opposition parties. By then, the National Congress for New Politics had 88 legislators and the United Liberal Democrats had 49 legislators. Except for one member belonging to the ULD, the members of the ruling party all voted to approve Kim Jong-pil as prime minister and by then the ruling party had managed to gain around 30 votes from the Grand National Party (*Segye Ilbo*, 18 August 1998).

The previous vote in February had shown that independent voting for legislators was not an option given the prevailing Korean political culture. The question arising here is of course how parties manage to control secret ballots. Considering that each party is home to different factions (e.g. regional basis, school ties), it is questionable how the party leaders discipline party members to coordinate party decisions very strictly. *Chosun Ilbo* (9 February 1998) reported that the committee of the Grand National Party announced that if any members voted to approve Kim as prime minister, the member(s) would be required to leave the party. This happened, for example, when the GNP member Lee Su-in expressed his approval of the prime minister by voting in public (raising his hand) against the party strategy and by not attending the meeting when the GNP party called for a vote to dismiss the minister of defence, Chun Yong-taek. He was finally dismissed. This was a rare exception as many legislators note instead that they do not have much choice but to follow party directives (*Chosun Ilbo*, 5 May 1998).

When Cho Sun and Lee Gi-taek, formerly leaders of the 'little' Democratic Party,[6] were excluded from standing as candidates in the 2000 elections, this confirmed Lee Hoe-chang's tendency to marginalize legislators holding dissenting views. This marginalization of dissent points to the lack of democracy in Korean party politics, where fear of not being allowed to stand again in elections acts as a powerful constraint on a deputy's behaviour. Although South Korea achieved electoral democracy nearly two decades ago, the country's political culture remains similar to that under the authoritarian regime. Under this strict political party culture, individual legislators could not play any active role in the process of law-making unless they followed the party line.

There seemed to be no margin for compromise or negotiation among party members belonging to different parties unless they defected from one party and joined another. Park No-cheol,[7] a chief secretary of Jeong Hee-su, the Seventeenth National Assembly member for the GNP, stated that:

> There are four different levels of punishment when the individual lawmaker does not follow the party's directives. The legislator who did something or anything against the party will be sanctioned by the party committee meetings and some of them may lose their position in the party organization and some of them will even have to leave the party. Especially when the legislators are not elected through the general elections but by proportional representation, they would not have any choice but to leave the party. If legislators who became members of the National Assembly through party lists leave the party they are not a member of the National Assembly any more. They simply lose their job. However, a legislator like Choi Yeon-hee[8] who resigned (or was expelled) from the party will still remain as a member of the National Assembly because he was directly elected by the vote of the people in the general election.

The debate and conflict over the approval vote shows that the coalition government could not control the legislature, because the size of the government was much smaller than that of the opposition party, as pointed out earlier, and also in light of the uncooperative political culture in the legislature. The monthly magazine *Monthly Chosun* (July 2001) pointed out that the Kim Dae-jung administration started off its office as a 'lame-duck', that is, as a minority ruling party and with a coalition partner. While the public blamed the opposition party for not compromising with the government, a large part of the responsibility for the deadlock lay in the weak leadership of the president. This is noteworthy as presidents in Korea are often referred to as '*Caesarean presidents*'.[9] Choi Jang-jip (2002: 143–151), however, argues that the Kim Dae-jung administration was a 'government without hegemony' compared to that of the former presidents, Roh Tae-woo and Kim Young-sam, who had effective hegemonic power. Choi points out that Kim Dae-jung did not have *Caesarean power* but authoritarian leadership which was built on a personalized party. The reason why the party could be personalized is not due to a powerful or authoritarian leadership style but due to a weak party without grassroots support. When a party is not linked to the grassroots, nobody can blame the party leaders who do not implement their political platform. Furthermore, when the government is trapped by the deadlocked legislature, this slows the procedure of introducing reform policies. To carry out reform policies, the government should be highly efficient, swift and constant in introducing them. Majority support is also essential for implementing policies. Mo Jong-ryn (2001: 3) argues that 'if the administration is unable to make prompt decisions and remains indecisive, people will lose confidence in government policy and the resulting uncertainty will have a negative effect on the economy.'

Too many bills, not enough votes

After Kim Dae-jung took office the legislature was supposed to deal with 300 law proposals, including bills on public subsidy, supplementary budget bills and social security bills. The bills included education funding such as student loans, housing subsidies and equalizing taxation. Of the 300 bills, only 49 were passed over eight meetings of the Assembly, and the Hearing on the Economy in the legislature was held only by the ruling parties while the opposition party was protesting outside (*Chosun Ilbo*, 4 February 1999).

The numerous conflicts and political crises in the legislature provided the Kim Dae-jung administration with the opportunity to legitimize its attempt to reorganize the whole party system. The ruling party was able to attract large numbers of defectors from the opposition parties and managed to gain 160 seats out of the total 293 seats facing the 133 seats of the opposition Grand National Party in September 1999. Because of the opposition party's boycott of the National Assembly, this was basically occupied by members of the ruling parties while the opposition party spent most of the time outside the National Assembly opposing the ruling parties and the government. As the National Assembly was obviously not functioning properly without the opposition party's attendance, the Assembly was labelled either the *vegetable assembly* when the chamber was totally empty and paralysed for a long term over the political stalemate on the vote to approve the prime minister or *bullet-proof assembly* as the Assembly was used to protect legislators of the GNP from being arrested.[10] When the ruling parties demanded action to investigate illegal political campaign contributions for the presidential election in 1997, to protect its legislators the Grand National Party ran the Assembly meeting on its own without the ruling parties' attendance (*Munwha Ilbo*, 17 August 1999). Until August 1999, the National Assembly meeting was held 19 times from the 189th National Assembly Extraordinary Session to the 207th National Assembly Session; however, about a half of the meetings were held either by the ruling parties or the opposition party. The meeting was held either by the ruling parties while the opposition party was protesting on the streets or by the opposition party in circumstances whereby the ruling parties considered that the reason for the meeting was nothing more than to protect the legislators' privileges. The ruling party suffered a crushing defeat in the following general election (*Seoul Sinmun*, 10 August 1999).

In the eyes of the public, the government just looked inefficient and unable to deliver reform policies. The civilian government appeared incapable of delivering political reform as legislators only looked interested in sharing power and subsequently engaged in particularistic infighting and blocked each other's bills. Bribing remained a popular method to mobilize voters and regional cleavages got even deeper than before (*Kyunghyang Sinmun*, 23 February 1999). A popular saying at the time was that '20 wins, 10 loses', meaning if the candidate spends one billion *won* in the electoral campaign he/she loses, but two billion *won*[11] will do (*Segye Ilbo*, 11 August 2000). A former news reporter, Lee Jung-hee,[12] notes that 'it costs about 1.5 million American dollars to win a seat in the general election'.

58 *Internal factors*

While the budget bill and related bills were waiting to be approved, on 3–13 October 1999 the Assembly Session was paralysed for ten days due to the conflict over the media reform report. There were 112 bills still awaiting approval, which were all related to reform policies including public subsidy bills, national security, human rights, etc. (*Kukmin Ilbo*, 4 November 1999). One of the most urgent bills was the national health insurance laws that were supposed to be implemented by 1 January 2000 but were all waiting for final approval in the legislature. The ruling party, however, was not only in conflict with the opposition party but also with the coalition partner ULD as well. In the following section I will discuss the internal conflicts within the coalition government.

Conflict of interests – fission and fusion of political actors

As the government finally became aware of public dissatisfaction with its political performance, the following year (2000) was spent preparing for the Sixteenth General Election. To keep the coalition agreement, the president was expected to amend the constitution before the end of 1999. Because the ruling parties found themselves unable to achieve a two-thirds majority in the assembly, another political deadlock followed.

Before proceeding further it should be recalled here that bamboo is one of four plants referred to as '*virtuous*'[13] and traditionally revered by Koreans because it is not flexible but 'lives with principle, straight and empty inside', thereby indicating the Confucian imperative of lack of greed. Kim Jong-pil's pivotal political role among the parties and flexible behaviour was not respected by the public. His political behaviour reminded many not of a bamboo but of the blackbird in Aesop's fable which changed its identity for the sake of convenience or interests. In fact, to the public Kim Jong-pil was always a key member in many administrations, not the first but the second in the political hierarchy for decades: under the Park Chung-hee administration as prime minister, under the Roh Tae-woo and Kim Young-sam administrations as a core member of the party merger, and under the Kim Dae-jung administration as prime minister and coalition partner. Perhaps that is why Kim Jong-pil seemed to prefer a parliamentary system. He was also referred to as a 'sunflower', following the sun (power) only. On the other hand, some scholars point out that he played a crucial role in the process of democratization (Kim 2001; Park 2003; *Seoul Sinmun*, 10 January 2000). Kim Jong-pil benefited from the support of those who believed the parliamentary system to be the most suitable system for Korea.

The ruling coalition parties' aim was to attract larger support in the Pohang region and therefore turn Kim Dae-jung's party into a nationwide party. Park Tae-jun, a founder of POSCO,[14] joined the ULD to support the presidential elections and the agreement was that Kim Jong-pil would become the prime minister and Park Tae-jun would become the chairman (*chongjae*) of the ULD, and the share of power would be divided according to a 4:4:2 power-sharing agreement, including appointment rights for the potential candidates in the general elections and the sharing of administration positions (*Sin Donga*,

January 1997). The rationale was set before they built a coalition with Park Tae-jun. *Donga Ilbo* noted the ratio will be shared by Kim Dae-jung, Kim Jong-pil, and whoever would join the coalition in January 1997; and, in November, Park Tae-jun was the 'whoever'. When they set the coalition ratio, Park Tae-jun was in Kim Dae-jung's plan already. In the previous year (1996) he sent his aide and suggested Park Tae-jun should be the first candidate on the NCNP proportional representatives list for the Fifteenth General Election in 1996. By electoral law, 30 per cent of the legislators are selected from the National Assembly, not directly on the basis of popular vote. Each party makes a list of the potential candidates and they can have numbers of legislators from the ratio of the seats they gain in the legislature during the elections. By then, Park Tae-jun refused to become a first candidate in the general election, saying 'it is not the right time', and later he was elected as a member of the National Assembly as a non-party-affiliated member in Pohang when there was by-elections[15] in 1997 (*Donga Ilbo*, 5 November 1997; *Hankyoreh Sinmun*, 19 January 1998).

The coalition between Kim Dae-jung, Kim Jong-pil and Park Tae-jun was thereafter referred to as the DJT coalition (*Donga Ilbo*, 5 November 1997; *Kyunghyang Sinmun*, 5 November 1997). The coalition was believed to bring more credibility to Kim Dae-jung's objective to widen support. Without the DJT coalition, the NCNP would look like a mere regional party based in Jeolla province only. Instead, attempting to widen support to make the NCNP a national party was a part of Kim Dae-jung's political strategy. The party leaders took advantage of regionalism in Korea and even played on regional divides to gain more support in their own region. They accused the government of marginalizing their own region politically but they were also pursuing ways of eliminating regional ties and the titles based on the regions such as 'Honam party' or 'Yeongnam party'.[16] From the birth of the administration, it was not difficult to forecast internal conflict within the coalition government and of course external conflict with an extremely antagonistic opposition GNP.

The ruling party was struggling over the political deadlock in the legislature and finally faced a conflict *within* the coalition government itself too. In August 1999, President Kim Dae-jung and Prime Minister Kim Jong-pil both agreed to delay the amendment of the constitution until the end of the presidency or at least until after the general election in 2000. Although the ruling coalition parties artificially enlarged the size of the parties in the legislature, without the opposition party's support it still remained hard to achieve two-thirds of the total votes in the legislature. After the meeting, both leaders stated that 'this is not the right time for amending the constitution in order to establish a parliamentary system' (*Segye Ilbo*, 21 January 1999). This became the third time that Kim Jong-pil was 'betrayed' by his political partners, the presidents Park Chung-hee,[17] Kim Young-sam and now Kim Dae-jung. One of the core members of the ULD, Kim Yong-hwan, vice-chairman of the party, left the ULD in December 1998 due to the breaking of the coalition agreement. Kim Yong-hwan founded Korea's New Party in January 2000 (see Figure 3.1).

60 *Internal factors*

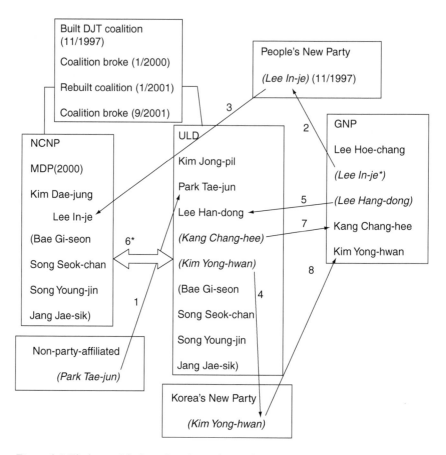

Figure 3.1 Fission and fusion of parties and party leaders (1997–2003) (source: author).

1 Park Tae-jun was elected as a National Assembly member in the supplementary by-election in May 1997 and joined the ULD in November 1997.
2 Lee In-je contested the result of the primary election and defected from the New Korea Party (the predecessor of the GNP) in November 1997. He founded the People's New Party.
3 Lee In-je joined the NCNP in August 1998.
4 Kim Yong-hwan, vice-chairman of the ULD, defected from the ULD in December 1998 and founded Korea's New Party in January 2000.
5 Lee Han-dong defected from the GNP and joined the ULD in December 1999. He became chairman of the ULD and later prime minister in June 2000.
6 Rented legislators to help the ULD qualify the quorum of the floor group from September to December 2000. Bae Gi-seon, Song Seok-chan, Song Young-jin and Jang Jae-sik defected from the MDP and joined the ULD in

				2000; however, they all returned back to the MDP when the coalition broke down in September 2001.
7			Kang Chang-hee, vice-chairman of the ULD, defected from the ULD and joined the GNP in October 2000.
8			Kim Yong-hwan, as the only legislator in the party, joined the GNP in October 2000.

The GNP itself was also suffering from factional conflicts, and Lee Han-dong, the vice-chairman (*bu-chongjae*) of the opposition party, also defected from the party and joined the ULD (*Donga Ilbo*, 30 December 1999), thereby becoming the chairman (*chongjae*) of the ULD. He actually became prime minister in the following year. Lee Han-dong was a core member of the Democratic Justice Party under the Chun Doo-hwan administration and was one of the faction leaders within the party. He was also once a colleague of Lee Hoe-chang at a time when they were prosecutors. In the lead-up to the 1997 presidential elections, he competed with Lee Hoe-chang in the primary election[18] to become a presidential candidate within the party, but lost to him. He lost again in the internal election to become a chairman of the GNP in 1998, being defeated by Lee Hoe-chang. A key problem here is that even if the party introduced a democratic process to select party leaders or representatives, the loser in the competition would not accept the rules of the game.

Questions may arise here as to why Lee Han-dong (or, even before, Lee In-je as a presidential candidate in 1997) did not accept the rules and defected from the party. As a pure office-seeker, it may be better to defect and join another party and secure his or her position within the party organization and future appointment as a candidate for the following general election. If one leader has appointment power in his hands, the competitor, Lee Han-dong, did not seem to accept Lee Hoe-chang's authority. This means it is likely that his position within the party would not be secured. Lee Gi-taek and Cho Sun were the cases being punished or marginalized by Lee Hoe-chang when they do not cooperate with the party leader (see pages 53–6). For Lee Han-dong, it would be better to deal with the ruling coalition parties to secure his position for the future and defect from the opposition Grand National Party. As Lee Han-dong succeeded in bargaining for his position with the ULD, he joined the ULD and later became chairman of the National Assembly and also prime minister when Park Tae-jun stepped down from his position over the suspicion of illegal land speculation (see pages 64–9).

The case shows that a lack of mechanisms for negotiation and compromise is not only a problem between the ruling parties and the opposition party, but also among individual political actors. This means that it is not only the level of institutionalization that matters but the internal environment or culture within the party. As the late scholar and US Senator Daniel Patrick Moynihan (cited in Huntington 2000: xiv) notes: '[t]he central conservative truth is that it is culture, not politics, that determines the success of a society. The central liberal truth is that politics can change a culture and save it from itself.' Although culture can also be cultivated by developing the level of institutionalization.

62 *Internal factors*

To prepare for the general election, Kim Dae-jung suggested merging the coalition parties into one. Kim Jong-pil refused to merge parties, for this meant he would officially agree not to amend the constitution, one of his key political goals. Kim Jong-pil stepped down from the position of prime minister to prepare for the following general election. To be a candidate in the general election, civil servants are required to resign from their position by law. To increase the ULD's seat numbers, Kim Jong-pil also had to be a candidate for the party. He did this by working for the party as honorary chairman of the ULD; the defector from the GNP, Lee Han-dong, became chairman (*chongjae*) of the ULD. The former chairman of the ULD, Park Tae-jun, then became prime minister in January 2000. To change the image of being a regional and old party for the next election, the NCNP changed its party name to the New Millennium Democratic Party (hereafter MDP). As mentioned, Kim Yong-hwan, who left the party and founded Korea's New Party, was also based in Chungcheong province (see Figure 3.1). This means that the ULD had to compete in the Sixteenth General Election with former party members from the same region with a different party name. This limited the party's appeal to the electorate. The ULD was unable to present a united front from the beginning of the electoral campaign.

The anti-candidate movement by civil organizations and coalition break-up

Another political storm hit the ULD in January 2000. Non-Government Organizations and other political actors in civil society embarked on an anti-candidate movement, although the extent to which the groups were spontaneous representations of the 'people's will' or simply manipulated by the government remains open to question. The anti-candidate movement was to campaign against the candidates allegedly involved in political corruption. The movement was viewed as indicative of a good democratic process by the president and some of the core members of the administration who themselves used to be members of civil organizations. As the first opposition party to have won an election and brought about a real change in the political make-up of the government, the MDP was sure to be less targeted (because it had a very short history of positions in power) than the former ruling parties who had enjoyed power and even illegal or unfair benefits for decades in the transition from the authoritarian to the civilian government, from 1960 to 1997. From the perspective of the 'anti-candidate movement', however, the MDP's error consisted of forging a coalition with the ULD, thereby becoming tarred with the same brush. If the citizen organizations were targeting old party politics, they would also target members of their coalition partner, the old, corrupt party that enjoyed privileges and long-term power.

For the ULD, the listing of the party leader, Kim Jong-pil, as one of the corrupt candidates came as a bolt from the blue. In the list of the anti-candidate movement, 66 names appeared of those who should be targeted in the Sixteenth General Election. Furious legislators of the ULD accused their coalition partner of conspiracy. They alleged that the MDP was involved in marginalizing the opposition party as well as the coalition partner, the ULD. On 27 January, the new party chairman (*Chongjae*) of the ULD, who had just joined the party from the GNP, Lee Han-dong, announced the end of the coalition with the MDP. A daily newspaper *Hankook Ilbo* pointed out that the real goal of this announcement was not to end the coalition but to boost public support for the ULD, especially in Chungcheong province, where the party traditionally had strong and loyal support (*Hankook Ilbo*, 28 January 2000). During Kim Young-sam's administration, when Kim Jong-pil was rejected by the main factions of Kim Young-sam he managed to gain a lot of support from Chungcheong province advocating *Chungcheongdo hatbaji* (Korean traditional underwear for men, see Chapter 2) and he actually achieved a relatively successful local election result in 1995.

A former legislator of the ULD, Lee Yang-hee,[19] contends that

> civil society should be purely independent of the government. If any civil society organization has financial support from the government, how can civil society act fairly against the government which acts against the interests of civil society? Civil society movements were run mainly through the subsidies of the government. This is wrong.

Lee Jin Seop,[20] a chief secretary of Na Kyung-won, the Seventeenth National Assembly member for the GNP, also notes that 'the role of civil society in South Korea is distorted. It is supposed to be close to citizens but not to power'. A recent study on the relationship between civil society and the government supports the above interviewee's point of view.

Yu Seok-chun and Wang Hye-suk (2006) report that 7 per cent (20 out of 313) of the former members of a civil organization, People's Solidarity for Participatory Democracy (*Chamyeoyeondae*), were appointed to high official positions during the Kim Young-sam administration, 36.1 per cent (113 out of 313) during the Kim Dae-jung administration and 50.5 per cent (158 out of 313) during that of Roh Moo-hyun (*Donga Ilbo*, 31 August 2006). *Donga Ilbo* (31 August 2006) reports that civil organizations are not civil but elite organizations. According to Yu and Wang's report on civil organizations, 40.9 per cent of the members (170 members) were lecturers or researchers out of 416 members in high positions in these civil organizations, 29 per cent were artists, 6.7 per cent religious leaders and chief executive officers, and 6.7 per cent civil movement activists. However, only 10.6 per cent of the respondents who held high positions in the civil organization were ordinary citizens. Yu (*Donga Ilbo*, 31 August 2006) argues that People's Solidarity for Participatory Democracy was hegemonized by a small number of elites. This suggests that the NGOs also cannot be free from the accusation of cronyism[21] indicated by the People's Solidarity for Participatory Democracy movement itself as being a deep-rooted problem of Korean society. A more serious problem, as the report notes, is that the high official members of the organization take part in the government's administration.

Civil society groups are not functioning but clinging to a patron–client relationship with the government (*Donga Ilbo*, 31 August 2006).

Despite the criticism of these civil organizations, their influence on ordinary citizens was remarkable. Before the election, each organization campaigned against voting for each of the listed candidates and the list of 'anti-candidates' was extended to 86 by April 2000. Over the Sixteenth General Election, 59 out of the 86 candidates failed to be elected (*Chosun Ilbo*, 20 April 2000). That was a 68.6 per cent success rate for the anti-voting campaign and this shows how much the voters were longing for a political system less pervaded by corruption and sleaze. In other words, this also shows how much the parties failed to link themselves to civil society.

Why do 'floor negotiation groups' matter?

The citizens did not grant majority status to any party again. This was due mainly to both the disaffection of the public with the political system and the existence of strong regionalism between the three main provinces: Jeolla, Chungcheong and Gyeongsang. Neither party could regard the general election as a success. The GNP remained the biggest opposition party, with 133 seats out of 273 and the MDP gained 115 seats and the ULD 17 seats. The Korea New Party gained only one seat, that of its founder, Kim Yong-hwan, who defected from the ULD; the People's Nation gained two seats and non-party-affiliated members gained five seats. It was a big failure for the ULD as it could not meet the minimum numbers to register as a negotiation group in the legislature, which requires a minimum of 20 seats. This triggered another disastrous political deadlock in the legislature as Kim Dae-jung tried to help the ULD so that he can rebuild coalition with Kim Jong-pil.

In the meantime, the prime minister, Park Tae-jun, resigned on 19 May 2000 amid allegations of illegal land speculation and accepting bribery in previous years. After he stepped down, President Kim Dae-jung offered him an alternative post. For the ruling party it was important to remain in a cooperative relationship with the ULD and the chairman of the ULD, one of the former elite members of the GNP, became the prime minister. The MDP and the ULD gained 136 votes, that is, three votes more than the total numbers of the ruling parties – Prime Minister Lee Han-dong was approved. The opposition party, GNP, had 133 seats and there were 130 votes against the vote of approval. This shows that there were three votes from the GNP that did not vote against the approval. Lee Hoe-chang, the leader of the GNP, was very disappointed over the 'uncooperative' three members that might be the ones who either gave up voting (two votes) or nullified their vote (*Hankook Kyungje*, 30 June 2000). Lee Hoe-chang was anxious about the party system having ruling coalition parties that had more seats (140 seats) than the GNP (133 seats) in the legislature (*Kyunghyang Sinmun*, 1 July 2000). It looked like the synergy effect could be really big if the ULD either remained in coalition with the ruling party or the GNP. What the ULD wanted was to be a 'floor group' to regain negotiation power among the summit meeting or the subvention that they could enjoy financially. Kim Jong-pil would support whoever would back that.

The MDP still needed to cooperate with the ULD and it was essential for the government to pass new laws and bills including those relating to the budget and other key pieces of legislation, revenues etc. Facing a big opposition party again, it was impossible for the government to continue without a coalition partner. The MDP had to rebuild the coalition with the ULD. If the ULD built a coalition or allied with the GNP, that meant the MDP would face even bigger opposition in the legislature. What the ULD wanted by then was to become a negotiation group. As the electoral result showed, the ULD with 17 seats could not qualify as a quorum for the negotiation group. It had three seats fewer than the minimum 20 seats required to be a negotiation group. The only way to qualify was to either pass a new law that would lower the quorum of the floor group to 17 or even 15 seats, or gain three more defectors from other parties. The ULD was enjoying considerable power as a coalition partner of the government. Superficially, therefore, the party's desperate attempt to gain this status seemed odd, but the party clearly had a number of points in mind.

First, parties able to gain the status of a floor group are provided with subventions from the state. The subvention is distributed to the parties by the ratio of popular votes or number of seats in the National Assembly. The parties able to meet the quorum for a floor meeting group are thereby entitled to receive a larger state subvention than smaller parties (i.e. those with fewer than 20 legislators). For example, as a small party with 17 seats, the ULD received 2.3 billion *won* a year, but as a member of a floor negotiation group the ULD would have been able to receive more than 5.6 billion *won* of subventions. The monthly subsidies as a floor group were nearly eight-times bigger than as a small party. They received 1.24 million *won* (600 pounds sterling, approximately) a month, but they could have gained 9.5 million *won* a month (about 5,000 pounds sterling) if they had qualified as a floor group. They could also put five members in the committee on national policy in the legislature. Therefore, for the ULD, the fact the party had only three seats fewer than the quorum of a floor group brought a financial loss of about 3.3 billion *won*. This law on subventions shows how the law-makers secured the interests of the big political parties institutionally by blocking any support for the emergence of new small parties.[22]

The ULD's second motivation for wanting to become a floor group was that most legislative decisions relating to bills, laws and budgets result from negotiation and compromise among floor group representative meetings that used to be held among Kim Dae-jung (or a party representative instead of him[23]), Lee Hoe-chang and Kim Jong-pil before the Sixteenth General Election. Kim Jong-pil was, however, no longer qualified to a seat in the floor group representative meeting as his party did not qualify as a quorum of the floor group. If the floor group leaders could not reach any decision after the core negotiation and compromise, then the ordinary legislators take part in the Assembly meeting as mobilized actors, either raising hands to approve or disapprove or, in an emergency, they even fight around the chairman's table to interrupt the announcement of the final decision.

66 *Internal factors*

The National Assembly sometimes fell into unseemly behaviour, as when legislators left their seats and congregated around the speaker, or even took the microphone away from the National Assembly chairman to disrupt the final announcement of a policy decision. Such behaviour is nothing new to Korean citizens.

Overall, the ULD could have received 3.3 billion Korean *won*[24] as a floor group; in fact, the financial loss was significant, simply because it lacked just three members to meet the quorum for a floor group. By July 2000, the two leaders from the MDP and the GNP could meet at the summit meeting to negotiate political problems. The problem was that most important decisions and negotiations were mainly discussed in summit meetings and the followers of the leaders either agreed to pass the bills and laws or boycotted the proposed laws. Kim Jong-pil could not play a casting vote role between the two leaders.

The ULD proposed to lower the quorum for the floor group from 20 to 10 or 15 seats so that the ULD could qualify to be a floor group. While the MDP was hesitating to amend the law to lower the quorum in June 2000, doing a favour for the ULD, Kim Jong-pil proposed coordinating with the opposition GNP. If the MDP lost the cooperation of the ULD and faced even bigger opposition, it would be impossible for the ruling party to function effectively, either as an administration or in the legislature. It was necessary for the MDP to embrace the ULD. In the meantime, the GNP also hinted to the ULD about the possibility of building a coalition. It was known that the former president, Kim Young-sam, once mentioned that the biggest mistake was to let Kim Jong-pil out of the coalition in 1995 (*Hankook Ilbo*, 23 July 2000). Lee Hoe-chang, the leader of the GNP, was also advised by Kim Young-sam to ally with Kim Jong-pil. On 22 July, after a meeting with Lee Hoe-chang, Kim Jong-pil said 'there is no eternal enemy in the political arena' and this gesture urged the ruling party to go further to pass the law on the quorum for a floor negotiation group (*Hankook Ilbo*, 23 July 2000). The ruling party, MDP, had to prevent any potential coalition between Kim Jong-pil and Lee Hoe-chang. The power that Kim Jong-pil could enjoy within the coalition was much more significant than the small size of his party (17 members) would have otherwise allowed him to enjoy.

On 24 July, struggles and combats among the law-makers were broadcast live on national television. The MDP and the ULD members passed a law lowering the quorum to 15 seats to qualify as a floor group at the National Assembly meeting. When the vice-speaker of the National Assembly was about to announce the passing of the law lowering the quorum to 15 members, the legislators of the GNP literally 'jumped up' onto the vice-chairman's table and took the microphone and the gavel he needed to end the meeting (*Segye Ilbo*, 25 July 2000). The legislators of the GNP occupied the Assembly's main chamber and began an overnight strike insisting that the bill was not valid. The GNP announced it would boycott cooperation with the ruling parties and occupied the Budget-settlement committee conference room in order to disrupt the passage of the supplementary budget. The MDP blamed the GNP for changing its decision as this sudden attack by the opposition was unexpected. The rational choice of the MDP was based on the assumption that the GNP and the ULD had agreed on the issue of lowering the quorum of the floor group in talks at a golf resort between Lee Hoe-chang and Kim Jong-pil. Lee Hoe-chang vigorously denied that there had been any talks on that and even dismissed one of his legislators in an executive position for leaking information on his meeting with Kim Jong-pil.

For the GNP, there was also another reason to object to this law. The GNP was still riddled with internal conflicts among the various factions. If the law was to be passed there would be the possibility for the factions to defect from the GNP and found their own independent factions and register as floor negotiation groups. The new law lowering the minimum number to become a floor group was, on the one hand, very democratic as this would also allow a small party to survive and represent alternative views. Due to lack of financial support, small parties with fewer than 20 members could hardly survive long-term in the Korean party system, and this was one of the reasons why the new parties such as the labour party representing the union could not emerge at an earlier stage. On the other hand, as far as the GNP was concerned, this new law would boost the number of small parties in the legislature. For example, each party has factions such as Donggyo faction, TK (Taegu-Kyoungsang) faction and PK (Pusan-Kyoungsang[25]) faction. If these factions leave their parties and found their own parties, with 15 seats they can still be financially secured as floor groups thus they no longer need to stay within the big parties. Factions with more than 15 members could simply leave the party and found their own party, building coalitions with other parties.

Apart from concerns over the emergence of numerous small parties, many scholars such as Sartori (1976), Mainwaring (1993), Cheibub (2002) and Tsebelis[26] (2002) argue that the effective number of parties in a multi-party system (five or more) would affect stable governability. Contrary to the widely believed assumption, Cheibub (2002: 299–300) argues that minority presidents do not face deadlock often. The probability of deadlock is one-third of the unstable cases under presidential regimes. Deadlock is not caused by the size of the government but by the characteristics of the party system. Cheibub contends that low or moderate (three or four parties) pluralism negatively affects presidential democracy. In other words, presidential democracies with more than five effective parties survive a lot longer than ones with fewer than five effective parties. For Cheibub, moderate pluralism (three or four equally effective parties) undermines the number of seats that the president can control in the legislature. Another explanation of moderate pluralism is that seats controlled by the president are not relevant to the survival of presidential democracy but, rather, the distribution of strength and seats controlled by equally effective moderate numbers of parties; thus, such situations produce stalemate. Therefore equally effective three- or four-party systems induce inherent instability in the process of compromise. When two parties agree on something, the third one can always offer something more to break the agreement between the two parties.

This has actually happened between the three parties in South Korea. Although the ULD had relatively fewer seats, the role the ULD played between the ruling MDP and the opposition GNP was equally effective. The GNP sought to break the coalition between the two ruling parties and the coalition partner, ULD, had known exactly how to react between the two parties. Cheibub argues that with more than five effective parties in the legislature, the hazard rates (of presidential democracy) are the lowest, though the share of seats controlled by the president is also reduced. Cheibub's argument leaves the possibility of lowering conflicts among parties in the legislature if the party system is changed to a multi-party system with more than five effective parties. Although the ULD was blamed for trying to lower the quorum for the sake of its own interests, the result of lowering the quorum may have brought about a very different party system in South Korea. There might have been a chance to institutionalize a different kind of mechanism of compromise and negotiation under multi-partyism. If the quorum was lowered to 15 seats in the legislature, as requested by the ULD, there was the possibility of breaking the existing moderate pluralism and turn it into a multi-party system. For the GNP, a major concern was whether factions would leave the party and found their own parties, as even small parties with 15 seats in the legislature could still gain considerable amounts of subventions from the government.

Although the GNP insisted no discussions about lowering the quorum with the ULD took place at the golf resort, it is noteworthy that Kim Jong-pil, who was at the core of the political strife, maintained a low profile at the time. He was very successful in making the MDP believe that the ULD and the GNP could build a coalition against the MDP, and urged the MDP to change the law on the quorum of a floor group from 20 to 15 seats. By helping the ULD, the MDP thought it could gain the cooperation of the ULD and thus prevent the party from building a coalition with the GNP. This was particularly important because at the time the coalition[27] between the MDP and the ULD had officially broken up. The GNP announced it would boycott any National Assembly Sessions and committee activities until the ruling parties nullified the new law and the president apologized for the sudden passage of the new law.

Another point is that both the ruling MDP and the opposition GNP wanted to attract the ULD to secure their own power in the legislature. The leader of the ULD, Kim Jong-pil, enjoyed the casting vote between the two parties in the political battles over power in the legislature. This indicates the power a small party can produce on its own.

It is obvious that all the parties were only interested in achieving a hegemonic position in the legislature. Most new policies remained dormant in the deadlocked legislature, including the crucial proposed reform of the medical and pharmaceutical system. At the time, 12 proposed laws, including the national budget, were waiting to be approved, but all the procedures were delayed again (*Donga Ilbo*, 25 July 2000; *Hankook Ilbo*, 25 July 2000). 24,000 billion *won* worth of supplementary budget was 'suspended' in the process after the 213th Extraordinary Session meeting in the National Assembly was guillotined (*Donga Ilbo*, 27 July 2000). Despite its approval in the legislature, the law on the quorum of a floor group was nullified by the Constitution Judge Committee in July 2000.

The ULD continued to press for lowering of the quorum, however. By the end of the year, three members of the MDP defected from the party and joined the ULD, thereby meeting the quorum of a floor negotiation group. The three members' reason to defect from the MDP was to help the Kim Dae-jung administration's governability. This means that the ULD 'borrowed' legislators from the coalition partner MDP and finally became a floor negotiation group. Having three more legislators, the ULD could finally qualify as a floor group and managed to gain all of the benefits this gave financially and politically in the legislature. The vice-chairman of the ULD, Kang Chang-hee, was opposed to such chicanery and later left the party and joined the GNP. He was joined by former vice-chairman Kim Yong-hwan, who was the only member of the Korea New Party (see Figure 3.1). A year later, one of the young legislators of the MDP recalled this as his worst moment in politics and felt ashamed of being a politician. The problem was that he followed the party leader due to his fear of retribution: non-cooperative action would mean he would not be appointed as a candidate in future general elections. Raising his own opinion against the party leader's decision would have meant the end of his political life (*Monthly Chosun*, January 2002).

Within a week, on 8 January 2001, the MDP and the ULD announced their decision to rebuild the coalition (*Kyunghyang sinmun*, 10 January 2001), nearly a year after the ULD pulled out of the previous coalition (27 January 2000). However, the second coalition lasted only until 3 September 2001 as the coalition broke up over disputes on dismissal of Im Dong-won, minister of the Ministry of Unification, and 'the rented legislators'[28] moved back to the MDP from the ULD in the same month. The ULD had 15 seats when the government was faced with charges of political corruption, represented by the four big 'gate scandals': Lee Yong-ho-gate, Yun Tae-sik-gate, Jin Seong-hyun-gate and Jung Hyun-jun-gate (*Hankook Ilbo*, 29 December 2001). The ruling party members and the son of President Kim Dae-jung were implicated in these cases of political corruption and the president entered a 'lame duck' period much earlier than normal as the government lacked legitimacy and support.

Size does not matter

In the above section I have revisited what happened in the legislature and why deadlock, in fact a series thereof, occurred from the very beginning of the administration. Coalition ruling parties struggled from the early stages of the Kim Dae-jung administration. This seems to suggest how deadlock and ungovernability are induced structurally by the size of the government under presidentialism as there are no mechanisms to resolve conflicts in the legislature. However, by looking at the intra-party politics and each party's rational choice, it is clear that there were other factors hindering compromise and negotiation. If the opposition party had been rather supportive of the ruling parties, the deadlocks and stalemates would not have occurred that often in the legislature. What actually hindered the mechanisms of compromise and negotiation was highly disciplined

– or better, rigid – party organization. Although a highly disciplined ruling party's organization induces the cohesiveness of the party organization if every party has a high level of discipline, this is problematic in gaining the support of the opposition parties. If individual legislators are not free to support other parties, but only to follow the party whips, the only way to avoid deadlock in the legislature is to attract defectors and enlarge the size of the ruling parties, and that was indeed what happened during the first six months from the start of the Kim Dae-jung administration.

I have shown that the enlarged ruling parties did not secure governability, as the opposition went on to protest outside of the National Assembly rather than attending the National Assembly meetings. One interesting thing to note is that when the MDP was the opposition party during the Kim Young-sam administration, the way they protested against the ruling party was very similar. For example, they protested outside the National Assembly and refused to attend National Assembly meetings (see Chapter 2). Thus Korean politics lacks space for compromise and negotiation in the political arena. From the case of the Kim Dae-jung administration I find that size alone cannot induce governability when the legislature lacks mechanisms for compromise and negotiation. To explain what would create an environment to enable negotiations to take place, it is essential to examine party organization in order to learn how the party is run and who rules the party, and what provides strong party discipline. In the following section I will examine the characteristics of party organization in South Korea.

The impact of governability: party organization

This section examines how parties are organized in Korea and tests the three hypotheses mentioned at the outset of the chapter on leadership, factionalism and funding as expressions of the level of linkage between the party and the citizens. Looking at the struggles the ruling party, MDP, had with the opposition party and with the coalition partner, the ULD's party organization (or the lack thereof) seems to be a central factor in explaining the party's electoral success and efficacy (in performance).

In order to carry out the above task, I draw on the concept of political party organization as theorized by Panebianco (1988). Panebianco points out that the survival and functioning of an organization depend on a series of party activities. A party's organizational activities can be categorized according to six main factors: competency, environmental relations, internal communication, formal rules, organizational financing and recruitment (Panebianco 1988: 33–35).

The first competency is 'the power of the expert' and 'fundamental resource of organizational power'. The expert with organizational power should have a specialized knowledge that is obtained by educational training and experience in management of the party's internal and external relations.

Second, environmental relations are as Panebianco contends, 'the primary source of uncertainty'. Organizations always face an uncertain external environment; however, to control this uncertainty, the party needs to be able to control 'a decisive zone of organizational uncertainty'. The tasks for environmental relations include stipulation, redefinition or solidification of alliances with other organizations and choice of issues, and those who are in charge of the tasks have two roles within the organization, on the one hand, and between the organization and the environment, on the other hand.

In terms of the third factor, communication, if a political actor within the party organization can distribute, manipulate, delay or suppress information, that means the actor holds a decisive resource in terms of power relations.

Fourth, as Downs also mentioned, rules are the institutionalization of deviation from the written norms. Panebianco emphasizes how formal rules enable the activists to strengthen their positions with respect to the other organizational actors. For Panebianco, 'to establish formal rules is to mold the "playing field", and to choose the terrain upon which confrontations, negotiations, and power games with other organizational actors will take place' (1988: 35). Parties in Korean politics show very low levels of institutionalization. High levels of fission and fusion among political actors, frequent party mergers or coalitions or break-ups show weakly institutionalized rules within the parties. If rules are not to be kept but to be applied only in certain cases, it is very easy for politicians not to abide by the rules and that is why, when politicians lose the primary election within the party, they often choose to leave the party. If there were certain rules to be kept by all members equally and strictly, this kind of phenomena would not happen.[29]

Fifth, Panebianco maintains 'money is indispensable to the life and functioning of every organization'. There are two main ways of financing political parties: external financiers, on the one hand, and many small contributions from membership dues or self-financing campaigns, on the other. External financiers control the zone of uncertainty and exercise a certain amount of power over the party organization, but in the case of many small contributors, the power belongs to the internal actors. For Panebianco, the reason why the British Labour Party is less institutionalized is that it has external financiers (the unions). In other words, due to the financial dependence of the party on the unions, it is more difficult for the internal actors to consolidate power and the internal cohesion of the party. For this reason, he argues that parties reliant on many small contributions from the membership and self-financing campaigns are more likely to be highly institutionalized.

Finally, the sixth crucial resource of organizational power derives from recruitment. Recruitment plays an important role in controlling organizational borders and the members' career opportunity structure (Panebianco 1988: 33–36). According to the six indicators Panebianco suggested, parties in Korea remain at a very low level of institutionalization.

Characteristics of party and organization: cadre or mass parties?

Parties in Korea are often characterized as cadre parties or mass bureaucratic parties. As Sartori (1976: 248) states, a mass party is 'a party open to all and/or followed by masses of people', that is, a mass party is based on wide public support. Such parties are rooted in social democratic parties, including workers, and extended to the public. A mass party is highly bureaucratized and the elites control the party organization; however, the party is based on the party members who regularly pay their dues and the elites provide the members with political education in support of political issues or policies. Duverger (1990: 41) characterizes a mass party in this way:

> it appeals to the public: to the paying public who make it possible for the electoral campaign to be free from capitalist pressures; to the listening, active public which receives a political education and learns how to intervene in the life of the state.

On the other hand, a cadre party is not based on the number of members but on a select group of influential persons. The small numbers of influential people support the candidate, conduct electoral campaigns and handle the finances of the party. Duverger argues that many American parties are cadre parties or semi-mass parties. With the system of 'closed primaries' it resembles a mass party; however, if the party does not have large numbers of due-paying, regular members it is no longer a mass party. As long as the electoral campaign relies on a cadre – that is, a small number of elites – it is not a mass party but a cadre party.

Are parties in Korea mass parties or cadre parties? Most parties in Korea do not have enough due-paying members to be regarded as mass parties. Most party members are mobilized by the staffs that are recruited to run the election campaigns. They are not party members who regularly pay dues but temporary electoral campaigners. Many members registered in the party are mobilized by the campaigners and quite a lot of them do not even know if they are members of the party (Jeong 2000: 239). Kim Yong-ho (2002: 299) notes 6,146,187 party members were registered in the political parties in 1999, but 6,122,300 members were recruited to carry out electoral campaigning and were paid for their effort. In fact, regular members paying dues amounted to only 23,889, that is, only 0.07 per cent of the total. That is very low compared to that of Austria, for example, with 17.66 per cent, and even the UK with 1.92 (see Table 3.1).

In terms of organization, however, parties in Korea show a mass-party structure. In other words, parties are organized in the central and peripheral sectors and they are all linked from the central to the local party offices. Parties have mass bureaucratic organizations with leaders; however, they do not have members. This would be, as Duverger notes, like a school with teachers but without pupils (1990: 41).

Do parties in Korea qualify as cadre parties? Many scholars note that parties in Korea can be characterized in this way (Kil 1990; Kim 2001; Park 2003). In terms of members who run electoral campaigns and support the candidates, parties appear to be closer to cadre parties than mass parties. However, in Korea the candidate in each electoral district bears most of the financial burden on his

Table 3.1 Numbers of party members in Korea and other countries

Country	Kind of party members	Total number of party members	Party member rates out of voters' rate (%)	Year
South Korea	Enlisted party members paying dues	23,887	0.07	1999
	Party officials	6,122,300	18.23	1999
	Total party members	6,146,187	18.30	1999
Austria		1,031,052	17.66	1999
Finland		400,615	9.65	1998
Greece		600,600	6.77	1998
Italy		1,974,040	4.05	1998
Spain		1,131,250	3.42	2000
Germany		1,780,173	2.93	1999
The Netherlands		294,469	2.51	1999
UK		840,000	1.92	1998
France		615,219	1.57	1999
Poland		326,500	1.15	2000
Average of EU 20 countries			4.99	1997–2000

Source: Kim (2002: 299).[30]

or her own, with some subsidy from the central party. In terms of the party, it is more likely that all candidates relied on the party leaders to raise funds. The party at both the central and local levels is highly concentrated around the leader. This is why the party is often called a one-man party or boss party. As the financial burden is on the shoulders of the party leaders, the right to nominate candidates is also concentrated on the leaders. Considering that the stakeholders in a mass party can be regarded as all of the members who share the financial burden for the functioning of the party by paying party dues, the ownership of Korean parties often seems to belong to the leaders. Herein lies the reason why, when the party leader leaves his/her own party, the party often collapses and is revived under another name with the same leader or disappears. This is another reason why it is easy to build a coalition without a consensus among the members of the party members but only among the leaders. Considering that a cadre party arises from a balance of power among cadre members, Korean parties can be said to be quite different from such parties, as Korean parties tend to be one-man centred (see Table 3.2).[31]

In terms of party type, Katz and Mair (1995: 8–19) note the emergence of the cartel party. The elite or cadre party was developed in nineteenth-century Europe and the committees of the party were both closely engaged with the state and the civil society. As working-class organizations emerged after industrialization and urbanization, the mass party appeared from the 1880s to the 1960s, making a link between the state and civil society. In the post-industrial era, the catch-all party developed from 1945 onwards with the emergence of the middle class; it cut across class boundaries. The ideology of parties increasingly converged towards the middle where they could attract a greater variety of voters. In this way, the mass party became closer to a 'catch-allistic' party.

Thus, the party organization has become more professional and politicians have become more office-oriented, acting as brokers between the state and civil society (see Figure 3.2). As brokers, party politicians appeal to the electorate in a professional manner, yet are also in a position to be able to manipulate the state. However Katz and Mair (ibid.: 14) warn that 'if a party can manipulate the state in the interests of its clients in civil society, it should also be able to manipulate the society in its own interests'. Jang Hoon (1997:16) points out that, fol-

Table 3.2 The stance of parties in Korea between the state and civil society during the Kim Dae-jung administration

		Civil society	
		Linked	Unlinked
State	One leader		One-leader party[32] (MDP, ULD, GNP)
	Small number of elites	Cadre party	Cartel party
	Mass	Mass party	

Source: author.

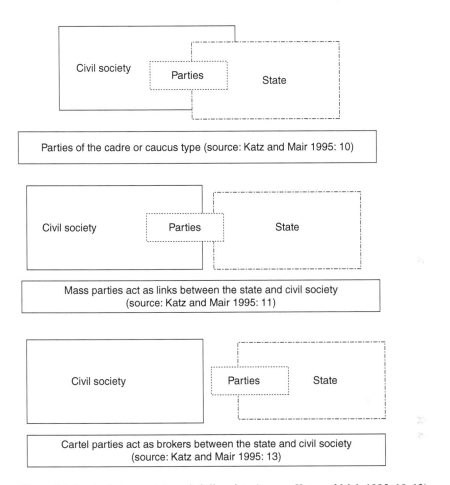

Figure 3.2 Parties between state and civil society (source: Katz and Mair 1995: 10–13).

lowing democratization, parties in Korea function as cartel parties between the state and civil society. One of the most salient characteristics of the cartel party is that such parties do not financially rely on party dues, but mainly on the state's subvention. This is also a feature of recent party politics in Korea.

As Figure 3.2 shows, the cartel party does not link the state with civil society. When the party does not link civil society with the state, and fails to represent civil society, it is more likely to represent a small number of elite interests and this eventually will lead to the erosion of legitimacy. Lawson (1988: 15) argues that:

> Participation, leadership recruitment, allocation of resources, the creation and propagation of values, the control of behaviour (through the control of

force and/or through educative communication) all require the creation of connections between different levels of aggregation. Creating linkages is itself an extremely important function of politics.

In other words, to secure a party's legitimacy and power in the legislature, the party must provide linkages between the state and the citizens. When the citizens are alienated from participation, resource allocation and developing policies, it is hardly likely to consolidate internal power with a wide range of support. No matter how the law-makers create a majority status through building coalitions, as long as elections are held for the party to be judged by the citizens, the ruling party will suffer from the punishment of the citizen. However, apart from the election, citizens and sometimes ordinary legislators are mainly excluded from the functions of party organization and the highly centralized power among the elites fails to provide the essential linkage between the state and the citizens. In this sense, the party in Korea is not functioning in a fundamental sense. The linkage role of the party matters for legitimacy: thus, when the government is engaged in reform policies, legitimacy comes into question. When the leadership is crippled, it is hard to establish stable governability.

Funding

According to the National Audit Report, the rate of dues paid by each party's membership is 0.5 per cent. In late 1997, just before Kim Dae-jung took office, the New Korea Party and then ruling party officially had 3,723,138 members; however, only 22,793 members paid their dues – that is, 0.6 per cent. The NCNP (by then led by Kim Dae-jung) had a 0.5 per cent rate among the party members; the Liberal Democratic Party had 0.03 per cent; and the People's Nation had a rate of 0.1 per cent (*Donga Ilbo*, 10 December 1998; Kim 1998: 15).

Most of the electoral campaign is funded by the individual party candidate, and the candidate mainly relies on self-generated funds, often from his or her own business or business supporters. This also limits the opportunity for the less-well-off but efficient human resource to enter politics. If the potential politician is without his or her own financial support, it is hardly likely he or she will run in the general election. There are thus a limited number of members who pay party dues, and at many local party offices no members pay their dues; rather, they are mobilized to attend electoral rallies and campaigns either through the use of gifts or bribes. When people work for the campaign, they are paid for their labour rather than acting as volunteer party members. If there are no incentives, the local voters do not even gather to listen to the candidates' policy proposals. This is due to the legacy of the political culture under authoritarian governments.[33] The population is not used to listening to electoral campaigning and policy proposals. Instead, the citizens are used to being mobilized by the government either by gifts or envelopes stuffed with money. The gifts include watches, towels, meals and sometimes tours to tourist spots (the candidate provides local voters with the tourist bus and other tour expenses). 'The more money or gifts, the more votes' is a popular saying in Korea. Citizens have no chance to play a more active role in politics because they have no opportunity to receive education and thus rely on the favours by local leaders, redistribution of gifts and funds. Cho Hong-gyu,[34] a former member of the National Assembly, contends that 'the level of civil society is lower than the political society. Politicians follow the preference of citizens to gain votes. Confucian culture based on family, friends and region is not always bad'.

According to *Chosun Ilbo*'s investigation, a candidate distributed envelopes with 100,000 *won*[35] in cash to 30 potential voters in a village meeting in Busan. Another candidate confessed that he had to give a minimum of 30,000 *won* in each envelop to try to woo potential voters; this goes up to 70,000 *won* near election day. He wryly noted that the only advantage of this kind of electoral campaign is that it feels like every four years Korea has the chance to redistribute wealth to the poor (*Chosun Ilbo*, 16 April 2000).

Subventions

At the central level, parties receive 800 *won* annually per voter as an ordinary subvention. In the year of the presidential election and general election, an additional 800 *won* subvention is granted per voter. When it is a year with local elections that are held on three levels (*Si/Do* Council Members, Autonomous *Gu/Si/Gun* Council Members, Education Board Members), the subvention is given three times so it amounts to 1,800 *won* per voter (Sim and Kim 2002: 157).

Half of the subventions are given to the floor negotiation groups equally divided, and the other half is given to the parties in the ratio of legislature seat numbers, percentage of the national votes each party gained at the general election and the percentage of votes each party gained at the local elections. The subvention is given to the central parties in the legislature.

Political donations to the National Election Commission

Political donations can be made by an individual or an organization. An individual can donate from 10,000 *won* to a hundred-million *won* or 5 per cent of the previous year's income. A company can donate 5-million *won* or 2 per cent of the previous year's income and organizations can donate 5-million *won* (Sim and Kim 2002: 157). The local party branches can raise dues, donations or can carry out some other activities to raise income; however, they can only be subsidized by the central party and cannot receive subventions from the state directly.

The problem is that most of the local branches do not rely on membership dues but on the legislator of the area who is the leader of the local branch: in most cases, he or she is the only source of finance. In terms of dues (in other words, membership fees), only a very small number of members pay. In 2000, only 9.6 per cent of the GNP's central income was from members' dues, 13.1 per cent from donations and 61.5 per cent from subventions out of a total income of about 34 billion *won*. The NCNP received 2.8 per cent from members' dues,

78 *Internal factors*

Table 3.3 Central party income (unit: million *won*) (%)

Party	Dues	Donation	Trust money	Subvention	Misc.	Total
GNP	3,310 (9.6)	4,505 (13.1)	0.4 (0.001)	21,046 (61.5)	5,338.6 (15.6)	34,200
NCNP	2,163 (2.8)	40,000 (53.1)	0.4 (0.0005)	18,417 (24.4)	14,665.6 (19.4)	75,246
ULD	477 (1.8)	7,815 (30.7)	0.2 (0.0007)	9,565 (37.6)	7,577.8 (29.7)	25,435
Total	5,950 (4.4)	52,320 (38.8)	1 (0.0007)	49,028 (36.3)	27,582 (20.4)	134,881

Source: modified from Sim and Kim (2002: 163).

53.1 per cent from donations and 24.4 per cent from subventions out of a total income of about 75 billion *won*. For the ULD, the ratio was 1.8 per cent from members' dues, 30.7 per cent from donations and 37.6 per cent from subventions out of a total income of about 25 billion *won* (ibid.: 163). Overall, parties relied on members' dues on average 4.4 per cent. As the ruling party, the NCNP had the biggest proportion of donations and the ULD, as its coalition partner, also seemed to enjoy more donations as well (see Table 3.3).

In terms of party income, the difference between the ruling party and the opposition party is significant. The GNP had the largest amount of subvention (about 21 billion *won*) as a result of the large number of legislature seats compared to that of the NCNP (about 18 billion *won*). However, the total income was nearly half of the NCNP's income. This shows political donors follow power and expect some benefit from their donations.

Sim and Kim (2002: 166) note that there is a higher rate of membership dues paid at the local branch of the party compared to the central party. But this results from donations by the members rather than from membership dues. In 2000, the GNP's 85,000 members paid 12.8 billion *won* in dues.[36] This means an individual member paid 1.5 million *won* each on average. The NCNP's 6,300 members paid ten billion won, that is, 1.6 million *won* per head. The ULD's 3,700 members paid 4.7 billion *won*, that is, 1.3 million *won* per head on average (see Table 3.3). In the local branch, the ratio of the subvention received from the central party is relatively low at 23.5 per cent for the GNP, 13.4 per cent for the NCNP and 4.5 per cent for the ULD (ibid.: 166).

As these figures show, the membership dues are not the same as the dues paid to so-called mass political parties in Western countries. In Korea, membership dues are paid by very small numbers of members, and parties are more likely to be dependent on legislators' personal sources of finance, donations and subventions. Overall, most of the party income is based on the small numbers of party leaders able to attract more donations at the party's central level and at the local level, as well as the subvention and their own personal financial resources. To raise donations, candidates at the general elections hold supporters' meetings (*Huwonhoe*). The supporters' meetings can be held in various forms, including inviting people to concerts,[37] a party for a book launch[38] or exhibition of the candidate's own calligraphy. Jang Seong-min,[39] a former legislator and radio presenter on current affairs, contends that:

It is a lot improved now but still supporters donate funds under the table. The interesting thing is that many supporters donate funds to prevent a change in the laws. The recent incident with the Private School Law is a case in point. Many involved in Private Schools donated funds to politicians to protect existing laws on Private Schools.[40]

The function of the local branch lies in recruiting potential candidates for the party, gathering the opinion of the local voters on the most important issues and educating voters. Staffs at the local branch are very active during the electoral campaign and take care of citizens' personal events such as the weddings or funerals of party supporters. Taking care of local voters' needs is a very important role played by the legislator who is the leader of the local branch. Each local branch spends an average of 10–30 million *won* a month on these sorts of things (*Kukmin Ilbo*, 11 May 1999; *Seoul Sinmun*, 10 May 1999). Apart from the maintenance of the office, including rent and utilities, the main expense for the local branch lies in taking care of the family events of local voters. Attending and sending money to a funeral or wedding is a part of traditional culture in Korea to help each other on a happy or sad day; however, most of the legislators who have local supporters in their areas spend more than two-thirds of their monthly expenses in taking care of the potential voters' family events.[41] Lee Yang-hee,[42] a former legislator, has stated that 'only a few who are in high positions have enough funds, especially in the ruling party. Ordinary legislators mainly rely on their very close relatives as supporters. Being a legislator does not have advantages economically'.

However, this comment actually contrasts with what was said by other legislators I interviewed. A former legislator[43] of the ruling party stated that:

> During the supporters' meeting many supporters come. Imagine one supporter donates 100 million *won* (about 100,000 US dollars) each. How much would it be? Yes, it costs 200 million *won* to 300 million *won* to run the local office where you are elected, but if you manage to have more than 10 supporters donating 100 million *won* each, you still have 700 million *won* in your pocket.

This shows how the funding channel is focused on a few politicians and how unequally the funding is allocated.

Examining one legislator's expenses at his local branch is illustrative. In this case, he spends about 20 million *won* a month to run his local branch office. Apart from rent and the wages of the staff, he spent two million *won* for sending flowers to the local citizens on special occasions, six million *won* for weddings and funerals and sometimes as much as nine million *won* for gifts in the months of the Lunar New Year's day and Thanksgiving day (*Seoul Sinmun*, 10 May 1999). This shows how Confucian culture functions in the political world: here, the local legislator acts as a representative of the area, a 'father figure' for the people. Many local citizens are members of the party in name only but they do not pay membership dues and subscriptions, but the legislator takes care of them in terms of family events. If the legislator does not take care of them, he is more likely to be criticized as one who does not know the custom or lacks manners, thereby risking loss of votes in the next elections. In return, the legislator receives loyal votes. In this system, the voters who have benefited from the legislator would vote for the legislator regardless of his or her policy orientation or party. Pye (1985: 67, cited in Helgesen 1998: 221) describes such leadership as follows:

> Korean rulers, like Korean fathers, are expected to be embattled, needing to prove themselves in adversary contacts; but they are also expected to be masterful at all times, for like the Chinese leader-father, the Korean is supposed to be an aloof, lonely authority figure, able to cope single-handedly with all of his wishes. Yet again like the Japanese leader-father, he is expected to be sympathetic, nurturing, and sensitive to the wishes of his followers' family, though at the same time vicious and aggressive in fighting external foes.

The father-figure leader is the same as in the central party. The party leader takes care of the ordinary legislators with subsidies to sustain the local branch and to carry out electoral campaigns or appointment of the candidate in the next election or executive position in the government in the case of the ruling parties. Strong loyalty is essential to gain those benefits from the party leaders. Power is centred almost exclusively on the party leaders.

As members normally do not pay membership dues, except for the few who offer big donations, members do not gain any education and do not have any power over decision-making at the local level. The legislator is mostly responsible for raising funds and a few members of staff and the legislator run the office based on a top-down hierarchy. This is also another reason why political parties in Korea fail to reflect the voices of the alienated citizens who are outside the mainstream: women, elderly citizens, under-paid labourers and so on. Nationwide, this is also why the central party loses the linkage between the state and society. Between the politicians and the interest groups, patron–client relationships developed during the history of modern Korea. Looking at the party system the main political figures have remained virtually the same all the way through. As Figure 3.3 shows, most of the parties have their origins in the Democratic Republic Party and the Democratic Party going back to 1960 (see Figure 3.3 and for more recent data see Figure 6.4).[44] Apart from the Democratic Republic Party, the Democratic Party has its root partly in the Korea Democratic Party of 1947.

When democratization is achieved through elite pacts, interest groups and the elites still dominate the party system and do not allow any new political groups to emerge. State subventions gave privileged rights to the parties of the existing political elites and these parties came to rely more on the leaders than on the grassroots; it is the leaders who raise the funds, not the ordinary members through paying party dues. Jang Seong-min,[45] a former legislator, points out that:

Internal factors 81

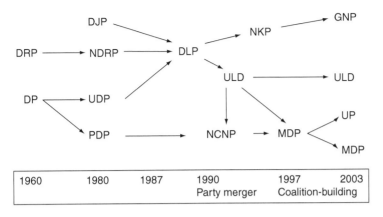

Figure 3.3 Coalition-building (1960–2003) Source: revised and simplified from Jang 2003: 40; Diamond and Kim 2000: 57; and author.

Party lists
DRP   Democratic Republican Party led by Kim Jong-pil (1963)
DP   Democratic Party led by Park Sun-cheon 1963 (later, New Democratic Party in 1964 and its former party of the New Korea Democratic Party (NKDP) in the 1980s led by Kim Young-sam and Kim Dae-jung)
DJP   Democratic Justice Party – ruling party led by Chun Doo-hwan (1980) and later by Roh Tae-Woo (1987)
NKDP   New Korea Democratic Party led by Kim Young-sam and Kim Dae-jung (1985)
UDP   Unification Democratic Party led by Kim Young-sam (1987)
NDRP   New Democratic Republican Party led by Kim Jong-pil (1987)
PDP   Peace Democratic Party led by Kim Dae-jung (1987)
DLP   Democratic Liberal Party after the three parties' merger (1990)
UPP   United People's Party led by Chung Ju-young (1992)
NKP   New Korea Party led by Kim Young-sam (1996)
PNP   People's New Party led by Lee In-je (1997)
GNP   Grand National Party led by Lee Hoe-chang (1997)
ULD   United Liberal Democrats led by Kim Jong-pil (1995)
KNP   Korea's New Party led by Kim Yong-hwan (2000)
NCNP   National Congress for New Politics led by Kim Dae-jung (1996)
MDP   New Millennium Democratic Party led by Kim Dae-jung, later Roh Moo-hyun (2000)
PP 21   People's Power 21 led by Chung Mong-joon (2002)
UP   Uri Party led by Roh Moo-hyun (2002)

There are three kinds of punishment if ordinary legislators do not follow the leaders of the party. First the allocation of the expenses for the local branch depends on the legislators' loyalty toward the leaders or elite members of the party. When a legislator does anything against the leaders' opinion the support funding for the local branch can be decreased right away. Second, when there is an important meeting among legislators in the party the less loyal legislators are not contacted. They are simply marginalized in the legislators' meeting in the party. Third there is no possibility of gaining a position within the party when he or she is not loyal to the leaders.

Another former legislator, Lee Yang-hee,[46] also mentioned that having a position in the party organization is very important for the next election. When the legislators are seen on TV, often as a representative of a party committee, the potential voters believe he or she is an efficient or hard-working politician. Party leaders are able to dominate their parties through authoritarian or charismatic leadership and attract strong supporters from their own regions. They do not have to be accountable or responsible for the platform used only for the electoral campaign. As long as they have loyal voters in their own regions, they are unlikely to be punished at the next election; therefore, they could seek hegemonic power. However, members of civil society are teaching themselves and communicating among themselves, calling for intervention in the life of the state and the legislature. With highly developed technology, civil society is opening its eyes without party elites' education, and the loyal voters in the three regions are gradually showing fracture in their party affiliation (see also Chapter 6).

Leadership

Party leadership is fundamentally based on perceptions of legitimacy and support from the majority of the followers. Panebianco (1988: 40) argues that the legitimacy of leadership relies in the control of public goods (collective incentives) and private goods (selective incentives). When the benefit is not distributed fairly enough, the legitimacy of the leadership will be undermined. Looking into the party system in Korea where the linkage between the state and civil society is limited, it is unlikely to achieve equal distribution of either public or private goods.

At the local branch level, the legislators fail to come up with policies reflecting the voices of the majority of the people but will tend to focus on some voters (generally relatives of other members) and not others. Thus there are a large number of alienated citizens or voters who do not enjoy the equal distribution of public goods. It is no different within the central party. The party is more interested in gaining power and, in order to do so, the leaders are mainly busy collecting funds from a few conglomerates or interest groups than in chasing after the small dues paid by the majority of the party's members. Ordinary members have been mobilized for elections by bribes and gifts over decades under the authoritarian governments – in essence, since the US military planted the democratic political system in 1947. Parties mostly converge to the right or centre of the ideological spectrum without any political education or major difference in policies between the parties. The ideological stance of the parties will be discussed in Chapter 5. It is highly likely voters would vote for their regional leaders. If the leader or especially party leaders won office with only regional support, the leaders lack legitimacy without the support of the majority in the nation.

Kim Dae-jung won office with only 40.3 per cent of the total votes. It was 1.6 per cent higher than his competitor, Lee Hoe-chang, who gained 38.7 per cent. The problem is that his supporters were concentrated in the Honam (or Jeolla)

Internal factors 83

region. Kim Dae-jung gained 90 per cent of the total votes in Jeolla province, 44.2 per cent in Seoul, 43 per cent in Chungcheong province but only 13 per cent in the Yeongnam (Gyeongsang) regions and 20 per cent in Gangwon province (*Donga Ilbo*, 19 December 1997). He gained relatively high votes compared to the previous presidential election in Chungcheong province, but this is due to the coalition partner. As scholars like Linz (1990), Stepan and Skach (1993) and Mainwaring and Shugart (1997) note, the dual legitimacy of the executive and the legislative branches of government structurally induces conflicts in the legislature. Kim Dae-jung gained legitimacy with a higher vote rate from the presidential election; however, the opposition GNP hardly sees itself as a loser but a winner as it received much higher votes in the general election and therefore became the party with the largest number of seats in the legislature. This dual legitimacy created strains in the legislature for the entire period of the Kim Dae-jung administration. With small numbers of supporters, the Kim Dae-jung administration started to govern, although the lack of legitimacy from the birth of the administration hindered the implementation of reform policies. The government was driven off track by the big opposition party nearly every time it tried to pass any new bills. At the same time, the coalition partner was not easy to control in order to make a cohesive organization. When the government wanted to implement reform policies, they had to be executed swiftly and decisively. If the government is unable to push through legislation as a result of resistance by the opposition party or even by its coalition partner, the wasted time provokes the emergence of major obstacles to implement policies in real life. Interest groups start to interfere for the sake of their own interests and, in the meantime, people who are actually suffering from the delayed policies become sceptical of the possibility of reform and blame the inefficient government.

Another significant problem for political leadership in Korea is that presidential power and the ruling party's elites are not equal; the party elites are subjugated by the president. When the parties are not separated from the power of the president, this can easily lead to delegated democracy with leadership highly concentrated on the president, and the president simply relying on his charismatic popular support to govern. This also leads to a lack of legitimacy in the legislature, especially when facing an opposition party or parties with more seats in the chamber. Decision-making procedures as well as the right to select the candidates are highly concentrated in the party leaders. If the leaders fail to gain agreement in committee meetings in the legislature, the ordinary legislators barely have the right to vote on his or her preference but are required to follow the decision of the leaders. In the case of ruling parties, the party chairmen (*Chongjae*) do not have much power but are more likely delegates of the original charismatic leaders: for NCNP, Kim Dae-jung and for ULD, Kim Jong-pil. For instance, if party chairmen attend the floor group leaders' meeting in the legislature, they may have reached agreement on certain issues. In the following days, if the actual leaders (Kim Dae-jung, Kim Jong-pil and Lee Hoe-chang) who were not in the meeting do not like the result of the agreement, it is hardly likely to materialize (see pages 87–91). In other words, the problem of so-called 'boss politics' lies in the concentration of power in the leader's hand. In the case of the MDP, the ultimate leader of the ruling party is the president. Therefore, above the party representative (mostly chairman, *Chongjae*) of the floor negotiation group, the president's decision is also crucial in the process of compromise and negotiation. Lee Yang-hee,[47] a former legislator of the ULD, pointed out that:

> The power of the president is bigger than that of a King under the Joseon Dynasty. Our constitutional laws allow too much power to the president. This is a disadvantage of the presidential system in South Korea. That is why we think the parliamentary system would work better in Korea. In the case of the US, if a republican or democratic president suggests a new policy, an individual legislator of the respective party is not required to follow the party whip in the legislature, as in the 'Westminster' system. Legislators can vote on their own preference. In the Korean system, however, if you do not follow the president's line a range of disadvantages will arise. This is particular the case if a legislator harbours ambitions to be the chairman, a position appointed by the president. If you are the chairman, you essentially have to listen to the president who appointed you. This is not doing politics but being controlled.

It also hinders party leaders from compromising flexibly with the opposition party. The legislature cannot play its original role of balancing power among the executive, judiciary and the legislature. The president occupies the pivotal role in the government and often dominates his own party. In the legislature, the ruling party is not free from the president's decision and this hinders negotiations and compromise among the parties. It seems more difficult to reach agreement, especially in relation to the balance of power. The opposition party, of course, would like to restrain the power of the executive but the ruling parties would not or could not reach agreement with the opposition on numerous pieces of legislation. This strict top-down hierarchy also matters in the process of negotiations and compromise. Once the decision has been made by the party leaders, the followers – that is, the ordinary legislators – would not vote against the party's decision. The reason is straightforward: to do so would mean no possibility to stand as a candidate for the following general election, no more promotion within the party and no more financial support from the party leader. In short, when legislators do not obey the party decision, they are punished in these and many other ways. Some are even forced to leave the party.

Parties in Korea represent peculiar cases in terms of leadership. Parties did not create the leaders; rather, leaders created the party. That is why voters vote for the person, his/her charisma and the candidate's region rather than the party or party ideology. Therefore parties in Korea do not belong to either the cadre party or mass party model evidenced in Western countries. Different levels of party organization, at central as well as local branch level, seem to suggest Korean parties are akin to the mass bureaucratic party. However, without any clear class division and ideology, including a wide range of parties gaining a large percentage of their funding from due-paying members, parties in Korea cannot be regarded as mass parties. Although the Cold War and the struggle with North Korea meant party ideology was mainly developed only on the right, as discussed in Chapter 5, Kim Dae-jung's party did move onto the centre ground with his reform policies, but the many decades of conservative hegemony meant the new ruling party faced widespread opposition in trying to push forward with reforms.

Another issue is that Korea is rather a classless society (Kil 1990: 51). In other words, the new rich class is open to the poor with education or whoever works hard to accumulate capital.[48] Under Japanese colonization, the royal family was deposed and, as a result of the Korean War and the land reform in the North and the South, most of the rich disappeared. Education became the most important social capital in Korea. The poor could gain an education and climb up the social ladder. For this reason a class-based mass party hardly developed in Korea, although the recent emergence of the Democratic Labour Party is worthy of attention.[49]

Lawson (1988) argues that linkage matters when the party fails. For Key (1964, cited in Lawson 1988: 14), linkage means 'interconnections between mass opinion and public decision'. Lawson emphasizes that creating linkages is essential in order to gain legitimacy and consolidate internal power. The party should remain in the core position between the state and the grassroots. Linkages between the two means that neither of them should be isolated from the other and the two should remain balanced. When the party wins office, the function of creating linkages between the government and civil society or citizens is crucial to gain legitimacy and wide support. If the party fails to link with the state and the citizens, the ruling party would hardly find wide and strong support from the people no matter how good the reform policies. The citizens would simply not know what is actually going on and, in the meantime, while the government is suffering political deadlock, the interest groups would gain their own interest rather than public goods. The Kim Dae-jung administration failed to link itself with civil society. Leadership without nationwide legitimacy undermined governability during his administration.

Factionalism

'Faction' refers here to a small group within a political party. In this section factionalism is considered with special regard to the dynamics within the coalition parties (which caused conflicts of interest between the NCNP (later, MDP) and the ULD). Further factional conflicts of interest will be discussed with respect to factionalism within the NCNP in the second part of this section. In this section, the allocation of resources to the factions will be discussed.

According to Panebianco (1988), an analysis of dominant coalitions can be carried out in terms of the degree of internal cohesion, degree of stability and the party's organizational power map. When the level of internal cohesiveness is low, the coalition is likely to be unstable. In the case of the Kim Dae-jung administration, this was not a dominant coalition in the Western parliamentary system, but a minority coalition facing a big opposition party under the semi-presidential system. So the government was not going to collapse as a result of investiture or a no-confidence vote and, no matter how much difficulty the government faced, it was highly unlikely to collapse during the term of the presidency. In other words, the period of political rule is institutionally secured. Apart from this terminal stability, however, the Kim Dae-jung administration seemed destined to cause ungovernability from the birth of the administration as a minority coalition government, not simply because of the big opposition party, but also due to internal factionalism within the coalition and even within Kim's own party. The previous section has demonstrated how the government provoked a deadlock of the legislature in order to maintain the coalition agreement – that is, to consolidate cohesiveness between the coalition parties. However, the ruling parties failed to negotiate with the opposition party and consolidate cohesiveness within the coalition as well as within Kim Dae-jung's own party.

Internal conflict within the coalition between the ULD and the NCNP

The Kim Dae-jung administration suffered from a lack of intra-party cohesiveness as well as a lack of cohesiveness with the coalition partner, as evidenced by the fact that the ULD left the coalition twice, in January 2000 and September 2001. As the president lacked legitimacy for his leadership, failing to gain wide support from the people, he entered the lame-duck period a lot earlier than expected. Before the local elections were held in 1998, the NCNP and the ULD were at loggerheads over the right to nominate candidates in the electoral districts. When the two leaders, Kim Dae-jung and Kim Jong-pil, were considering nominations from each party in certain regions such as Gangwon province, competition between the two leaders became intense. For instance, Kim Dae-jung wanted to appoint his favourite candidate as the mayor in Gangwon province and Kim Jong-pil insisted on putting forward his own favourite candidate – a politician expected to be loyal to him after winning the election. In Gangwon province, the ULD nominated nine candidates from the ULD and the NCNP nominated 14 candidates for the education board and for the autonomous local elections. Therefore, the coalition parties had to compete against each other in at least seven electoral districts (*Segye Ilbo*, 25 May 1998).

As far as the candidate for the Mayor of Gangwon province is concerned, the NCNP gave way to the ULD after internal conflict between the two parties: thus, the NCNP decided not to appoint any candidate from the NCNP but help the ULD's candidate (Han Ho-sun) in the local elections. On the other hand, apart from the party's decision, the local candidate from the NCNP, Lee Sang-ryong, was not prepared to accept his failure to be selected as a candidate to run in the election. He finally defected from the NCNP and took part in the election as an independent (not party-affiliated) candidate. Eventually, conflict between the coalition partners confused voters in the province and the fracture of supporters

Internal factors 87

for former NCNP members and the ULD gave the GNP candidate a chance to win the election. In the end, the confused voters cast their ballots for the opposition party candidate, Kim Jin-sun, and the coalition parties lost the election. After the election result became known, some of the NCNP laid the blame for their failure at the door of the ULD, insisting that, if the candidate from the NCNP had taken part in the election, he could have won.

This points to two main problems. The nomination of the candidate was based on undemocratic procedures. While the two leaders were competing over the right to nominate candidates, their action undermined any potential candidate who would bring more support from the provinces. The ruling parties could have recruited professional candidates who could attract the most voters instead of focusing on who would be loyal to which party leader – the main focus of the two leaders. If the two parties are in negotiation to provide one strong candidate in certain districts, the candidate could be selected by primary election from the two parties. If they had such rules, it would be more reasonable for the loser to accept their loss in the primary election or any fair process of selecting candidates. A former legislator[50] recalls his experience in being nominated as a candidate in the Fourteenth General Election:

> People around me told me to bring a bottle of good whisky to the party leader. At that time I was very innocent to understand what was going on among politicians. I had just come back from the US after living many years there. I simply brought a bottle of whisky; however, I found out later that a bottle of whisky carton box can contain 20 million *won* [20,000 US dollars] cash.

Although that was the situation a couple of decades ago in early 1990s, the example shows the relationship between the leader and the would-be candidates. When the way the candidate is selected is undemocratic and does not garner wide-range public support, the party can hardly be expected to win the election. Too much competition between the two coalition parties blinded both parties to adopting the right strategy to win the election. This is just one illustration of the many conflicts within the coalition government. The two parties had struggled over who should be appointed in the administration and the committees of the legislature, rather than concentrated on winning the election.

Factional conflict within the ruling party NCNP (later MDP)

The NCNP itself also consists of factions. The oldest group is the so-called *Donggyo-dong*[51] faction. The members have all been secretaries or colleagues of Kim Dae-jung since the beginning of his political life. When the government was launched, four out of eight executive members of the NCNP were from the *Donggyo-dong* faction, two were former lawyers, one was a businessman and the other was a journalist. The leaders of the NCNP were mainly from the *Donggyo-dong* faction and played dominant roles within the party. The party was neither highly institutionalized nor democratically run by the ordinary members.

Munhwa Ilbo (24 July 1998) indicates two issues that can shed light on the *Donggyo* faction. The NCNP leaders were highly dependent on President Kim Dae-jung and this relationship acted as a barrier in reaching an intra-party consensus. The strong loyalty of the party leader towards the president undermines powerful leadership within the NCNP. The dependency of the *Donggyo* faction on the president means the party is dependent on the president. It is also a fundamental reason for the personalized characteristics of the party. If the leader disappears, so does the party. In other words, loyal leadership within the party to the president would undermine not only the internal cohesiveness of the party, but also the balance of power between the legislature and the administration. This also hinders creating mechanisms of compromise in order to address conflicts with the opposition party and coalition partner. Furthermore, party members who are less loyal to the president or a party leader who feels alienated from the president will become less cooperative within the party.

Another problem with the *Donggyo* faction is that it was not professional in terms of developing policies. Many members of the faction were appointed in the administration and in the legislative committees. When recruitment is not carried out professionally, but as a consequence of personal factions, it is difficult to develop reform policies. In January 2002, one of the progressive legislators from the MDP (previously NCNP) interviewed in *Monthly Chosun* said:

> The *Donggyo* faction eventually ruined the MDP because the *Donggyo* faction appointed scarecrow [powerless] leaders of the party and dominated most of the leading positions in the party. They were not efficient and professional, and as a result, members or potential members who could actually lead the party in a better direction were alienated. Last summer, the majority of the legislators insisted that the party leader should be a person who actually has power within the party. However, the *Donggyo* faction sent Han Kwang-ok, one of the *Donggyo* faction members, to be the chairman (*Chongjae*) of the MDP.
>
> (*Monthly Chosun*, January 2002)

Eventually, factionalism caused inefficient organization within the party and the administration.

The factions were also divided according to high school alumni networks. As Kim Dae-jung was from Jeolla province, certain high schools' alumni from the province were appointed to senior positions in the administration. Compared to the previous administration, it was nothing new but seemed quite natural among Korean politicians. It was not until the late-1970s that high schools were equalized and students were sent to high school based on their region not by exam result. Before the late-1970s, high schools in Korea were highly divided by the grades of the students. Therefore, there were a few elite high schools and junior high schools taking the most-able students from the primary schools through to highly competitive entrance examinations to high school and university. Once students were allowed into a certain high school, the majority of the students were admitted to highly reputed universities, such as Seoul National University, which produced large numbers of public servants who passed the government exams such as the bar examination, administrative public service examination and diplomatic service examination. Once students enter the university they often gather together based on their own high school alumni. The high school alumni are strongly connected to their seniors who are now in important positions. That is where most of the young students at the university collect information for job vacancies after graduation.

During the Kim Young-sam presidency, Gyeonggi high school (based in Seoul) and Gyeong-nam high school (based in Busan, Gyeongsang province) alumni enjoyed high status and positions in the administration as well as in the judiciary and legislature. Under Kim Dae-jung it was Gwangju high school, Gwangju Il high school and Jeonju high school. For the Sixteenth General Elections, all of the Jeonju high school alumni of the MDP members were selected as candidates by the MDP leader. People who failed to be candidates for the election criticized the faction from Jeonju high school, calling it the *Jeonju Mafia* (*Sindonga*, April 2000). Within the ruling party, the high school factions were divided by Jeonju, Gwangju Il and Gwangju high schools alumni factions. These factions competed over leading positions in the administration, judiciary and legislature, candidates for the elections, and even in the army. When there was competition over the positions for the president of Kukmin bank and Gwangju bank, the competition between Gwangju high school faction and Gwangju Il high school faction was intense and caused many complaints over appointments in the administration (*Sindonga*, April 2000: 3).

During the Kim Young-sam presidency in February 1998, the Blue House had 60 official secretaries: 12 were from Gyeonggi high school, seven from Seoul High school, four from Gyeongnam high school, another four from Gyeongbok high school (located in Seoul) and three from Gyeongbook high school. Therefore 19 officials (31 per cent) were from Gyeongsang province and there was one each from Gwangju high school and Gwangju Il high school that are located in Jeolla province. On the other hand, under the Kim Dae-jung presidency, the Blue House had 48 secretaries in February 2000. There were five from Gwangju Il high school, three from Jeonju high school, three from Gyeongbok high school, three from Seoul high school and two respectively from Gwangju high school, Mokpo[52] high school, Incheon high school and Jungdong high school. Overall, fewer than 30 per cent were from Jeolla province (*Sindonga*, April 2000:3) and there was one from Gyeongnam high school located in Gyeongsang province. This shows the emergence of officials from Jeolla, as with the president, and the decline of high school factions from Gyeongsang province, due to the demise of Yeongnam (Gyeongsang province) hegemony. The remaining officials from Gyeongsang province were mainly those who survived through the coalition or defected from the previous ruling party.

90 *Internal factors*

These factional appointments to high official positions were criticized by the opposition party and used to boost regional cleavages in the electoral campaign. The opposition GNP published books and pamphlets revealing the unfair appointments made by the government of people from Honam (Jeolla province). The material insists that the government favoured people from Honam region when appointing to administrative positions. However, a report by *Sindonga* comparing the Kim Dae-jung administration with that of Kim Young-sam suggests the proportion of such appointments was not as high as in the case of the previous government. It counter-argued that the government was giving fair opportunity to those who had been alienated during the Yeongnam hegemony for decades in the past. As most of the previous presidents were from Yeongnam region, high officials were mainly from Yeongnam. After the start of the Kim Dae-jung administration, the power of the Yeongnam factions fell and that of the Honam factions rose (*Sindonga* 2000: 8). This personnel policy seemed fair to those who have been alienated for a long time and now finally had a chance to be selected for high official positions, especially to the people from Jeolla province. However, the new administration could not avoid being blamed for such unfair appointments, as many officials from Yeongnam in high positions were replaced by people from Honam. In theory, it was finally equalizing the unfair personnel policy from the previous administrations. However, it was easy for the opposition party to target regionalism and the GNP's strategy during the electoral campaign. This actually boosted a strong sense of regionalism, especially in Yeongnam.

As a result, the unfair personnel policy of the Kim Dae-jung administration undermined the efficiency of the organization and came under criticism by the opposition party.[53] Kim Pan-seok argues that official appointments were concentrated in the president's hands and there was no professional human resource department in the party able to suggest highly competent personnel. During the Kim Dae-jung administration, each minister kept his/her post for an average period of 10.54 months – that is the lowest average, compared to 11.45 months for the Kim Young-sam administration, 12.88 months for the Roh Tae-woo administration, 17.11 months for the Chun Doo-hwan administration and 24.54 months for the Park Chung-hee administration (Kim 2004b: 392). This also illustrates that the Kim Dae-jung administration did not hold hegemonic power. The government could not back up its ministers against the opposition party or public opinion in the case of political disputes. It is obvious that, if the government cannot secure the position of a minister for even a year, the minister can hardly implement new policies. It was not only the short period of the minister's tenure that illustrates this point; the chief executives' positions could not be secured for more than 14 months (ibid.: 392).

The process of personnel appointment was not open and institutionalized but carried out through either factional connections to the president or party leaders. Therefore, the persons selected were not professional and the government could not also secure positions for the persons appointed as ministers or executive officers, but replaced another person whenever the government faced severe criticism regarding such personnel. Another problem was that the government won office through the coalition with the ULD which mostly enjoyed hegemonic power from the previous administrations: some of the politicians were from the Park Chung-hee administration and some from the Chun Doo-hwan, Roh Tae-woo and Kim Young-sam administrations. When the personnel were selected through negotiations between coalition partners, the person selected was easily targeted as a corrupt politician. Kim Tae-jeong, the former minister of the Ministry of Justice, stepped down within six months as his wife was implicated in the clothing lobby[54] incident. Ju Yang-ja, a minister of the Ministry of Health and Welfare, also resigned after she was criticized over her personal assets acquired through land speculation. Within a year of the Kim Dae-jung administration, eight ministers were accused of a range of culpable offences by the opposition GNP, and ministers of the departments of foreign affairs, environment, public health and justice were forced to step down from their positions. It was due to their personal mistakes or corruption; however, when core ministers such as these resign, this naturally affects the government's ability to implement new policies in these departments.

Kim Pan-seok argues that the problems of personnel appointment lie in three factors. First, the Central Personnel Committee does not have sufficient and reliable information on the potential personnel. Second, the appointments were carried out through personal or family connections, regional or school ties, and the main factor in the final decision was in the person's loyalty to the leader. Finally, the selection of the most suitable personnel was not systematically and fairly processed by the personnel department. In other words, the human resource department is not professional in recruiting the right personnel (Kim 2004b: 393–395). When the government lacks infrastructure, it is hard to develop and implement reform policies. As reform has to be carried out at the right moment and rapidly if the government is not to lose the momentum, action is of the essence, otherwise interest groups will gain time to resist and interfere with the implementation of any new policies likely to harm their interests. While the government struggles with the interest groups, the public will also start to become sceptical of the new policies and withdraw their support. One of the examples of reform policies that met with difficulties was the divisions over medical and pharmaceutical work. Although the reform policy was planned even in the previous administrations, the government failed to gain wide support for the policy. In this way, strong factionalism was another reason for undermining governability during the Kim Dae-jung administration.

Summary

This chapter examined what happened in the legislature and how and why deadlock occurred from the start of the Kim Dae-jung administration. This eventually legitimized the ruling parties' political reorganization by attracting numerous defectors from the opposition parties. As shown in this chapter, however, the enlarged size of the government did not secure governability, and failed to gain wide support from the people. As a result, the ruling parties lost seats in the elections following the Sixteenth General Election in April 2000. This demonstrates two things: first, that the parties were not linked with the citizens; and second, that enlarging the size of the government was not the will of the masses. The coalition parties also suffered from internal conflict of interests. Although the attempt to lower the quorum of the floor negotiation group as the ULD requested ended in failure, and the ULD was widely blamed for this outcome, bringing multi-partyism into the legislature by lowering the quorum might have created a completely different party system, where mechanisms of negotiation and compromise played a greater role and a small number of parties would no longer have been able to occupy large numbers of seats in the legislature. This means the percentage of legislative seats occupied by the president's party can be decreased at the same time as the number of opposition parties increases. In this situation, the ruling party would have the margin to negotiate with the opposition parties. Therefore, multi-partyism can be said to induce mechanisms of compromise and negotiation, and thereby reduce potential conflicts in the legislature.

I then examined party organization in South Korea. As mentioned, the formation and size of government lie at the centre of scholarly attention and, especially in Korean scholarship, there has been a (mainstream) focus on the problems or peculiar characteristics of party politics in Korea such as ideas as 'one-man party', 'conservative party' and 'boss party', particularly compared to Western countries. Scholars have suggested introducing democratic institutions, grassroots-based parties and issue- or policy-oriented parties as a means to develop the level of institutionalization of the parties. All these suggestions simply overlook the reality of the party organization in Korea, and also overlook the history and the culture of the voters. In other words, Korea was ideologically tilted to the right in the Cold War era, with strong anti-communism, and the political party was created by the elites during the American military occupation, not by the grassroots (see Chapters 2 and 5). Leftist ideology was taboo in Korean politics, and many opposition politicians were politically or even physically marginalized. In some cases, even though they did not have any leftist ideology, the government took advantage of the National Security Law to get rid of political opponents.[55] Anti-communism became the only viable political ideology. For over half-a-century, voters were mobilized by party cadres sometimes with bribe and gifts, and asked to vote for the party through personal or regional ties. Given this situation, how realistic is it to suggest that parties should grow out of issues and policies or that parties should be organized by the people, the grassroots?

Korea has not had the historical and cultural environment to develop a democratic and highly institutionalized political party system. Where Confucianism is embedded not only in the political culture but also in civil society, it seems that political elites are the first in need of reform in order to consolidate democracy, and that is how a majority of voters, who are tired of political corruption, conceive politics in Korea. Civil society, however, cannot avoid responsibility for its share in perpetuating a system based on patron-client relations.

Particularly, when leaders lack legitimacy, the government is unlikely to succeed in implementing reform policies. When the leadership failed to provide mechanisms for compromise with the opposition party, and the ruling party faced deadlock in the legislature, governability was undermined as a result. Failure by the ruling party to consolidate the cohesiveness of the party organization contributed to factionalism within the party as well as the coalition, and increased conflict with the coalition partner. Without party consolidation within the ruling parties, the government was unable to implement reform policies. As we have seen, the administration rapidly entered the lame-duck period as a result.

Overall, the fundamental problem of party organization in Korea, as seen in the case of the Kim Dae-jung administration, is that the ruling party failed to play its main role of linking the state and civil society. When the party fails to represent the majority of the people, it is unlikely to gain legitimacy, even if it manages to win office through its electoral strategy. The Kim Dae-jung administration failed to widen its support base, despite embarking on a comprehensive political reorganization that allowed it to attract defectors from the opposition party. The party eventually failed to connect with civil society in terms of gathering members, educating them and developing new policies. When parties fail to make a link between the state and society, it is highly unlikely to be able to implement new policies and consolidate overall government stability.

4 Regionalism and the reform of the electoral law

Introduction

One of the main reforms undertaken by the Kim Dae-jung administration involved changing those electoral laws that had traditionally created minority governments (or at least, were perceived to do so) and emphasized regional cleavages. The post-authoritarian governments struggled to secure majority status and this resulted in the three-party merger of 1990 and the formation of a coalition between the National Congress for New Politics (NCNP)[1] and the United Liberal Democrats (ULD) in 1997. When building a coalition did not suffice to allow the winning party to achieve a majority in the legislature, the Kim Dae-jung administration started to reorganize the party system by attracting defectors from the opposition parties. During Kim Dae-jung's administration, the change of party affiliation (defection) from members of the opposition parties reached the highest level since democratization.

The question that this chapter seeks to answer is, therefore, whether the government's majority status secured governability after Kim Dae-jung's political reorganization. Though the coalition government managed to reach majority status, the chapter shows that struggles within and outside the party (with coalition partners and opposition parties) did not end. Stable governability does not simply seem to come from the size of government. Arguing that the internal cohesiveness of the organization matters, this chapter focuses on the process of the reform of the electoral laws and conflicts of interest in the legislature.

When the Kim Dae-jung administration introduced reform policies, a major emphasis was placed on the change of electoral law. The government tried to introduce new electoral laws, and the three main parties (the NCNP, the ULD and the GNP) put forward different proposals, none of which actually met with favour from the public. They only showed, it is argued here, the rational choices of pure office-seeking politicians.

Hence, this chapter seeks to explore the political stances of the three main parties on the reform of the electoral laws, and what is embedded behind the politicians' rational choices on this issue. In doing so, this chapter aims to test the following hypotheses:

Regionalism and the reform of the electoral law

1 Stronger regional cleavages negatively affect governability.
2 The degree of cohesiveness of party organization affects governability.

The chapter starts by illustrating how regionalism has been shaped after democratization, and how regional cleavages and regional support for the parties affected the legislators' behaviour while negotiating and compromising on reform of the electoral law. I will first focus on regional cleavages through the electoral results of the general elections from 1996 to 2000 and of the presidential elections from 1963 to 1997. I will then explain how regionalism affected each party's stance over reform of the electoral laws while they were still under negotiation. The chapter suggests that when a party is strongly tied to a regional constituency it fails to gain nationwide support, thereby weakening governability, as the battle over implementing reform policies clearly shows.

Regionalism

It is often argued that regional division in South Korea dates back to when Kim Dae-jung and Park Chung-hee competed in the presidential elections of 1970, as highlighted in Chapter 2, with some such as Lee Byung-hyu (1991) and Shin Bokryong (1996) even maintaining that it originated in the late three kingdoms' era (Baekje, Koguryo and Shilla) dating back to AD 890s (Lee 1998: 53). Either way, this does not explain the strong regional party affiliation or even why regional cleavages intensified after democratization, as the results of both general and presidential elections show. Political leaders have merged parties or built coalitions prior to the presidential elections and succeeded in winning office; however, in the following general elections voters have voted in divided or minority governments with large opposition parties as a result of strong regional voting in the general elections.

Many parties emerged and faded with different names after democratization. Nevertheless, the three main parties can be identified with the three Kims (Kim Young-sam, Kim Dae-jung and Kim Jong-pil). This is often referred to as the 'three Kims era' (Im 2004). Each leader can be associated with a particular region, which has provided loyal support during the various electoral campaigns. In Korea it is possible to identify three main regions that have played a crucial role in the country's political life: Gyeongsang province, Jeolla province and Chungcheong province. These three areas have provided very strong electoral support bases for all the leaders who have played the main roles of charismatic leadership in the history of political parties in Korea. The former presidents Park Chung-hee, who is known as the military coup president; Chun Du-hwan, who became president following the Gwangju Massacre after President Park's assassination; Roh Tae-woo, who continued the military government; and Kim Young-sam (YS), who was the first civilian president, are all from Gyeongsang province. Kim Jong-pil (JP), the leader of the United Liberal Democrats, is from Chungcheong province and Kim Dae-jung (DJ), the president from 1998 to 2003, comes from Jeolla province.

A major question arising here is whether the regionally structured support for the three political party leaders is a consequence of regional divisions or whether

96 *Regionalism and the reform of the electoral law*

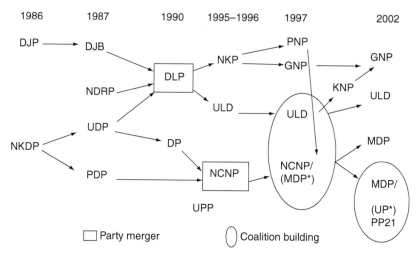

Figure 4.1 Coalition-building since democratization (source: author).

Party lists

DJP   Democratic Justice Party, ruling party led by Chun Doo-hwan (1980) and later by Roh Tae-woo (1987)
NKDP New Korea Democratic Party, led by Kim Young-sam and Kim Dae-jung (1985)
UDP   Unification Democratic Party, led by Kim Young-sam (1987)
NDRP New Democratic Republican Party, led by Kim Jong-pil (1987)
PDP   Peace Democratic Party, led by Kim Dae-jung (1987)
DLP   Democratic Liberal Party after the three parties' merger (1990)
DP   Democratic Party, led by Lee Gi-taek (1990)
UPP   United People's Party, led by Chung Ju-young (1992)
NKP   New Korea Party, led by Kim Young-sam (1996)
PNP   People's New Party, led by Lee In-je (1997)
GNP   Grand National Party, led by Lee Hoe-chang (1997)
ULD   United Liberal Democrats, led by Kim Jong-pil (1995)
KNP   Korea's New Party, led by Kim Yong-hwan (2000)
NCNP National Congress for New Politics, led by Kim Dae-jung (1996)
MDP   New Millennium Democratic Party, led by Kim Dae-jung, and later by Roh Moo-hyun (2000)
PP 21 People's Power 21, led by Chung Mong-joon (2002)
UP   Uri Party, led by Roh Moo-hyun (2003)

these have instead been created and manipulated ad hoc by the leaders themselves who rely on and actually encourage this cleavage. If the latter is the case, how do the political leaders create such support in their own hometown regions and what are the crucial factors behind such mechanisms? In order to answer these questions this section focuses on the following factors: (1) political elites and (2) voters' behaviour.

Political elites

As already noted in Chapter 2, since 1948 Korea has experienced four decades of authoritarian government, until the fifth republic under President Chun Doo-hwan (1980–1987). This also signalled the rise of Gyeongsang province[2] in national politics, known in popular discourse as the 'T-K faction' (see Chapters 2 and 3): Taegu, the capital of North Gyeongsang province and Gyeongsang (Chun Doo-hwan was originally from Taegu and Park Chung-hee from the southern area of Gyeongsang province). They both privileged the development of the Gyeongsang province (also known as the Yeongnam region) which also turned out to be a political resource as it created a system of patronage based on the distribution of power, privileges and positions in the administration. This led to an increase in inter-regional tensions, especially with Jeolla province, as the inequality in the distribution of resources and wealth became deeper. The tensions between these two regions were reflected at the electoral level, and the national vote split along regional lines.

In the meantime, the result of rapid economic development increased the demands for democracy from civil rights movements and, eventually, nation-wide demonstrations brought the authoritarian regime of the Chun presidency to an end. The following presidential candidate, Roh Tae-woo, announced the '6.29 declaration' on 29 June 1987 with which he accepted competitive and fair presidential elections. Despite his unpopularity (as he was still essentially authoritarian), Roh Tae-woo succeeded in the presidential elections of December 1987, and practically continued a military government despite his claims of being a 'man of the street'.

With electoral democracy, however, also came 'a crisis of success' (Diamond and Kim 2000; Im 1997; Kim 2001) in Korean politics. As was pointed out in Chapter 1, since the start of democratization coalition-building was a constant phenomenon in presidential elections and a fundamental part of political and party life in the country. In fact the procedure for succeeding to the Roh Tae-woo presidency lay in building a coalition with the opposition parties. Although widely unpopular due to continuous party merges and splits, coalition-building gradually forced the military regime into a process of bargaining and compromise. The ruling party (Democratic Justice) merged with two opposition parties: the Unification Democratic Party led by Kim Young-sam and the Democratic Republic Party led by Kim Jong-pil. The merger of these parties influenced regional divisions as Roh Tae-woo and Kim Young-sam both represented Gyeongsang province and Kim Jong-pil Chungcheong province. By then, the party system started to be articulated around a split between the Honam (Jeolla) region and the Non-Honam region (representing Chungcheong and Yeongnam (Gyeongsang) provinces, thereby isolating Honam supporters as well as party leader Kim Dae-Jung in the party system. The three merged parties later renamed themselves as the Democratic Liberal Party and agreed to nominate Kim Young-sam as presidential candidate for the then-approaching elections in February 1990 (see Chapter 2). The politics of coalition-building was successful and led to the electoral success of Kim Young-sam, who became the first president not belonging to the military establishment after a long period of authoritarian military rule.

A second moment where coalition-building seemed to be decisive in Korea's political life was before the 1997 presidential elections. The opposition party leader, Kim Dae-jung, entered an alliance with Kim Jong-pil, the party leader of the United Liberal Democrats (ULD). This coalition created different party affiliations in the following elections: Non-Yeongnam (Honam and Chungcheong) province versus Yeongnam province.

More recently, in 2002, Roh Moo-hyun, the presidential candidate of the New Millennium Democratic Party (MDP), also built a coalition before the presidential election with Chung Mong-joon[3] of the People's Power 21 Party, although Chung Mong-joon announced the break-up of the coalition only eight hours before the presidential election. Therefore, Roh Moo-hyun won office without a coalition, though he still obviously benefited from the previous coalition with Chung Mong-joon. A serious drawback, as will be shown later, is represented by the fact that electoral success is no guarantee of effective governability. As a matter of fact, this has been constantly undermined by permanent factionalism internal to the coalition and to the parties themselves, as already examined in Chapter 3.

Voters' behaviour

After democratization, a clear political, personal and regional cleavage started to emerge in the presidential elections. The two Kims (Kim Young-sam and Kim Dae-jung) had built charismatic leadership within the anti-authoritarian movement as opposition party leaders during the military government, as I have shown in Chapter 2. When South Korea finally achieved electoral democracy, the population, expecting a major political change from authoritarian rule, hoped that the two Kims would cooperate in the presidential elections and compete against Roh Tae-woo, the presidential candidate from the ruling Democratic Justice Party. Kim Dae-jung announced he would not take part in the electoral competition so as to leave a single candidate from the biggest opposition party (the then-New Korea Democratic Party) to compete with the ruling party. Due to the internal competition between the two leaders within the NKDP, however, Kim Dae-jung left the party and announced he would become a presidential candidate. As voters in favour of a change of government were split into two camps, Roh Tae-woo won the presidential election. Opposition figures Kim Dae-jung and Kim Young-sam were severely criticized by the public for losing the chance of shifting power from the authoritarian government to a civilian one because of their personal rivalry (Kim 2001: 234).

Both Kims gained high support from their own respective hometowns: Kim Dae-jung from Honam and Kim Young-sam from Yeongnam respectively. In essence, the conflict between the two over power was nothing new and could also be used strategically by other competing parties. In fact, the ruling party seemed to fuel the rivalry between the two leaders. One of the ruling party's evident strategies to hinder the integration of the opposition parties, especially between the two Kims, emerged when the politicians took part in the discussions on revising the constitution after the 6.29 declaration (Kim 2001: 226–227). The ruling and opposition parties had different opinions on many articles of the constitution based on their own interests. For example, when they finally agreed to set five years as the term of a single presidency, the next issue consisted of introducing the position of vice-president into the presidential system. This meant that, should the opposition New Democratic Party win the election, the two Kims would share the posts of president and vice-president in the first term and switch roles in the next presidential election without any power struggles. This new institutional framework could have helped the opposition party integrate more than before. Had the two integrated within the same party and succeeded in the election with a president and vice-president institutional format, the party system in South Korea would presumably have been different, and a new social cleavage rather than regionalism may have emerged. On the other hand, as the post of vice-president was not introduced, the two Kims' struggle over becoming the presidential candidate became obvious. The conflict between the two Kims was just what the ruling party wanted to achieve for the continuance of their own power and they were very successful in this strategy.

The largest opposition party (New Korea Democratic Party) eventually split when Kim Dae-jung left the party and formed a new party called the Peace Democratic Party. Kim Young-sam later also founded the Unification Democratic

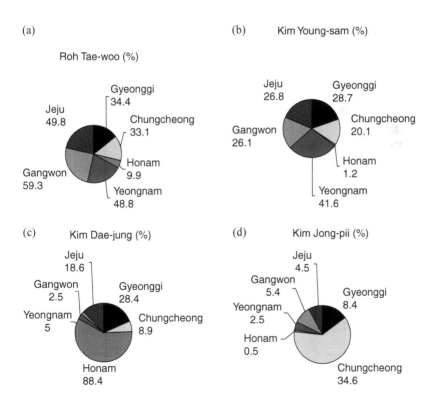

Figure 4.2 Regional distributions of votes in the Thirteenth Presidential Election (source: author – data from National Election Commission).

Party in 1987. The integration of the opposition parties proved difficult as the two Kims' apparent ambition to gain power prevented them from compromise and negotiations. By this time (after the 6.29 declaration), Kim Jong-pil had founded the New Democratic Republican Party and was a candidate in the presidential elections. The emergence of four presidential candidates led the people to draw on regional affiliations in deciding their vote: Roh Tae-woo from North Gyeongsang province (Gyeongsangbuk-do), Kim Young-sam from South Gyeongsang province (Gyeongsangnam-do), Kim Dae-jung from Jeolla and Kim Jong-pil from Chungcheong province.

Before the 6.29 declaration, voting behaviour was defined by a democratic versus anti-democratic cleavage, or *Yeochonyado* (與村若都). This overlapped with the urban/rural one (Lee 1998: 29). This meant that the more-educated urban population tended to vote for the opposition party (demanding democracy), whereas the less-educated people from the rural areas tended to support the ruling party. After democratization, the democratic versus anti-democratic cleavage became less relevant, as people believed that democratization already had been achieved in 1987, and was apparently replaced by the regional cleavage. Scholars such as Choi Jang-jip (2002) and Lee Gap-yun (1998) note that this new phenomenon had its origins in the early period of democratization. As Kim Dae-jung believed he lost the presidential election due to unfair electoral competition from the authoritarian government in 1970, when he competed with former president Park Chung-hee, he drew on strong support from his home regions where he was popular due to decades of political campaigning against the authoritarian government. As noted before, Kim Dae-jung and Kim Young-sam were at loggerheads with the authoritarian regime and cooperated in demanding democracy, but split the opposition front by competing in elections against each other.

Lee (1998: 114–117) argues that the two Kims' decision to run separately in the upcoming presidential elections was not a rational choice in terms of maximizing power for the New Korea Democratic Party. Though the personal popularity of each candidate was considerable, it was not large enough to successfully overcome the power of the ruling party. Furthermore, they did not recognize that a majority of the people preferred stability over sudden change and also, most Korean voters showed a continued support for a conservative right-wing ideology.

Political parties aimed at achieving political power in the legislature and eventually winning office. Considering that the two Kims cooperated within the party rather than defecting from it, the opposition New Democratic Party could have won the presidential elections given that Roh Tae-woo gained only one third of the votes and won office. If cooperation between the two Kims had led to electoral victory, they could have succeeded one another in the post through a power-sharing agreement. This shows the personalized and factionalized nature of the opposition party.

In fact, factionalism among opposition party leaders did not do them any good in their competition with the authoritarian ruling party, considering the latter's relatively stronger degree of institutionalization following decades of ruling experience and sufficient financial support from the government and other funding sources such as the *Jaebeols*. In terms of candidate recruitment for the general election, moreover, the ruling party could rely on more highly qualified candidates than the opposition parties. Opposition parties continuously formed and dissolved according to the circumstances. Furthermore, the parties' strategies were mostly shaped not by ideology or grassroots support but by the leaders. While it is understandable that under authoritarian rule opposition parties were less organized and showed a lower degree of institutionalization, in terms of party members or electoral candidate recruitment and financial support, the result was a struggle over power among the party leaders, and ultimately four leaders were competing in the presidential elections.

Voting behaviour along regional lines has nearly doubled since democratization. Lee Gap-yun (1998: 83) argues that the two opposition party leaders influenced voters to mobilize along regional lines. As the two political leaders share a very similar background in terms of political careers, ideology and political platform, the only difference would lie in the regional background of the candidates. That is why strong regional cleavages started to develop after democratization as the two mainly played important roles in the post-democratization era. Kim Jong-pil (the 'third Kim' in the 'three Kims era') also played a pivotal role in the competition between the two after the democratization of the party system. The electoral results in the Thirteenth Presidential Election in 1987 show that Roh Tae-woo gained 34.4 per cent of the votes from Gyeonggi province where Seoul is located, and Kim Young-sam gained 28.7 per cent, Kim Dae-jung 28.4 per cent and Kim Jong-pil 8.4 per cent; therefore, this does not show much voting along regional lines in Gyeonggi province. However, regional support from the party leaders' provinces shows a clear cleavage. Roh Tae-woo achieved 68.1 per cent of the votes from North Gyeongsang province, Kim Young-sam, 53.7 per cent from South Gyeongsang province, Kim Dae-jung 88.4 per cent from Jeolla province and Kim Jong-pil 34.6 per cent from Chungcheong province (see Table 4.1).

Lee (1998: 4) notes that the party system in the 'three Kims era' has 'deteriorated' as personalized factions rather than parties have grown in importance. During that period, party members joined and left political parties following the party leaders' decisions.

This could be ascribed to the Confucian culture embedded in Korean society. Party members followed their leaders when they built coalitions or defected from parties. Parties are divided into factional groupings by high schools, universities or regional or family ties. Most of the recruitment for the electoral candidates was done through regional or alumni ties, or personal or family connections. Furthermore, candidacies were not approved by ordinary party members through any democratic process (bottom-up) but by the party leaders (top-down). To candidates willing to take part in the electoral competition, it appeared a rational choice to follow their party leaders. Clearly, parties during the 'three Kims era' were more personalized and less organized internally. In Korea, democracy was

Table 4.1 Electoral votes from the presidential elections

Presidential elections	Presidential candidates	Gyeonggi	Chungcheong	Jeolla	Gyeongsang (North)	Gyeongsang (South)	Gangwon	Jeju	Total
The Fifth 1963	Park Chung-hee	31.6	40.9	54.3	55.7	57.6	39.6	69.9	46.7
	Yun Bo-sun	61.1	49.2	38.1	36.1	35.3	49.1	22.3	45.1
The Sixth 1967	Park Chung-hee	43.1	45.8	43.7	64.0	67.3	51.3	56.5	51.4
	Yun Bo-sun	51.9	45.7	47.4	26.4	25.5	41.7	32.1	40.9
The Seventh 1971	Park Chung-hee	43.6	54.8	34.8	75.8	66.9	59.9	56.9	51.1
	Kim Dae-jung	55.3	43.1	62.3	23.4	32.1	38.8	41.8	43.5
The Thirteenth 1987	Roh Tae-woo	34.4	33.1	9.9	68.1	36.6	59.3	49.8	38.6
	Kim Young-sam	28.7	20.1	1.2	26.6	53.7	26.1	26.8	28.0
	Kim Dae-jung	28.4	8.9	88.4	2.5	6.9	8.8	18.6	27.1
	Kim Jong-pil	8.4	34.6	0.5	2.4	2.6	5.4	4.5	8.1
The Fourteenth 1992	Kim Young-sam	36.0	36.2	4.2	61.6	72.1	40.8	15.2	42.0
	Kim Dae-jung	34.8	27.3	91.0	8.7	10.8	15.2	32.9	33.8
	Chung ju-young	19.8	23.8	2.3	17.0	8.8	33.5	15.4	16.3
The Fifteenth 1997	Lee Hoe-chang	37.8	25.7	3.2	65.7	53	42.4	35.9	38.15
	Kim Dae-jung	41.4	43	93	12.9	13.4	23.3	39.8	39.65
	Lee In-je	18	26.1	1.5	17.4	29.5	30.4	20.7	18.91

Source: Lee and author – remade from Lee Gap-yun (1998: 32) until the Fourteenth Presidential Elections and added the results of the Fifteenth Presidential Elections from the National Election Commission.

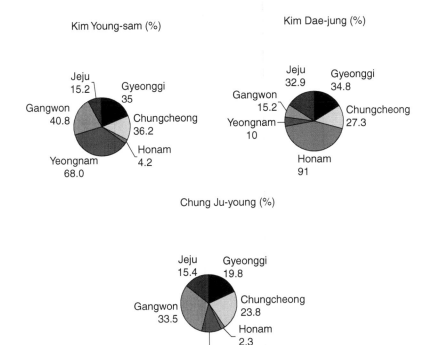

Figure 4.3 Regional distributions of votes in the Fourteenth Presidential Election (source: author – data from National Election Commission[4]).

Note
Numbers in the charts are actual rates of vote from each region.

achieved more rapidly in a relatively bloodless way compared to the longer and more tortuous democratization process in the West. Scholars like Choi Jang-jip argue that this is due to South Korea being a 'premature' democracy. Electoral democracy was achieved through popular demands and demonstrations, though the democratization process barely moved beyond that (i.e. electoral democracy). If factional party politics becomes a goal in itself, played out by the political elites struggling over power, this raises questions over the truly democratic nature of the whole process, no matter how democratically the elites were elected. Choi Jang-jip (2002: 120) argues that the opposition parties ultimately showed a very low level of organization as the parties became personalized factions representing small numbers of elites and their followers' interests. When the opposition parties took office after democratization in 1992 and 1997, it appeared to be a good moment to consolidate democracy. In fact, the government failed to bridge the various gaps and cleavages existing in Korean society.

In the Fifteenth Presidential Election, Kim Dae-jung won office, gaining 39.65 per cent of the total votes, and the opposition leader Lee Hoe-chang gained 38.15

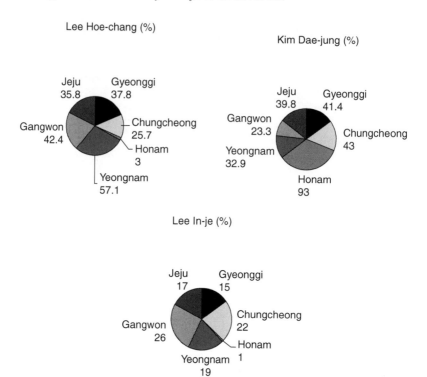

Figure 4.4 Regional distributions of votes in the Fifteenth Presidential Election (source: author – data from National Election Commission).

per cent. Kim Dae-jung won office with only 1.5 per cent more of the vote than Lee Hoe-chang. Regional cleavage was also evident in the Honam and Yeongnam regions. Kim Dae-jung gained 96.3 per cent of votes in Gwangju (the capital of south Jeolla province), 92.9 per cent in South Jeolla province and 90.65 per cent in North Jeolla province. On the other hand, Lee Hoe-chang gained 71.6 per cent in Daegu (the capital of North Gyeongsang province), 60.55 per cent in North Gyeongsang province and 52.6 per cent in Busan (*Munhwa Ilbo*, 19 December 1997; National Election Commission;[5] *Seoul Economy*, 20 December 1997).

Two years into the Kim Dae-jung presidency, the results of the Sixteenth General Election showed that the regional cleavage had deepened. Despite the ruling coalition parties' effort to maximize the number of seats in the legislature through political reorganization, the opposition Grand National Party became the largest party, gaining 112 seats, and the New Millennium Democratic Party (hereafter MDP) won 96 seats and the United Liberal Democrats 12 seats (*Seoul Sinmun*, 15 April 2000). As the seats in the legislature consisted of 227 district members and 46 members by proportional representation, the GNP gained 21 proportional representation seats and, in total, the GNP won 133 out of 273 total seats in the legislature. The MDP gained 115 seats including proportional representation seats and the

ULD won a total of 17 seats. However, the GNP won 65 legislative seats out of a total of 65 districts in Yeongnam (Gyeongsang) province and the MDP won 25 legislative seats out of 29 districts in Honam (Jeolla) province. Four legislators without party affiliation in the Honam region openly declared during the electoral campaign that they would join the MDP if elected. The Honam region also supported all the legislators of the MDP. The salient difference from the previous election in 1996 is that the voters in Honam produced 36 legislators for the NCNP out of 37 districts (97.3 per cent) in 1996 but 25 legislators for the MDP out of 29 districts[6] (86.2 per cent) in 2000. The United Liberal Democrats only gained 11 seats in the legislature out of 24 districts (45.8 per cent) in the Chungcheong region in 2000 in comparison to 24 seats out of 28 districts (85.7 per cent) in 1996. However, in the case of the Yeongnam region, voters produced 51 legislators for the New Korea Party out of 76 districts (67.1 per cent) in 1996, while producing 64 legislators for the GNP out of 65 districts (98.5 per cent) in 2000 (Kim and Kim 2000: 8).

The GNP gained 39 per cent of the total votes, the MDP 35.9 per cent and the ULD 9.8 per cent. Regional patterns of voting are also clear here. The GNP gained 62.5 per cent of the votes from the Yeongnam region (Busan, Daegu, Gyeongsang buk (north)-do and Gyeongsang nam (south)-do) and the MDP gained 66.8 per cent from the Honam region (Gwangju, Jeolla buk-do, Jeolla nam-do) and the ULD 34.8 per cent from the Chungcheong region (Daejeon, Chungcheong buk-do, Chungchung nam-do) (see Table 4.2).

A comparison with the votes of the previous general election in 1996 shows a more marked regional voting in the Yeongnam region. In 1996, the New Korea Party (the former core group of the Grand National Party) achieved 42.4 per cent of total votes in Yeongnam region, whereas in 2000 the GNP achieved 62.5 per cent of the total votes in the region. As for the National Congress for the New Politics and the United Liberal Democrats, votes were relatively scattered in the Honam and Chungcheong regions. The NCNP gained a lower rate of votes (66.8 per cent) in 2000 than in 1996 (71.6 per cent) in the Honam region. The ULD votes decreased to 34.8 per cent in 2000 from 47 per cent in 1996 in the Chungcheong region. However, considering the seats each party gained through the election in each region, the results still show that regionalism had deepened.

Table 4.2 Votes gained in the Sixteenth General Elections on 13 April 2000

Regions	Total votes	GNP	MDP	ULD
Nationwide	18,904,740	7,365,359 (39%)	6,780,629 (35.9%)	1,859,331 (9.8%)
Gyeonggi	8,285,039	41.4	42.9	8.6
Chungcheong	1,939,185	23.2	30	34.8
Honam	2,344,026	3.7	66.8	2
Yeongnam	5,398,726	62.5	14.6	7.3
Gangwon	689,907	38.6	36.5	10.2
Jeju	247,857	44.2	49.4	0.6

Source: author – data from National Election Commission.

Table 4.3 Votes gained in the Fifteenth General Elections on 11 April 1996

Regions	Total votes	NKP	NCNP	ULD
Nationwide	19,653,073	6,783,730 (34.5 %)	4,971,961 (25.3 %)	3,178,474 (16.2 %)
Gyeonggi	8,569,380	35.4	31.7	8.5
Chungcheong	2,028,444	27.8	8.4	47
Honam	2,458,285	17.6	71.6	0.7
Yeongnam	5,641,438	42.4	3.67	15.7
Gangwon	710,803	37.3	6.7	23.6
Jeju	244,703	37.2	29.4	1.2

Source: author – data from National Election Commission.

A blurred ideological division has also been a main feature of party politics in Korea: the ideology of the parties mostly clusters on the right of the political spectrum, as I will discuss in Chapter 5. The threat posed by North Korea has long cast a shadow on South Korean domestic politics. However, the last decade has seen an apparent change, especially since the ascent of Kim Dae-jung to the presidency. Under his presidency, policies have begun to shift from the right towards the centre. Kim Dae-jung's MDP party mainly represents, in his own words:

> the middle and lower classes; it is the party of productive welfare, providing equal opportunities and happiness for all; it is the party of reform that will bring all regions, generations, classes and genders together; it is the party that promotes inter-Korean reconciliation and unification; and it is a modern party that creates new politics.
> (New Millennium Democratic Party agenda 1997)

Based on wide public support, the Kim Dae-jung administration was able to overcome the Asian crisis of 1997, and made inter-Korean reconciliation (and re-unification) one of the cornerstones of the administration's mandate. Kim Dae-jung's presidency faced major opposition when it tried to carry out policies based on this policy platform (e.g. on public health, tax reform and labour policies under IMF restructuring schemes).

This factor interplayed with regionalism. In the political arena, this translated into reliance on strong party leadership and regional constituencies that constitute strongholds on which to draw for electoral success and to which to redistribute powerful positions in the aftermath of success. Electoral support is highly based on the regions where the party leaders are from. The centre often relies on the regions in a search for support.

A look at how development plans have affected the regions differently shows that regional divides are much deeper than any ideological stand-off between conservatives and reformists. A major divide is between the Gyeongsang and Jeolla provinces. Former presidents focused on developing the Yeongnam region, thus the Honam region has been marginalized. This made people from rural areas in

Jeolla province more resentful towards state policies, emphasizing divisions between the centre and periphery, industrial and agricultural areas, rich and poor areas, as well as the Gyeongsang province (former presidents) and the Jeolla province (where Kim Dae-jung is from). The regional cleavage has also manifested itself as an urban versus rural division rather than an East versus West cleavage, as most resources are rather concentrated in Seoul and the Gyeonggi province, causing resentment among the people from Jeolla and Gyeongsang provinces. Choi and Kim (2000: 70–90) argue that regionalism is a consequence of the government's focus on the economic development of the capital, Seoul, and the metropolitan areas. The Gangwon and Chungcheong provinces are relatively closer to the centre and these two regions traditionally showed strong support for the ruling parties. Honam and Yeongnam, by contrast, were both relatively isolated from the political and economic centre. In terms of economic and political struggles, both regions have suffered isolation or discrimination from the centre. If local leaders manage to successfully put across the message that their region is marginalized (in terms of economic investment) as a result of the fact that the region did not produce the ruling party in the legislature, voters are likely to respond by supporting the local leaders and legislators, hoping this would yield some change at the economic level. Therefore, regionalism shows up clearly in the electoral results.

Another area where the regional cleavage is evident is the elite recruitment patterns in both parties and the government. Along with the president, elite recruitment illustrates a deep division along regional lines, as shown in Chapter 3. For example, under the Kim Young-sam presidency, most of the elites within the ruling party and the government were from Gyeongsang province, and the same seems to be true for Kim Dae-jung: most party elites came from Jeolla province. During the electoral campaign for the Sixteenth General Election, the GNP provided *Insabaekseo* 人士百書 (*Recruitment report of the Kim Dae-jung administration*) emphasizing how more people from the Jeolla region were appointed in the administration and how people from Gyeongsang province were discriminated against.

Regionalism or patron-client relations – which are a major feature of the South Korean social system – used to be considered as a serious barrier to developing a democratic political environment. However, Kang (2003) points out that strong regionalism is not a barrier to consolidating democracy, but rather a phenomenon that arises out of the voters expressing their self-interest, thereby showing their rationality. Voters believe that voting for the leaders from their own region will focus attention on their own region's development. In his study of voting behaviour since democratization, Kang argues that this is based on rational choice rather than emotional or personal ties. Therefore it is the parties and not the voters that undermine democratic consolidation by continuously switching party allegiance. As this section has shown, Confucianism creates a typical political culture in the elites and voters alike; however, when parties fail to implement reform policies as a result of facing big opposition parties, the elites are likely to indicate regionalism and low levels of party institutionalization as the main culprit, rather than Confucian culture itself.

In the case of the party system in South Korea, not only each individual party but the party system itself is weakly institutionalized. In fact, a salient issue emerging from the evidence of regionalism is how this demonstrates a low level of institutionalization in the party system as a whole. As Randall and Svåsand (2002) point out, if a single party is identified with certain groups, this undermines the level of institutionalization of the party system. Randall and Svåsand maintain that an institutionalized party is not always compatible with that of the party system. As the Korean case shows, each party is strongly identified with a leader and the region where he or she is from. This is evident from the electoral results: Kim Dae-jung and his party NCNP (later MDP) is identified with Honam, Kim Jong-pil and ULD with Chungcheong and Kim Young-sam (later, Lee Hoe-chang), and the NKP (later GNP) with Yeongnam supporters. When a party monopolizes a region, this undermines fair competition in the election in the region, as I touched on in Chapter 1. Scholars, politicians and voters are all aware of this problem; however, when it comes to efforts made to resolve the problem, all the politicians who actually could change the law to help address the problem associated with regionalism by redrawing the boundaries of the electoral districts fall prey to seeking their own interests in the legislature. This is not in itself surprising, given that they are pure office-seeking politicians acting on the basis of their own rational choice. No mechanism for managing party interests and internal conflicts within the party, or even within the coalition, was in place; hence this permanent conflict led to a failure to introduce any reform policies.

The following section will explore factionalism and Confucian culture to illustrate how factionalism within the parties and between the coalition parties hinders political parties from functioning efficiently and how the legislators' role works in the local district in terms of the performance of the party organization.

The reform of the electoral law: the process of compromise and negotiation and the rational choice of the political actors

The Kim Dae-jung administration embarked on restructuring the 'high cost, low efficient political system' and introducing reform policies that included the reform of the political parties and electoral institutions. The main reform policies the government sought to implement within the party system were in electoral law. This section focuses on how the ruling coalition parties struggled to introduce reform policies, experiencing difficulties within the party and with the coalition partner, as well as with the opposition parties. To answer the question raised, I start by examining each party's political stance including the lawmakers' rational choices and elucidate how their choices caused severe conflicts of interest among the parties and legislators and influenced the outcome of the passage of the newly proposed electoral law.

The parties' stances

As the Kim Dae-jung administration started office in the aftermath of the Asian crisis, the Korean economy was mostly under the guidance of the IMF's restructuring plan and this also influenced the political arena. The government and the legislature sought to restructure the political party system and its institutions. The main political reform focused on restructuring the political system, particularly addressing the issue of regionalism. As parties gained support in their own regions, it was highly unlikely that they would gain nationwide support from the people as a whole. This obviously obstructed the possibility of implementing reform policies. As shown in Chapter 3, when the GNP was unable to hold negotiations in the legislature, party legislators gathered together outside the National Assembly, or more often in Gyeongsang province. This actually appealed to regional support when the opposition party leaders gathered in Gyeongsang province to lay the blame for the political impasse on the present government.

The main coalition leaders – President Kim Dae-jung, Kim Jong-pil (honorary party leader of the ULD) and Park Tae-jun (leader of the ULD) – agreed on a progressive restructuring of political institutions in the legislature. The restructuring plan included a reduction in the number of legislators in the National Assembly and the number of council members in local council (*Jibanguiwon*); the restructuring of the electoral districts and the party system; and, finally, the introduction of a closed party list for the elections. The proposal was to reduce the total number of legislators in the National Assembly to either 150 or 200 from the present number of 299. The opposition GNP also suggested reducing the number of legislators to 200 and also to reduce the number of council members in the local governments (*Gwangyeokuiwon*) to two-thirds of the then-current number, from 960 to 650, and council members at ward level (*Gichouiwon*) to just over half of the present number, from 4,540 to 3,000 (*Segye Ilbo*, 1 February 1998).

Furthermore, the legislature established a special committee on political reform consisting of eight legislators of the NCNP, four of the ULD and 12 of the GNP. The committee announced that the main issue to negotiate among the members would be the reduction of the size of the legislature and the introduction of a Mixed Member Proportional Representation System, also known as a German-style mixed electoral system, with a closed party list (*Korea Economics*, 10 December 1998). The German system includes two ways of electing the national assembly members: half of the national assembly members are elected in single-member districts and the other half are elected by a proportional representation system in six large electoral districts.[7] Each voter can express two preferences: one for a legislator in a single-member district and the other for a party among listed parties in the ballot. A small party can win seats if it gains 5 per cent of the votes overall in the closed party list votes or three seats from single member districts in the legislature.

If the legislators adopt this new electoral law, the party adopting these new electoral bills would bring major changes to the electoral results in the following general election. The following section discusses what each party proposed or objected to, and what the rational calculation of each party was based on.

The NCNP: a German-style, mixed electoral system with a closed party list

The NCNP was home to contrasting opinions vis-à-vis the restructuring plan, the main division being among leading members who mainly followed the president and the ruling leaders' opinion, and the ordinary assembly members. President Kim Dae-jung often referred to the possibility of introducing a closed party list system and a new electoral law that would change the present system to a German-style, mixed electoral system early in his presidency (*Weekly Donga*, 17 July 1998). The electoral reform policy the government pursued also included reducing the size of the legislature. This meant some National Assembly members would lose the possibility of being re-elected in their previous local district as the district would have either disappeared or been combined with other districts.

It was not decided then whether the party would insist on continuing with the present electoral system electing a single member on a winner-takes-all basis within the small local district or would change the electoral district to a larger district that elects two or three members on the basis of plurality rules. The leaders of the NCNP later showed a preference for the multi-member districts; however, whether it is a single member district or multi-member district, if the size of the legislature is to be reduced to 150 or 200 from the present 299 National Assembly members, it is obvious that 149 or 99 legislators would lose their potential positions as electoral candidates for the forthcoming Sixteenth General Election in 2000. When the reform policies were a threat to the existing ruling elites' positions, it clearly would have been hard to gain any support within the party and the coalition partner for such policies. The reform policies were popular among the people and civil society. However, when the ruling parties consist mainly of elites who gained privileges from the existing system, it is not hard to imagine conflicts arising in the legislature from an early stage.

Another proposal from the NCNP was to increase the number of voters in the district. This means that whether a single member district or a multi-member district system is adopted, by increasing the number of voters in a district the number of districts would be decreased, especially when the legislators are elected within a multi-member system. It would also foreshadow severe internal competition among legislators to become an electoral candidate. The then-electoral districts were settled before the Fifteenth General Election in 1996 by three parties: the New Korea Party (predecessor of the GNP), the NCNP and the ULD. The parties agreed that an electoral district should not have fewer than 75,000 voters or more than 300,000 voters. This means that the smallest number of voters in a district such as a rural area would be 75,000, and the largest number of voters in the urban district would be 300,000. The Imsil-Sunchang district in the Southern Jeolla province, for example, had about 78,000 voters for the Sixteenth General Election and Jeju district had 266,000 voters. In other words, one vote in Imsil-Sunchang district was worth approximately four votes in the Jeju district. For instance, Jeong Se-gyun for the MDP, a National Assembly member, won his seat in the legislature gaining 34,165 votes in the electoral district (Jinan, Muju and Jangsu), with 70,912 potential voters during the Sixteenth General Election in April 2000. On the other hand, a candidate for the MDP, Jeong Dae-gwon, lost the election receiving 49,508 votes in his district (Jeju city) with 184,294 potential voters. His competitor, Hyun Gyeong-dae (for the GNP) won the election with 53,264 votes. As illustrated by these examples, the value of one vote in a rural district with a small voting population is worth more than three-times that of a vote in a big district with a large number of voters. In July 1995, the constitutional court ruled that the present electoral districts did not allow equal elections to be conducted (*Weekly Donga*, 17 July 1998). As a result of this ruling, the boundaries of the electoral districts had to be redrawn.

If the earlier proposal to increase the minimum number of voters to about 100,000 based on the results of the national census in 1998 were accepted, seven districts in Honam would have been combined or would have disappeared and six districts in Yeongnam. This would have resulted in 37 districts in Honam and 76 districts in Yeongnam, so both regions would have lost similar numbers of electoral districts. If the minimum number was increased to 150,000, Honam would lose one more district in Kwangju and four more districts in North Jeolla and most of the districts except Mokpo-Sinan district and Yeosu district in South Jeolla. The Yeongnam region would also have 22 districts to be reallocated. This reorganization of the electoral districts would have fundamentally changed the existing voting basis for the three parties and strong regional votes would have disappeared.

In the case of Seoul, and the Seoul metropolitan area, increasing the number of minimum voters would not impact on the number of districts, even if the minimum were 150,000 voters in a district. In other words, increasing the minimum number of voters in the district would have decreased the number of electoral districts in the rural areas such as Honam, Yeongnam and Chungcheong provinces, but the same number of districts in Seoul and its metropolitan areas would have been retained. Therefore the reorganization of the electoral districts would have ameliorated the regional cleavage. Traditionally, the NCNP has received weak support from Gangwon province and relatively more support from the Seoul metropolitan area. Therefore, if the number of districts were to be decreased in Gangwon province, the NCNP would not lose any votes from Gangwon and still enjoy similar support from the metropolitan areas as the new districts would not influence the urban areas. Although the NCNP could not have guaranteed becoming the majority party reaching more than 50 per cent of the total seats in the legislature, by decreasing the number of districts this would at least ensure that the NCNP would be the largest party.

Weekly Donga (17 July 1998) presented a hypothetical outcome applying the German-style electoral system using the results of the Fifteenth General Election in 1996. If the German-style system had been introduced, the New Korea Party would have gained 24 fewer seats than the original 139 seats (original seats gained from the single member plurality votes), falling to 115 seats. The Democratic Party won 15 seats in the Fifteenth General Election but under the proposed system it could have gained 40 seats. This shows that the electoral institution matters in terms of the size of government or ruling parties. This hypothetical calculation also implies the existing electoral laws favoured the present major parties and discriminated against existing small parties or the emergence of new small parties. Under the single member plurality voting system, the number of votes for the Democratic Party has been disregarded in the metropolitan districts and less popular areas such as Yeongnam. This suggests that the votes are not equal as it failed to show some minority voters' opinions. Applying the new electoral system, the NCNP could have won 81 seats instead of 79, and the ULD may have gained 49 seats instead of 50. Clearly, the impact would have been minimal on the NCNP and the ULD, but at least both could have benefited from otherwise wasted votes in the Yeongnam or Gangwon provinces.

The *Hankyoreh* daily newspaper (16 April 1999) also calculated the potential result of multi-member districts with a closed party list, applying it to the results of the 1998 local elections. If the local elections had taken place with multi-member districts based on a closed party list system, the NCNP could have lost one seat from the then-total of 105 seats and the GNP would have lost 32 seats from the original 134 seats; the ULD would have lost 14 seats out of the 54 seats it previously gained. Therefore, both the ruling coalition parties would have lost 15 seats and the opposition GNP 32 seats. It is obvious from these results that the GNP would not be interested in the new system and the NCNP would have benefited the most. According to research conducted by the *Hankyoreh* daily newspaper on 6 April 1999 on party support among the people, the NCNP gained 30.1 per cent, the GNP 17.6 per cent and the ULD 4.6 per cent. If the electoral system were changed to a two-vote system with a closed party list, even the NCNP, which still would not win any seats from the first vote for the legislator in the Yeongnam areas, would gain support for the party from the second vote as the new electoral system would mean the voters would cast two votes: one for the candidate and the other for the party. Considering this party affiliation support and the result of the local elections in the previous year, the NCNP might have reached the conclusion that it could gain 117 seats, the GNP 96 seats and the ULD 34 seats in the following Sixteenth General Election (*Hankyoreh Sinmun*, 16 April 1999). This assumption shows that the NCNP would have benefitted the most among all the parties if reform of the voting system had been implemented.

President Kim Dae-jung strongly favoured transforming the Korean electoral system into a German-style one (a Mixed Member Proportional Representation System). He stated that 'strong regionalism is a short cut to ruin the whole nation. This situation has to be changed by introducing new electoral institutions' (*Segye Ilbo*, 1 February 1998; *Hankyoreh Sinmun*, 17 November 1999). As regionalism created a problematic party system, President Kim Dae-jung appealed to the public, gaining wide support. But considering that the decision-making on the reform policies was in the hands of pure office-seekers in the legislature, it was hard for legislators to negotiate and compromise when they had a stake in the outcome of the process. Had the German-style electoral system been introduced, this new arrangement would also have increased the possibility of the emergence of many small parties that would also be considered as a cause of a potentially unstable party system. However, many scholars such as Mainwaring (1993), Cheibub and Limongi (2002) contend that multi-partyism induces stable governability, as discussed in Chapter 2. In light of the number of factions within each party (e.g. the *Donggyo* faction, the TK faction and the PK[8] faction), the system would have hardly given way to moderate multi-partyism, but more likely to a more fragmented multi-party system like that of Italy. For instance, the PK and TK factions would have presumably established their own parties, which would have enabled them to aspire to create a floor negotiation group (that requires 20 seats in the legislature). If the general election had produced many smaller parties, the NCNP would have had no need to stay in coalition with the ULD only, but could have explored the possibility of building coalitions with other newly emerged parties (*Weekly Donga*, 17 July 1998).

These potential new scenarios, however, were not welcomed by either the National Assembly members or by the NCNP. Many legislators of the NCNP based in Honam province were concerned that the decreased size of the electoral district would mean them losing their voting base. Some members would have been more interested in the new electoral system as they hoped to win seats in metropolitan districts and even in districts of Yeongnam. However, some based in Honam were not satisfied with the main flow of party opinion as it reflected that of the party leaders and President Kim Dae-jung. The beneficiaries would be those in more senior positions – e.g. those who have previously participated in and won elections. It is these politicians who can win the internal competition to become a candidate, either in the district or proportional representative seats. On the other hand, a new politician or someone with strong regional support would be at risk in the internal competition to be a candidate for the general election. That is inevitable in order to avoid internal conflict among the members even within the NCNP. This means that the NCNP structurally lacked internal solidarity on this issue between those who would enjoy the new system and those who would lose the possibility of winning a seat in the legislature.

The ULD: single member district versus multi-member district

As a ruling coalition partner, the ULD was not positioned to be actively engaged in introducing reform policies. In the early stages of restructuring, the electoral system the ULD leader Kim Jong-pil and Park Tae-jun agreed with the policies of its coalition partner, the NCNP. However, except for a few senior legislators, most of the legislators of the ULD would be at risk of losing their electoral base in Chungcheong province if the electoral districts were to be either separated or combined.[9] The ULD also contained the 'TK faction', based in the Yeongnam area. Park Tae-jun, the leader of the ULD (later, prime minister from 1999–2000), did not have an electoral base in the Chungcheong province but in Ulsan, Yeongnam. As regional cleavages deepened after the Kim Dae-jung administration, regional tensions in the Yeongnam area also increased. Some members based in the Yeongnam area pushed strongly for changes to the electoral law to multi-member districts after they visited their electoral districts in Yeongnam area, given the existence of strong regionalism in Yeongnam.

When the announcement that the reforms would be delayed was made in April 1999, internal dissatisfaction with the leaders grew rapidly. In the meantime, the ULD lost its vice-chairman, Kim Young-hwan, who left the party when the coalition agreement on the parliamentary system was delayed in December 1998, as seen in Chapter 3. In the case of a strongly hierarchical political culture, there is little margin to solve conflicts among political actors, as mechanisms of negotiation and compromise are lacking. Political actors either accept the rules or leave the party. Kim Jong-pil had to reconcile the Chungcheong faction in the ULD revoking his previous agreement on electoral law with President Kim Dae-jung and the ULD chairman (*Chongjae*) Park Tae-jun. Before he reached the agreement with the other leaders, it would have been more efficient if he had garnered a majority of voices within the party and made decisions. When the decision-making process is made from the top down, the leadership risks its legitimacy within the party. Realizing that there were many dissatisfied legislators within the ULD, Kim Jong-pil promised to keep the present single member plurality voting system rather than change it to a multi-member district system (*Chosun Ilbo*, 31 August 1999).

It seems that the ULD also suffered from disputes between the Chungcheong and TK factions. When the opinion within the ULD did not emerge as the TK faction expected, it announced that if the ULD did not introduce the two-vote system with a closed party list, the members of the TK faction[10] would leave the party and found another party (*Hankyoreh Sinmun*, 17 November 1999; *Hankook Ilbo*, 10 December 1999). This means that if they had run on the ULD ticket, with the party not originally from Yeongnam but Chungcheong, there would be very little chance of winning elections. The actual votes in the Sixteenth General Election in April 2000 showed exactly what the TK faction was concerned about: the ULD won no seats in Yeongnam. The TK faction gathered signatures from among the legislators of the ULD in order to promote new electoral laws. The party leader, Park Tae-jun, also addressed the importance of a two-vote system with a closed party list when he visited Gyeongsang province. Park Tae-jun even insisted on passing the new electoral law among the ruling parties only when they all could not reach agreement with those who did not agree with the new system. It is nevertheless questionable whether the coalition parties would have managed to pass the new law by gaining over 50 per cent of the legislative vote, even if the ruling coalition parties held the National Assembly meeting without the presence of the opposition GNP. By then, if the NCNP and the ULD shared a common view on the electoral law within the coalition parties, the size of coalition parties in the legislature actually allowed them to pass the new law, albeit without the presence of the opposition party, and this would matter in terms of the legitimacy of the new law. As shown, each coalition party (the NCNP and the ULD) was struggling to consolidate internal opinion with respect to the new electoral system. The conflict of interest among the law-makers did not allow the ruling coalition parties to put forward consistent reform policies with regard to the electoral law. It seemed that both agreed on a closed party list system but not on the multi-member district system, as many National Assembly members would be in danger of losing their seats in the next general election. This highlights the distance between internal opinion among the legislators in the ULD as well as in the NCNP. If a party fails to consolidate internal solidarity, it is hardly likely to be able to implement reform policies even though it started out with the wide support of the ordinary people and civil society.

The GNP: proportional representation with large districts

The GNP disagreed with this new electoral system as the leader declared it to be part of the ruling party's plot to enlarge the size of the party itself. In light of the close ties between the voters in the Honam region, a closed party list would only benefit the NCNP and this would eventually affect regionalism. The GNP also noted that the present hierarchical political culture combined with the new electoral system would strengthen the leader's power. Following the German-style electoral system, half of the legislature seats would be selected by the party list system. This means that half of the National Assembly members would be selected by appointment from the party, mainly from the party leaders; the other half would be selected by a plurality of ordinary voters. As mentioned earlier, if the calculation of the proposed electoral system failed to show an increase of power and size for the GNP, there would be no apparent reason for the party to consider reforming the electoral law.

The GNP also suffered from internal conflicts among members and did not have a clear opinion in the party. Some of the senior National Assembly members would have preferred to introduce multi-member districts, for they believed that, if the coalition partners did not cooperate in the electoral campaign, it would be hard for them to be elected in a small single member district (*Hankyoreh Sinmun*, 17 November 1999). This means that in a larger district, if two or three members of the National Assembly were to be elected, there would be the possibility for some politicians to be elected in the election even in a less-popular region such as Jeolla or Chungcheong provinces.

When the regional cleavage is as apparent as in the case of Korea, it is not difficult to make predictions as to who would win in a particular electoral district. When Roh Moo-hyun campaigned for the presidential elections in 2002, his title was '*Babo* [Idiot] Roh Moo-hyun' because he was a candidate for the MDP in Busan where most voters would vote for the GNP (see also Chapter 6). Although he is from Busan, strong regionalism means that everybody knows he was perceived to lack foresight in becoming a candidate for the MDP in Busan, whereas actually he insisted on being a candidate in Busan in order to fight against regionalism. In fact, Yeongnam regions did not support any candidate for the MDP but mostly for the GNP, 64 candidates, and one candidate was non-party-affiliated showing 98.5 per cent support for the GNP. Roh Moo-hyun failed in the election. However, the very fact that he campaigned despite knowing he would lose granted him the image of being stubborn and not flexible, but also that he was strongly principled, which is reminiscent of the quality of bamboo, something widely respected in Confucian culture (see Chapter 3).

If the number of politicians elected by proportional representation was increased to half of the total seats in the legislature, it would be easier for a legislator with seniority to be appointed as a candidate for the proportional representative seat. Also in the larger district, if two or three members are to be elected, it is still possible to win an election even though opposition politicians are able to garner local support. Therefore, the influence of regionalism can be reduced by adopting a 'multi-members in a large district system'.

Conflict of interests and the outcome of the new electoral laws

Partial law amendment and the aftermath

In April 1998, the legislature passed a number of amendments to ensure that elections and electoral campaigns would be run in a fair manner. Legislators would be no longer allowed to act as officials[11] at a wedding ceremony and/or to send small 'comfort money' for funerals or money gifts to a wedding or any other family events. As mentioned in Chapter 3, the role of legislators in the electoral district is that of a 'father figure' in the community, taking care of potential voters' family events. To change a highly expensive and inefficient political structure, it was a necessary first step to change the costly system at the local level. Taking care of potential voters' family events in the electoral district took most of the funds required to run the branch office of each party. Over the weekend when most weddings are held, one legislator reported that he attended three or four weddings on the weekend and seven or eight times during the national holidays in his/her official role. Sending a gift of money has been a big financial burden to the legislators and they do not spend much time developing policies or listening to the voice of the people in the local district (*Hankook Ilbo*, 2 April 1998). Some legislators, however, see that this gesture would not change much of the political culture as voters still expect them to be the same and the legislators can also send money in their secretary's name or that of some other distant relative. Another legislator mentioned that he 'still sends flowers instead of a gift of money though he does not attend wedding ceremonies as an officiator' (*Hankook Ilbo*, 2 July 1998).

After the amendment was approved, the negotiations and compromise within and between the parties did not proceed smoothly. It took nearly 13 months to reach any further agreement on possible proposals to change the electoral system. After a long wait, the Structural Reform Special Committee of the National Assembly came to agree as follows on 16 January 2000.

- The legislature would introduce hearings on appointment of high-ranking public servants such as a prime minister or high officials.
- National Assembly law: (1) will introduce an electronic voting system during the assembly meetings in the legislature so that the voters' name will show on the board in the meeting room; (2) the National Assembly's regular meeting will start from 1 September every year and the ad hoc meetings will be held on the 1 February, April and June every year.
- Political funding law: subvention was increased by 50 per cent from 800 won to 1,200 won per voter.
- Candidates are allowed to be appointed in both electoral systems at the same time: one in the single member district and at the same time he or she can also be in the list of candidates for the proportional representative seats.

Criticism of the gerrymandering agreement and the new electoral law

Despite continuous negotiations (and conflict), the outcome of the debate over the electoral law was hardly satisfactory to anyone. The public, as well as scholars and the media, severely criticized this agreement of the special committee as a typical result of gerrymandering among pure office-seekers – that is, a deliberate attempt to reorganize the electoral districts in order to influence the outcome of elections. The plan to reduce the size of the legislature was abandoned, even though it was one of the main reform plans to restructure the high cost of politics aimed at reducing the seat numbers from 299 total seats to either 200 or 150. However, the agreement on reform of the electoral law meant that single member districts were increased by only five districts. In other words, the number of seats in the legislature was increased by five seats from 253 to 258, and the proportional representative seats were decreased by five seats from 46 to 41.

In some districts, applying up-to-date population figures would risk changing the electoral districts. For instance, if the census result of November 1999 was used, *Gap* and *Eul* districts in Busan *Nam-gu* were to be combined as one district and Gure in South Jeolla province and Changneoung in South Gyeongsang province would have to be combined with other districts, but the districts were all retained as they were. To save these districts, the law-makers applied the September 1999 census result which showed an increase or decrease in the population. This was considered of dubious legality as the most recent census should have been used. That means the October or November census result was supposed to be used to decide whether the districts are to be combined or separated. If the maximum 300,000 voters rule is applied, some other bigger districts in Gyeongju, Wonju and Kunsan had to be divided but remained the same. Thus, these three areas were designated as special districts so that they could be allowed a maximum of 250,000 voters in those districts only (*Seoul Sinmun*, 17 January 2000).

Under the current law, if legislators had broken the electoral law, they could have been taken to court within six months of the offence taking place; however, the proposed law would have shortened this term to four months. Civil society organizations campaigned for changes to the Electoral Campaign Law Act 87 which does not allow civil society movements to be involved in anti-candidate activity or anti-appointment activities. Civil society organizations announced that they would continue the anti-candidate campaign regardless of its legality. The Citizens' Coalition for Economic Justice publicly announced the names of the 164 potential candidates who should not be appointed as candidates in the Sixteenth General Election on 11 January 2000.

In 1998, the legislature opened the National Assembly for 296 days but the meeting was actually held only for 54 days for the entire year, and the period the special committee was held was extended seven times without reaching any positive compromise. The special reform committee suggested 44 amendments to the reform law. However, two proposals were rejected and only two were passed, and the rest of the 38 proposed laws were left waiting to be considered (*Donga Ilbo*, 17 January 2000). The special committee suggested that women candidates were to be protected by a 30 per cent quota in the proportional representative seats. However, in the process of negotiation, the issue was not discussed.

Scholars such as Yang Seung-mok and Ham Seong-deuk argued that the agreement needed to be re-negotiated in order to introduce more reform policies (*Donga Ilbo* 17 January 2000; *Kyunghyang Sinmun*, 17 January 2000). The press also reported that each party reached agreement on the basis of its own rational choice. Eventually the NCNP gained one seat more in North Jeolla and lost one seat in South Jeolla. At the GNP's request, some districts were not combined and in return it obtained an agreement on introducing the two votes system. However, four seats were reduced in the proportional representative seats. In this sense the NCNP lost some potential seats. The ULD lost one seat in Daejun in South Chungcheong and gained one seat in Heungdeok in North Chungcheong. This seems to suggest that the changes were zero sum. However, Seochun in South Chungcheong was saved as a district by keeping 75,000 as the minimum threshold for being considered as a separate district. The Seochun district, with a voting population of 78,614, was the main vote base for Lee Geong-gyu who was the representative of the reform special committee and director (*chongmu*) of the ULD (*Weekly Donga*, 27 January 2000). If the proposed reform policies on increasing the number of the minimum voters in a district were implemented, the district could have been combined with neighbouring districts. A district, Younki in Chungcheong province, was also saved in favour of Kim Go-seong, vice-director (*bu-chongmu*) of the ULD. As it had 81,138 voters in the district, applying the proposed electoral law meant the district was in danger of disappearing to become part of a bigger district. The ULD is the smallest party among the three main parties but it managed to secure its interests during the process of negotiation and compromise.

The GNP benefited from the agreement the most, as not many changes were made after the negotiations were completed. It saved four seats that were in danger of being lost as it had the maximum 300,000 voters in the Dongrae-gu districts and Changnyeong with about 75,000 voters was also saved along with the Wonju and Gyeongju districts. It also saved seven districts in the metropolitan areas such as Gyeonggi Dukyang, Ilsan, Bundang, Yongin, Eujeongbu,

Suwon Gwonseon and Namyangju districts (*Kyunghyang Sinmun*, 17 January 2000). Those districts supported the GNP candidates in the previous Fifteenth General Election in 1996. The double candidate system was also put under scrutiny as it was only used to save candidates who failed to gain seats in the single member districts so that they can have another chance to be elected as a proportional representative legislator.

As far as the popular criticism of the gerrymandering agreement is concerned, the party leader of the GNP, Lee Hoe-chang, publicly apologized and the president also showed disappointment at the result after the long deliberations of the reform special committee. President Kim Dae-jung ordered a discussion on abolishing Act 87 that did not allow freedom of citizens' electoral campaigns and expressed the possibility of joining with civil organizations as political reform partners. Lee Hoe-chang did not think of groups in civil society as representing the voices of the people but simply those of strong interest groups and was sceptical about these civil groups being related to or doing a favour for the government. He also viewed pandering to civil society groups as being a typical type of populism. Secretaries of the Seventeenth National Assembly members for the GNP, Im Tae-hee, Jeong Hee-su, Na Gyeong-won and Park Hyeong-jun, unanimously pointed out that civil organizations in South Korea are distorted as they sprung up suddenly and with the government's support. Cho Hong-gyu, a former legislator of the NCNP, mentioned that

> civil society is too big and powerful. It should develop in both quantity and quality but there are so many gigantic civil groups with a large amount of social power; however, its function is not working properly considering its size.[12]

On the other hand, President Kim pursued institutional changes to allow civil groups to be involved in politics. Seo Young-hoon, for example, was involved as a life-long member in the civil movement and became chairman of the New Millennium Democratic Party. There were a few positions in the Blue House filled by civil movement campaigners[13] (*Munhwa Ilbo*, 22 January 2000). When Kim Jong-pil appeared on the list of the anti-candidate movement, the ULD also became suspicious about the relationship between the ruling party and the civil groups. It was a crucial point as the coalition broke up before the election, and when the committee agreed to a 'one voter, one vote' system, the two coalition parties could not ally together as they needed to compete in the same districts. The new electoral law was finally passed on 8 February 2000 just two months before the general election, as follows:

- The total seats in the legislature were decreased from 299 to 273.
- One voter, one vote system continues, and the double candidate system for the single member districts and the proportional representative seats is abolished.
- Act 87 was modified to allow civil groups to meet with politicians and for members of civil society to hold discussions with them.

- Subvention is retained as in the present system of 800 won per voters. Each party can gain subvention according to its size in the legislature.

As shown after the turmoil of compromise and negotiation over a year of introducing reform policies, the special reform committee did not or could not make much progress.

Chronology of the process of electoral laws

9/12/1998	Establishment of the first political structural reform special committee consisting of representatives from each party
25/5/1999	DJT meeting: the president Kim Dae-jung and the prime minister Kim Jong-pil and the Chairman of ULD agreed on multi-member districts (*Jungseongeoguje*) with a closed party list system (*Jeongdang Myeongbuje*)
16/7/1999	Dissolved the first reform special committee
2/8/1999	Established the second reform special committee
30/11/1999	Dissolved the second reform committee
17/12/1999	Established the third reform committee
24/12/1999	Dissolved the third reform committee
28/12/1999	Established the fourth reform committee
29/12/1999	Dissolved the fourth reform committee
30/12/1999	Established the fifth reform committee
3/1/2000	DJT meeting returned to the single member district
13/1/2000	Three parties' directors (*Chongmu*) substantially agreed to one voter for two votes in a single district
15/1/2000	Legislators resisted passage of the electoral law
22/1/2000	Civilians participated in committee to decide electoral districts
8/2/2000	National Assembly finally passed the electoral law (*Pyogyeolcheory*)

Summary

This chapter has shown that, through the political reorganization of the party system, the coalition ruling parties outsized the opposition parties. This means that – on paper, at least – they could have passed an electoral law as the law can be passed by a qualified majority (50 plus 1 per cent of legislators, providing half of the total legislators took part in the vote). This process would not have been without problems, though. First, the introduction of new structural reform policies by the ruling coalition parties, with the opposition party not participating in the work of the assembly, would have harmed the legitimacy of the government's proposed reforms. In other words, the NCNP and the ULD by then reached the majority status after the political reorganization (*Jeonggye Gyepyeon*) in the legislature; therefore, the ruling parties were able to pass the electoral law as proposed by themselves. This would cause more problems,

Regionalism and the reform of the electoral law 121

however, with strong opposition from the GNP as well as the public. This shows majority status (size) does not secure governability. Second, the ruling coalition parties themselves were unable to develop and sustain cohesive support within their own ranks. In this way, both the NCNP and ULD were suffering from the conflicts of interest among the legislators in trying to introduce reform.

The whole process of negotiation and compromise shows that political actors were decisively pure office-seekers, more interested in preserving power and ultimately their seats in the next election for the legislature rather than in introducing reforms that would address the challenges and problems that had emerged in the aftermath of democratization. The present electoral law privileges the existing parties, on the one hand, while, on the other hand, hindering the emergence of new, smaller parties. Strong regional support developed as voters loyally followed the leaders rooted in their regions. This fundamentally undermined the development of nationwide support for a ruling party (or for the opposition, for that matter). If the party system is institutionally based on regional support, the chances that a minority or divided government facing large opposition could successfully introduce its own policies are small at best from the very outset of the administration.

Furthermore, it has shown that the ruling parties also failed to consolidate the internal cohesiveness of the party organization. The Kim Dae-jung administration was then unable to introduce new electoral law reforms that could have mitigated strong regionalism institutionally. Korean political actors have clung to achieving the majority status for the government since democratization. However, this chapter shows that it is not only the size of government that matters and that negatively affects governability. In fact, both hypotheses outlined at the start are confirmed by the discussion of the negotiations over the introduction of the new electoral law. The regional cleavage has deepened in Korea since democratization and this has made the formation of a national politics and party system flawed from the outset, thereby affecting the country's governability. In addition, the parties' internal factionalism has also contributed to undermine the formation of cohesive political organizations.

5 Ideological cleavages and the debate over the National Security Law

Introduction

It is often noted that South Korean parties are mainly located on the right of the ideological spectrum as a result of the Korean War and the Cold War (Choi 2002; Kang 2005; Kim 1999a; Kim *et al.* 1999). Alongside these broader structural constraints, however, there are also contingent factors that have shaped the ideological debate in the country, namely the National Security Law (see Chapter 2).

Every post-authoritarian administration in Korea sought, to different extents, to introduce political reforms; however, it was not until the Kim Dae-jung administration that more progressive reform policies, that would bring structural changes to the society, were introduced – or, at least, there was the intention to introduce them. In particular, the Kim Dae-jung administration tried to implement reforms that would benefit the wider citizenry and not just a narrow circle of elites. To bring about such changes, a crucial move was the attempt to abolish one of the country's most controversial pieces of legislation: the National Security Law (NSL). The NSL had traditionally been used by the government as a means to repress opposition activists under both military *and* civilian rule. Accused of contravening the NSL, people considered as deviant because they held socialist, pro-North Korean or anti-American views had to serve long terms in prison, and were often subject to torture. This ideological polarization between North and South and the convergence towards the right in the South continued throughout the Cold War and the democratization process that began in 1987. A critical point that threatened to derail South Korea's right-wing ideological consensus was reached under the Kim Dae-jung administration, as the former president faced severely ideologically motivated opposition over his determination to introduce the so-called 'Sunshine Policy' towards North Korea (Son 2006), and to act accordingly in the domestic scene by abolishing the National Security Law. As the Kim Dae-jung administration won office through coalition-building with one of the opposition parties, the United Liberal Democrats, it was not easy to maintain a cohesive position within the ruling coalition parties, especially when it came to such a thorny issue as North Korea and particularly so when it came to abolishing the National Security Law.

In this chapter I seek to explain why and how the political actors failed to introduce reform policies that a wide range of people, including the progressive civil rights movement activists and young politicians as well as the then-president Kim Dae-jung himself, demanded. By using the debate over the abolition of the National Security Law as a case study, I seek to explain the role played by ideological cleavages in the party system and how it affected governability. The chapter focuses on the members of the ruling coalition and opposition party, and examines how they were affected by the internal conflicts over the NSL debate. In so doing, I also discuss the extent to which it is not only ideological difference that matters in Korean politics but also political culture. I go on to ask whether and how the institutionalization of the party system would increase the possibilities for negotiating across party lines.

The Kim Dae-jung administration was certainly affected by ideological divides in what came to be referred to as a 'South–South conflict'.[1] Using survey data provided by the East Asia Institute in Seoul, I examine public attitudes with regard to aid to North Korea, the proposed abolition of the National Security Law and the respondents' ideological stance. A cross-tabulation was carried out in order to measure the correlation between the opinions on the questions of aid to North Korea and the abolition of the National Security Law, and the respondents' provinces of origin. The chapter will test the following hypothesis:

> A deep ideological cleavage is likely to undermine governability in implementing new laws.

I will first discuss the ideological difference among people and parties to provide an overview of the ideological spectrum in Korea. Second, I move on to examine the case of the National Security Law and its influence on party ideology. Third, I examine how ideological conflicts were manifest both between the ruling coalition and the opposition, as well as within the ruling coalition itself, thereby undermining its capability to undertake reforms and change the above-mentioned laws. This seems to confirm the argument advanced by policy-oriented scholars who see politicians as policy-oriented actors (Axelrod 1970; De Swaan 1973; Dodd 1976). This ensures the presence of ideological conflicts among coalition partners associated with governability or the duration of a coalition and its termination. More recently, theories on policy dimensions also show that a median party gains a more powerful bargaining position (Baron 1991; Budge *et al.* 2001; Schofield 1993) or parties at the centre of the political spectrum are likely to form a government and also gain a stronger bargaining position. Finally, I conclude that people in South Korea are not deeply divided along ideological lines, although this is widely believed. Ideological conflict is rather the result of the low level of party institutionalization: this allows political elites to mobilize support exploiting policy differences.

Ideological differences among voters and parties

Scholars often note that there is no ideological difference among political parties in South Korea, and that most, if not all, parties are ideologically right-wing or conservative.[2] Others even make a further argument that, because most parties are conservative, 'there is no ideology in conservatism in South Korea' (Kim 1999a; Seo 1999). This seems to suggest that measuring party ideology in Korea, as most of the parties share very similar views, may be of questionable use. Especially when most of the parties turn out to be run by professional electoral strategists, parties are more likely to be catch-all parties pursuing votes and party platforms run across a left-to-right spectrum converging more towards the centre. Choi Jang-jip (2002) argues that South Korea is characterized by a conservative hegemony derived from a decades-old threat coming from the North, a threat reinforced over many decades of authoritarian rule. This obviously does not mean that the threat did not exist, but that the extent thereof also served as a means of self-legitimating the authoritarian governments. Choi notes that anticommunist ideology during the Cold War systematically funnelled or 'caged' most parties towards the right end of the ideological spectrum, ultimately establishing a conservative hegemony. Despite the important role of anti-authoritarian movements (1980 in Gwangju and 1987 nationwide[3]), South Korea was democratized through a pact between the ruling elites. As a consequence, Choi argues, a conservative hegemony (of the elites) has continued to play a crucial role in ensuring that the few ruling groups' interests would be protected.

As discussed in Chapters 2 and 4, during the Kim Dae-jung presidency regionalism deepened between the Yeongnam and Honam regions, creating what is known as the East–West conflict. Yet, in addition to these regional differences, I should note the existence of severe ideological debates over the suggestion made by progressive law-makers to abolish the National Security Law, and the Sunshine Policy (or engagement policy) towards North Korea when Kim Dae-jung tried to relax tensions between South and North Korea. This gave rise to the 'South–South conflict', which also built on regional differences: the Yeongnam region is commonly regarded as conservative, whereas Honam is referred to as progressive (*Hankyoreh Sinmun*, 3 June 2002). When the region is strongly linked to a certain political party, the ideology of the people in that region also seems to correlate with the ideological orientation of that party. For instance, 90 per cent of the citizens in Gwangju (capital of south Honam province) supported the proposal to abolish the NSL, according to opinion poll data (*Jungang Ilbo*, 3 January 2001). Another opinion poll[4] shows that 71.6 per cent of Gwangju citizens supported sending aid to North Korea, while citizens in Gangwon expressed the lowest level of support (44.9 per cent) for offering aid to North Korea. In this opinion poll, citizens in Gwangju and Jeolla provinces expressed relatively progressive opinions on the NSL or the issue of aid to North Korea; on the other hand, citizens in Gangwon and Chungcheong provinces expressed relatively conservative opinions (*Hankyoreh Sinmun*, 3 June 2002). Interestingly, 73 per cent of people who supported the potential presidential candidate for the MDP, Roh Moo-hyun, expressed support for sending aid to North Korea, and 52 per cent of Lee Hoe-chang's supporters for the following presidential election disagreed with offering aid to the North. On the issue of whether or not to abolish or amend the National Security Law, 58 per cent of Roh Moo-hyun's supporters agreed with abolishing the NSL, while 59 per cent of Lee Hoe-chang's supporters favoured maintaining the law. The preference of the supporter for the presidential candidate is also divided by regions. Roh Moo-hyun had 52 per cent support from the Honam region and Lee Hoe-chang had 38 per cent of support from the Yeongnam region, while Roh Moo-hyun received 18.4 per cent of support in Yeongnam region (*Hankyoreh Sinmun*, 3 June 2002). Overall, 58 per cent of people nationwide supported abolishing the NSL and 55 per cent agreed to support the policy of sending aid to North Korea (*Hankyoreh Sinmun*, 4 June 2002).

To identify the relationship between the regions and policy preferences, I looked at the EAI Political and Social Survey (2002) conducted by the Seoul-based East Asia Institute in 2002. The survey was conducted over the phone with 1,008 respondents who had the right to vote in national elections. Among the 20 research questions of the survey, I focus on question 1 ('What is your opinion about the aid policy toward North Korea?'), question 2 ('What do you think about the issue of amending the National Security Law?') and question 14 ('Where would you place yourself on the ideological stance from progressive (0) to conservative (10)?'). On the first question, 16.6 per cent of respondents agreed that aid should stop, and 23.3 per cent answered they agree with limited support; 44.1 per cent agreed that the aid should continue, and 15 per cent of respondents agreed that it should be extended (see Figure 5.1).

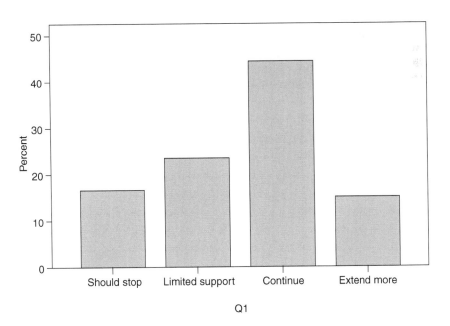

Figure 5.1 Opinion on aid to North Korea (source: author. Raw data supplied by East Asia Institute; EAI Political and Social Survey 1, May 2002).

126 *The debate over the National Security Law*

As to question 2, 7.3 per cent of respondents agreed that the NSL should be abolished immediately, and 34.5 per cent of respondents agreed it should be replaced with a new law; 40.4 per cent of respondents agreed to amend the NSL partially, and 12.2 per cent agreed to maintain the law (see Figure 5.2).

Examining the relationship between the regional support and policy preference over aid to North Korea and amending the National Security Law yields interesting results. As mentioned earlier, previous surveys reported in the *Hankyoreh* daily newspaper in June 2002 hinted at the strong regional difference in support for the National Security Law as well as support for the abolition of the law. Apart from the assumption of a strong relationship between the regional support and policy preference on aid to North Korea and abolishing the National Security Law, the results showed a relatively weak association (Cramer's V^5 0.131 and 0.081 respectively) (see Tables 5.2 and 5.4). Looking at the cross-tabulation of the respondents' province and their preference towards North Korea. Cramer's V 0.131 showed that there is a relatively weak association between the provinces and the preference of aid to North Korea (see Tables 5.1 and 5.2).

I also examined how respondents in different provinces answered with regard to the issue of abolishing the National Security Law. Examining Cramer's V 0.081 also showed a weak association between the provinces and the position on the NSL issue (see Tables 5.3 and 5.4). Although respondents in Jeolla showed a higher preference in that the NSL should be replaced with a new law that would not harm human rights, preferences at the national level

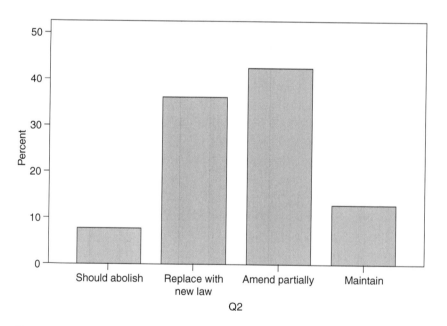

Figure 5.2 Opinion on the National Security Law (source: author. Raw data supplied by East Asia Institute; EAI Political and Social Survey 1, May 2002).

The debate over the National Security Law 127

also showed similar patterns. Therefore the relationship between the province and the National Security Law issue showed a weak correlation between the two.

On the question of their ideological stance, 38.6 per cent of the respondents perceived themselves as belonging to the centre. As Figure 5.3 shows, there is clear ideological convergence towards the centre, with the number of those identifying with the right slightly higher than those on the left.

What are the main ideological tenets of Korean political parties? What are the dividing lines and issues separating conservatives from progressives? It seems problematic to define a party's ideological stance along a left–right axis in South Korea. One wonders, however, what is meant by a 'conservative ideology' and how that manifests itself in Korea. Unlike ideologies like socialism, Marxism or liberalism, conservatism represents more a tendency than a precise set of objectives and goals. As Budge *et al.* (2004) underline, conservatism is primarily about 'preserving what is thought best in traditional society' and 'opposes radical change'. Rather than having one clearly defined set of ideological precepts, conservatives can be characterized by their opposition to radical change and their desire to preserve traditions. Most Western countries are home to one or more political parties that could be broadly defined as conservative. Other countries, typically post-authoritarian and democratizing ones, happen to have more 'unusual' party systems, where on the surface all parties

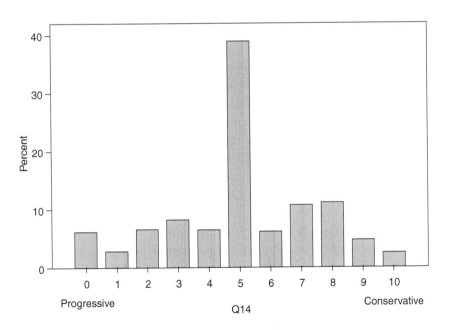

Figure 5.3 Respondents' ideological stance (source: author. Raw data supplied by East Asia Institute; EAI Political and Social Survey 1, May 2002).

Table 5.1 Province and aid to North Korea: cross-tabulation

			Aid to North Korea				Total
			1 Should stop	2 Limited support	3 Continue	4 Extend more	
Province	Gyeonggi	Count	75	105	218	63	461
		Expected count	77.1	108.6	205.6	69.8	461.0
		% within aid to North Korea	44.9	44.7	49.0	41.7	46.2
		Residual	−2.1	−3.6	12.4	−6.8	
		Adjusted residual	−0.4	−0.5	1.6	−1.2	
	Gangwon	Count	6	3	18	5	32
		Expected count	5.4	7.5	14.3	4.8	32.0
		% within aid to North Korea	3.6	1.3	4.0	3.3	3.2
		Residual	0.6	−4.5	3.7	0.2	
		Adjusted residual	0.3	−1.9	1.3	0.1	
	Chungcheong	Count	14	26	47	15	102
		Expected count	17.1	24.0	45.5	15.4	102.0
		% within aid to North Korea	8.4	11.1	10.6	9.9	10.2
		Residual	−3.1	2.0	1.5	−0.4	
		Adjusted residual	−0.9	0.5	0.3	−0.1	
	Jeolla	Count	29	44	33	5	111
		Expected count	18.6	26.1	49.5	16.8	111.0
		% within aid to North Korea	17.4	18.7	7.4	3.3	11.1
		Residual	10.4	17.9	−16.5	−11.8	
		Adjusted residual	2.8	4.2	−3.3	−3.3	
	Gyeongsang	Count	41	57	123	61	282
		Expected count	47.2	66.4	125.7	42.7	282.0
		% within aid to North Korea	24.6	24.3	27.6	40.4	28.3
		Residual	−6.2	−9.4	−2.7	18.3	
		Adjusted residual	−1.2	−1.6	−0.4	3.6	
	Jeju	Count	2	0	6	2	10
		Expected count	1.7	2.4	4.5	1.5	10.0
		% within aid to North Korea	1.2	0.0	1.3	1.3	1.0
		Residual	0.3	−2.4	1.5	0.5	
		Adjusted Residual	0.3	−1.8	1.0	0.4	
Total		Count	167	235	445	151	998
		Expected count	167.0	235.0	445.0	151.0	998.0
		% within aid to North Korea	100.0	100.0	100.0	100.0	100.0

Source: author. Raw data supplied by East Asia Institute; EAI Political and Social Survey 1, May 2002.

The debate over the National Security Law 129

Table 5.2 Measures of association between province and aid to North Korea

		Value	Approx. Sig.
Nominal by nominal	Phi	0.226	0.000
	Cramer's V	0.131	0.000
Number of valid cases		998	

Source: author. Raw data supplied by East Asia Institute; EAI Political and Social Survey 1, May 2002.

Notes
a Not assuming the null hypothesis.
b Using the asymptotic standard error assuming the null hypothesis.

seem to be located on the right-wing of the political spectrum and could be broadly defined as conservative. So what are the common features of these parties? Is it correct to refer to them as 'conservative'? And what defines their ideological stance?

Comparing Korea to Western political systems would suggest that Korean conservatives have no ideology. First, in terms of keeping tradition, Confucianism would be the tradition that the conservatives would like to preserve. However, due to the colonial period and the Korean War, such traditionalists/ would-be conservatives were totally eradicated as a result of the radical changes in Korean history. In fact, Confucian scholars and the aristocrats were considered to be the main factor behind the *Joseon* Dynasty's demise and the resulting colonization by Japan.[6] The Cold War then crystallized the ideological polarization between the two Koreas, with a socialist North and pro-Western South. During the American-led reconstruction process in the South, most left-wing activists were either physically eliminated (executed or forced to serve long-term prison sentences) or went to North Korea in line with their ideological beliefs. In the absence of leftist ideology, South Korean political actors developed as hybrids of the left and right ideology in terms of their policy preferences. The so-called conservative and progressive parties are in fact all on the right or centre-right. The MDP, which might be referred to as a centre-right party, is criticized as a socialist party by the opposition, whereas the GNP or the ULD are seen by the MDP as reactionaries. Looking at their policies, Kim Dae-jung introduced neo-liberal economic policies seeking to dismantle the *Jaebeol* system under the IMF restructuring guidelines in the early years of his presidency, while his labour policies were seeking the third way, akin to that of the British Labour Party (*Munhwa Ilbo*, 13 August 2001). People also show hybrid views on their policy preferences. According to an opinion poll conducted by the Korean Social Science Data Centre, 68.9 per cent of respondents agreed that the government should pay more attention to economic growth than distribution of wealth, and 68.2 per cent agreed to sending children to school based on their financial ability or on the child's ability rather than the present standardized system. The poll also showed that 64.3 per cent agreed that the government

Table 5.3 Province and National Security Law: cross-tabulation

			National Security Law				Total
			Should abolish	Replace new law	Amend partially	Maintain	
Province	Gyeonggi	Count	37	157	204	43	441
		Expected count	34.3	161.2	188.5	57.0	441.0
		% within National Security Law	50.0	45.1	50.1	35.0	46.3
		Residual	2.7	−4.2	15.5	−14.0	
		Adjusted residual	0.7	−0.6	2.0	−2.7	
	Gangwon	Count	1	8	13	4	26
		Expected count	2.0	9.5	11.1	3.4	26.0
		% within National Security Law	1.4	2.3	3.2	3.3	2.7
		Residual	−1.0	−1.5	1.9	0.6	
		Adjusted residual	−0.8	−0.6	0.8	0.4	
	Chungcheong	Count	6	36	40	14	96
		Expected count	7.5	35.1	41.0	12.4	96.0
		% within National Security Law	8.1	10.3	9.8	11.4	10.1
		Residual	−1.5	0.9	−1.0	1.6	
		Adjusted residual	−0.6	0.2	−0.2	0.5	
	Jeolla	Count	9	49	41	14	113
		Expected count	8.8	41.3	48.3	14.6	113.0
		% within National Security Law	12.2	14.1	10.1	11.4	11.9
		Residual	0.2	7.7	−7.3	−0.6	
		Adjusted residual	0.1	1.6	−1.5	−0.2	
	Gyeongsang	Count	20	92	106	48	266
		Expected count	20.7	97.2	113.7	34.4	266.0
		% within National Security Law	27.0	26.4	26.0	39.0	27.9
		Residual	−0.7	−5.2	−7.7	13.6	
		Adjusted residual	−0.2	−0.8	−1.1	2.9	
	Jeju	Count	1	6	3	0	10
		Expected count	0.8	3.7	4.3	1.3	10.0
		% within National Security Law	1.4	1.7	0.7	0.0	1.1
		Residual	0.2	2.3	−1.3	−1.3	
		Adjusted residual	0.3	1.5	−0.8	−1.2	
Total		Count	74	348	407	123	952
		Expected count	74.0	348.0	407.0	123.0	952.0
		% within National Security Law	100.0	100.0	100.0	100.0	100.0

Source: Author. Raw data supplied by East Asia Institute; EAI Political and Social Survey 1, May 2002.

Table 5.4 Measures of association between province and National Security Law

		Value	Approx. Sig.
Nominal by nominal	Phi	0.141	0.223
	Cramer's V	0.081	0.223
Number of valid cases		952	

Source: author. Raw data supplied by East Asia Institute; EAI Political and Social Survey 1, May 2002.

Notes
a Not assuming the null hypothesis.
b Using the asymptotic standard error assuming the null hypothesis.

should continue its own policies regardless of the opposition of the people. However, 53.6 per cent agreed to abolishing the NSL and 70 per cent agreed that the government should raise taxes to distribute them to the poor (*Hankyoreh Sinmun*, 3 June 2002). As the poll shows, Korean's ideological perspectives are all 'mixed up'. They are very conservative in terms of growth, state authority and privatization; on the other hand, they are also progressive in respect of issues like the National Security Law or taxation.

The NSL played a crucial role in 'pushing' ideological preferences to the right as it does not allow the legal existence of any socialist organizations. The South Korean legislature passed the National Security Law in 1948, a law which in essence made anti-communism the South's ideology (Choi 2002). Many of those who opposed the NSL were later arrested (under the NSL) in 1949. Right-wing nationalists established the South Korean government with the crucial support of the US military and preserved the authoritarian regime for decades. By then, most of those on the left of the political spectrum were also politically marginalized. At that point in history, though, there was little remaining to be kept in terms of tradition. Recent history has seen colonization, liberation and then a growing ideological conflict with the North. Conservatives are regarded as seeking to preserve tradition; however, this factor is less valued among the conservatives in South Korea (Kim 1999a: 34). The modern history of Korean politics since the *Joseon* Dynasty has witnessed radical changes. Economically, South Korea was also very different from Western systems as no welfare system was in place or even conceived. Instead, Korea had a state-led development strategy and therefore rapid development was the pre-eminent value and so came before human rights or social welfare.[7]

The opposition was not ideological, as the cleavage was between the ruling authoritarian elites and the opposition striving to introduce democratic reforms. Conservatives here were those who enjoyed privileges during the authoritarian governments, including bureaucrats, *Jaebeol* leaders and media entrepreneurs. As most of the parties were advocating and pursuing democracy, they were mostly on the right or centre of the ideological spectrum. There could obviously be individuals with left-leaning tendencies, but no organization or political group

132 The debate over the National Security Law

exhibiting this orientation was allowed to survive (Chae 2004; Han 2001). Such groups were banned under the National Security Law.

Anti-communism was the glue keeping the parties together, and because of the structure of the international system during the Cold War, this was the only ideological position allowed to exist (Choi 2002; Han 2001; Kim 1999a; Seo 1999). It is clear, then, that anti-communism shaped the party system's ideological divide, basically eliminating the divide itself and creating a convergence towards the right. This point is relatively unproblematic, but this does not explain why parties would be in conflict over different issues like the policy towards North Korea if there were really such an ideological consensus (voluntary or imposed). What is necessary, therefore, is a measure of ideological distance between the parties. How far apart are they on specific issues, and why?

Hyun (2004) examined the parties' platforms and positions on several issues from 1952 to 2000 by using ECPR (European Consortium for Political Research) data and measured the difference between, and the evolution of, party ideologies over the decades. Hyun argues that there was an actual difference on issues among political parties. Under the authoritarian governments, the polarization of ideology was from 1 to 2.3; after democratization, however, polarization on issues is 0.5. This suggests that, with the democratization process, political parties showed an ideological convergence. During the period of authoritarian governments, the ruling parties and the opposition parties viewed each other as enemies, whereas after democratization the parties looked at each other as adversaries, with which they could compete in the political arena. This implies that the main cleavage under authoritarian rule was that between the ruling elites versus the democratic opposition, but after democratization the parties' position on issues converged to the centre and the main cleavages emerged around the attitude towards North Korea (ibid.: 207–211). The North Korean policy became the dividing line in South Korean politics. Although Hyun's research focuses on the period up to 2000, it shows that this ideological cleavage was amplified over the Sunshine Policy, leading to a South–South ideological conflict.

Kang (2005) points out that ideological conflicts in South Korea are fundamentally different from those in the West. According to Kang, a conservative–progressive cleavage can be examined by looking at four different dimensions. First, left and right can be distinguished by examining the parties' position on issues like equality and efficiency, nation and market, distribution and growth, labour and capital. It can also be divided by looking at the stance on authority and liberalism, with conservatives being more concerned with law and order, authority and tradition, while progressives appear more focused on individual freedoms, human rights, and political and social equality. For Kang, the third dimension is that distinguishing between modern and post-modern values. Conservatives tend to hold modern values such as control of immigration, strong concern over national security issues – for example, anti-terror laws – and low taxes, and attempt to decrease the presence of the state in the economy and society, while progressives tend to pay more attention to environmental issues, human rights, including gay rights, and race relations. Kang argues that these three dimensions (left/right, authority/liberalism and modern/postmodern values) are universally applicable to define either conservatives or progressives on the ideological spectrum. However, using only three universal dimensions is unlikely to explain ideological difference among parties in South Korea. The most crucial difference that can be added to distinguish conservatives and progressives in South Korea lies in the conflict over the anti-communist issue (ibid.: 2–3). Kang argues that the fourth dimension is:

> The fact that these differences over the North Korean issue is of a more profound significance than that of a mere disagreement over the course of 'political or military' relations. Thus, a defence strategy that incorporates North Korean policy, U.S. relations, and the National Security Law forms a key axis which delineates the ideological conflicts within Korean society, in that, these rifts represent not only the political preferences of society, but also more fundamental differences over individual value systems.
>
> (ibid.: 3)

Drawing on a survey conducted with the members of the Sixteenth National Assembly, Kang sought to measure their ideological stance. In Kang's research, the main divide between parties concerns the policy towards North Korea and the more or less firm opposition to communist ideology, and the North's regime as a threat to the peace of South Korea. Table 5.5 shows a strong division over the National Security Law and aid to North Korea between the ruling party (MDP) and the opposition party (GNP). While both parties converge to the centre with regard to relations with the US, showing a difference of absolute value 1.11, the difference over the issue of abolishing the National Security Law is more marked, with a 2.17 value. Similarly, and even more pronounced, is the issue of aid to North Korea, with a 4.34 value (see Table 5.5).

The core of the conflict over the Sunshine Policy lies in how one should deal with North Korea, either as a threat to be contained or deterred, or even being forced to collapse, or as a potentially cooperative regime. Aid to North Korea was often criticized by the opposition party, GNP, as this helps North Korea by allowing it to arm to defeat South Korea or prepare for a future war.

Table 5.5 Rejection versus acceptance of anti-communist ideology

Issue	MDP	GNP	Difference (absolute value)	T value
US relations	4.70	5.81	1.11	3.92
National Security Law	3.28	5.45	2.17	8.24
Aid to North Korea	1.86	6.20	4.34	18.22

Source: remade from Kang (2005: 5).

Note
For all figures, 0=most progressive, 5=moderate, 10=most conservative.

On other issues, such as the *Jaebeol* reform, a class-action lawsuit system, expansion of welfare policy and educational equalization, the two parties show differences ranging from a marginal 0.03 to 1.42. On some issues, such as a system for class-action lawsuits, both parties could be located on the left of the political spectrum, while both parties would appear on the right-wing with respect to *Jaebeol* reform. On this basis, Kang concludes that the most serious conflict in the Korean party system is ideological, and manifests itself most clearly in the shape of anti-communist ideology. In regard to the distribution of economic resources, moreover, the two parties do not show much difference on the left versus right ideological dimension. Kang concludes that 'the most serious ideological conflicts, in the political sector and among the general public, are related to the "rejection vs. acceptance of anti-communist ideology" and "authoritarianism vs. liberalism" dimensions' (2005: 12).

Another survey conducted by the *Hankook Ilbo* (7–8 June 2002) also shows that Western-style categorizations, which see conservatives more concerned with economic growth and progressives with redistribution of wealth, do not seem applicable to and do not explain party divisions in Korea. Ideology in South Korea has been influenced by two radical events in modern history since its foundation in 1947: the Korean War from 1950 to 1953 and the Gwangju uprising in 1980. The Korean War placed most of the politicians and people on the right, with a strong anti-communist orientation. The National Security Law made establishing socialist groups illegal. The Gwangju incident influenced citizens in Gwangju to mobilize vigorously for the protection of human rights and to abolish the National Security Law, resulting in 71.6 per cent support to abolish the NSL. When the population protested and demanded democracy in May 1980, the new military government of Chun Du-hwan clamped down on the demonstration, causing a large number of deaths. The Gwangju 5.18 civil movement resulted in about 3,586 total victims, including the death of 207 civilians.[8] The fact that people in Gwangju witnessed their families and acquaintances dying at the hands of the military – sent by the government under the National Security Law – explains their strong anti-authoritarian sentiments.

These experiences also made the strong regional divisions clearly evident in voting behaviour. Choi (2002) argues that regionalism is not a problem of division between Yeongnam and Honam but it is rather a problem of Honam with its own political experience. As a matter of fact, Yeongnam's[9] residents are likely to hold strong anti-communist and conservative attitudes. On the other hand, with the great loss of participants in the civil movement in Gwangju and the dreadful memories of the deaths of family members and friends, they could be expected to hold more progressive views against authoritarianism, the National Security Law and in favour of human rights. Under the authoritarian governments, being against the government was simply understood as a threat to national security, especially when facing North Korea's threat. The survey shows that respondents did not split over questions of economic growth or taxation, but over issues of human rights, the abolition of the National Security Law, the policy towards North Korea, aid to the North, or even the broader question of the unification of North and South. Another finding was that views on human rights and policies towards North Korea do not correlate with conservatives and progressives, as some high-income earners expressed conservative views on North Korean policies, but were very progressive with regard to human rights. On the other hand, those who considered themselves as progressives would favour abolishing the National Security Law, while showing negative views on the reunification of the North and the South.

In the survey conducted by the East Asia Institute in May 2002, question 3 asked the respondents for their opinion on a possible reunification with North Korea. In total, 15.2 per cent of respondents agreed that they should achieve reunification regardless of social and economic costs, and 51.6 per cent of the respondents agreed they should take time considering the circumstances. On the other hand, 28.7 per cent of respondents agreed that there is no need to be in a hurry if social and economic sacrifice is crucial, and only 4.3 per cent agreed that there is no need for reunification (see Table 5.6).

Overall, 80.3 per cent of respondents agreed that reunification should go forward considering the social and economic environment (see Table 5.6), and 74.9 per cent of the respondents agreed that the National Security Law should be replaced with a new law that would not harm human rights, or should be amended partially (see Figure 5.2). In running a cross-tabulation between those who favour abolishing the National Security Law and those favouring reunification, Cramer's V 0.119 shows that there is a relatively weak association between the two opinions (see Table 5.8). Of respondents who favoured abolishing the National Security Law, 16.2 per cent agreed that reunification should be achieved regardless of social and economic sacrifice. However, people who favour either 'replacing the NSL with a new law' or 'amending it partially' were scattered rather evenly between those who answered either 'should achieve reunification', 'should take time' or 'no need to be in a hurry and no need for reunification' (see Table 5.7). The survey result shows people's ideological preferences are all mixed up.

The ideological debate over the policies towards North Korea does not appear to be about ideology but is more related to the Kim Dae-jung administration and the opposition party's political struggles over the Sunshine Policy and abolishing the National Security Law. *Sin Donga*, a monthly magazine (1 September 2001), notes that the political conflicts in South Korea are mainly over regionalism, North Korean policies, taxation or media laws between the ruling party and the opposition party. The ideological debate also follows the leader as well. For many, supporting Kim Dae-jung was synonymous with holding progressive ideas and opposing him was equated with conservative ideas (see Table 2.1).

What is taking place is a political conflict over power between the ruling party and the opposition party on specific issues. Kim Byong-ik, a literary critic, argues that 'the conservatives are pervasive but it is hard to see anyone with conservatism and there are many individual progressives but no progressives as a social group' (*Hankyoreh 21*, 2 August 2001). In practice, this means that an

Table 5.6 Respondents' opinion on reunification

Question 3. What do you think about the reunification of Korea?

		Frequency	%	Valid %	Cumulative %
Valid	Should achieve reunification regardless of social and economic sacrifice	153	15.2	15.2	15.2
	Should take time considering circumstances	520	51.6	51.7	67.0
	No need to be in a hurry if social and economic sacrifice is crucial	289	28.7	28.8	95.7
	No need for reunification	43	4.3	4.3	100.0
	Total	1,005	99.7	100.0	
Missing	System	3	0.3		
Total		1,008	100.0		

Source: Author. Raw data supplied by East Asia Institute; EAI Political and Social Survey 1, May 2002.

Table 5.7 Cross-tabulation of opinion on the National Security Law and reunification

Q2 on the National Security Law and Q3 reunification crosstabulation

			Q3				Total
			Should achieve reunification regardless of social and economic sacrifice	Should take time considering circumstances	No need to be in a hurry if social and economic sacrifice is crucial	No need for reunification	
Q2	Should abolish immediately	Count	23	42	8	0	73
		% within Q3	16.2	8.6	2.9	0.0	7.7
		Residual	12.1	4.4	−13.3	−3.2	
		Adjusted residual	4.1	1.1	−3.6	−1.9	
	Replace with new law	Count	54	184	97	13	348
		% within Q3	38.0	37.6	35.0	31.7	36.7
		Residual	1.9	4.7	−4.6	−2.0	
		Adjusted residual	0.4	0.6	−0.7	−0.7	
	Amend partially	Count	44	213	131	18	406
		% within Q3	31.0	43.6	47.3	43.9	42.8
		Residual	−16.8	3.8	12.5	0.5	
		Adjusted residual	−3.1	0.5	1.8	0.1	
	Maintain	Count	21	50	41	10	122
		% within Q3	14.8	10.2	14.8	24.4	12.9
		Residual	2.7	−12.9	5.4	4.7	
		Adjusted residual	0.7	−2.5	1.1	2.3	
Total		Count	142	489	277	41	949
		% within Q3	100.0	100.0	100.0	100.0	100.0

Source: Author. Raw Data supplied by East Asia Institute; EAI Political and social survey 1, May 2002.

Table 5.8 Measures of association between the National Security Law and reunification

		Value	Asymp. Std. Error[a]	Approx. T[b]	Approx. Sig.
Nominal by nominal	Phi	0.206			0.000
	Cramer's V	0.119			0.000
Interval by interval	Pearson's R	0.150	0.033	4.673	0.000[c]
Ordinal by ordinal	Spearman correlation	0.141	0.033	4.372	0.000[c]
Number of valid cases		949			

Source: Author. Raw data supplied by East Asia Institute; EAI Political and Social Survey 1, May 2002.

Notes
a Not assuming the null hypothesis.
b Using the asymptotic standard error assuming the null hypothesis.
c Based on normal approximation.

individual can be a socialist privately but cannot organize any group legally. Conservatives in South Korea are often criticized as they do not hold traditional conservative values but are rather reactionary, thereby implying that they would rather abolish democratic reforms and return to authoritarian rule. Jin Jung-kwon argues 'there are no conservatives but reactionaries who disguise themselves as conservatives.... The true conservatives would hold patriotism and pursue traditional values' (*Hankyoreh 21*, 2 August 2001). Meanwhile, the conservatives also accused the ruling party of being a leftist party and a threat to social stability in South Korea by wasting people's taxes for the good of North Korea.

On the other hand, whether the progressives actually hold any leftist ideology also appears debatable. A particularly interesting case is that of a social and political group called *Jaeya*,[10] which comprised civilians who have played a part in social movements against the authoritarian governments since the 1970s. Kim Dae-jung was politically indebted to these *Jaeya* groups for finally achieving political power after decades in opposition. Priests, ministers or monks holding different religious beliefs played a very important role and remain the strength of the *Jaeya* groups. *Jaeya* can be considered as one of the leading progressive groups in South Korea. *Sin Donga*, a monthly magazine, argues that the leaders of *Jaeya* have their roots on the right. Jang Jun-ha was a politician and one of the high-ranking officials of the far-right group, the National Young Society. He also published a monthly magazine called *The World of Thought* (*Sasanggye*) but the magazine was later abolished under the National Security Law. Members of the group include Ham Seok-heon, an authorative philosopher and campaigner who led the demonstrations against communists in Sinuiju, North Korea; Mun Ik-hwan, a minister who was jailed after visiting North Korea in 1989 and who was an American army interpreter; Kim Su-young, a poet who chose to come to South Korea where he was a communist prisoner; and Lee Young-hee, a social scientist, who was a Korean army officer (*Sin Donga*, September 2001). As a study of the careers and personal background of all of these *Jaeya* leaders shows, and as *Sin Donga* notes, the roots of *Jaeya* are not on the left, but rather they have fought to preserve traditional conservative values against authoritarian governments.

The so-called progressives in South Korea are not really on the left of the ideological spectrum but arguably on the centre-right too (*Sin Donga*, September 2001). When Korea was divided into two countries, South Korea was established around a fierce anti-communist ideology. However, the conflicts between the conservatives and the progressives during the Kim Dae-jung administration lie in the disputes over policies such as abolishing the National Security Law or the Sunshine (or engagement) policy towards North Korea. In other words, conflicts among political parties are over very specific issues, namely policies affecting the North Korean question. In the following section I will discuss how these two laws (the NSL and the Anti-Communist Law) shaped the parties' and people's ideologies.

The National Security Law's influence on party ideology

Since the National Security Law was passed, it has played a major role in allowing the authoritarian regime to 'get rid of unwelcome people', namely those involved in socialist groups, and opposition groups more generally. Many political opponents were arrested or executed on the basis of this law. For the authoritarian government, any opposition or pro-North Korea sentiment was seen as bringing instability to the nation. Especially after the tragic experience of war, strong anti-communism was embraced by the majority of people as well as by North Koreans who fled from the North after losing most of their property over the land reform that was carried out by the North Korean regime. For the authoritarian government, it was also easy to repress political opponents accusing them of holding leftist views or trying to contact North Korea. The National Security Law provided the political mechanism to get rid of not only leftists but also of political opponents who would allegedly break the peace and stability of the government.

It also legitimized the government's closing of publishing companies that published novels, poetry or columns that contained any form of criticism of the government's actions. Many books were banned and the writers and publishers were imprisoned for long terms or, in the early years of the republic, executed. Jo Yong-su, a publisher of a daily newspaper, *Minjok Ilbo* (*Nation Daily*), was arrested and executed in 1961 as he was accused of receiving funding from North Korean spies, though it was not proven.

A particularly dramatic event happened in 1949 when 13 members of the National Assembly were arrested under the National Security Law, being accused of contacting North Korean spies (see Chapter 2). The 13 legislators had previously opposed the approval of the National Security Law and announced the 'seven principles for the peaceful unification of the South and the North' that included the withdrawal of any foreign troops, the release of North and South political prisoners, the introduction of fair parliamentary elections, punishing anti-nationalists, and reinforcing national defence forces. They were mostly sentenced from two to twelve years, but during the Korean War ten of them went to North Korea. This seemed to prove that the government was right about their alleged leftist ideology. Scholar Seo Jung-seok notes that the South Joseon Labour Party was legal until June 1949. The 13 members were accused of being spies as they contacted members of the South Joseon Labour Party. Seo (*Voice of People*, 15 November 2005) argues that they were accused because of their critical views. In November 1956, the first Progressive Party was founded by Jo Bong-am who competed twice in the presidential elections with Rhee Syngman, in 1952 and 1956. Jo Bong-am gained more than 2,160,000 votes during the presidential election in 1956. In early 1958, many members of the Progressive Party were arrested under the National Security Law. The party policy on peaceful unification was against Rhee Syng-man administration's policy. Over a year of court procedures, the party leader Jo Bong-am was sentenced to a number of years in prison and the rest of the members were declared innocent. In a later suit, however, Jo Bong-am was sentenced to the death penalty and executed within 20 hours of the court decision in 1959. The rest of the members were sentenced to ten to twenty years in prison. However, this was mainly considered an artificially manipulated incident by anti-communists to get rid of political competitors or opponents before the general election in April 1958 (*Voice of People*, 15 November 2005).

Over the series of arrests of political opponents and leftists, the National Security Law became known as the *Makgeolli* (rice wine) Security law during the Rhee administration (*Hankyoreh 21*, 2 February 2002). There were many civilians arrested under the National Security Law as they expressed their opinions against the government while they were drinking *Makgeolli* with their neighbours or friends in the neighbourhood. Some of them were jailed for at least three years just for verbally abusing the Rhee government. During Park Chung-hee's administration, the Anti-Communist Law was passed in July 1961 and the law forbade any praise of communism. Under the Anti-Communist Law, whoever praised or admired the Kim Il-sung administration or leftist ideology was sent to prison. From 1961 to 1979 under the Park administration the number of people violating the Anti-Communist Law was twice that of the National Security Law. This new law also gained the nickname *Makgeolli* Anti-Communist Law (*Hankyoreh 21*, 2 February 2002).

Since then the two laws played a major role in oppressing political opponents and whoever contacted North Korea or expressed different views on the Korean War or leftist ideologies. When an artist, Sin Hak-cheol, sent a slide depicting farmers working in the rice field in North Korea, where the international students' festival was held in Pyongyang in 1989, he was also arrested under the National Security Law. In 1994 the human rights committee of the UN concluded that his case represented the suppression of freedom of expression. In November 2002, the constitutional court also decided that the death penalty for other violators of the National Security Law was against the constitution. Many social scientists were also arrested under the National Security Law or Anti-Communist Law. According to the report of the National Security Law published by civil society organizations, the Lawyers' Society for Democracy (*Minbyeon*) and the Society for Democratization Activists' Family Association (*Mingahyeoup*), there were 454 people in 1998, 299 in 1999 and 128 in 2000 arrested under the National Security Law. In other words, the rate of arrested people under the National Security Law decreased from 66 per cent in 1998 to 58.7 per cent in 1999, and 51.1 per cent in 2000. In the following year, 128 persons were arrested under the National Security Law, with 117 of those arrested under Act 7 of the National Security Law, that is, the Act that punishes people who admire or praise North Korea or communism. That means 91.8 per cent (117 out of 128 persons) were arrested simply for having different thoughts or ideological perspectives (*Seoul Sinmun*, 18 June 2001; *Hankook Ilbo*, 30 July 2001).

As shown in this section, the National Security Law and the Anti-Communist Law crucially forced popular ideology to converge to the centre or right. The laws created a division of policy preference between the old who experienced the Korean War and the young who experienced fighting against authoritarian governments, and also further divided people between those who experienced the 'Gwangju democratization movement' in 1980 and those who did not. This is linked with regional division between Yeongnam and Honam in South Korea. Introducing the Sunshine Policy brought further social conflicts within the party, and with the coalition partner as well as the opposition party. When the government could not gather wide support and could not abolish the so-called 'evil law' (NSL) to further boost the Sunshine Policy, 80 members who attended the 15 August Liberation Festival in Pyongyang were arrested under the National Security Law. Sending people from South to North Korea was also a part of the Sunshine Policy to bring harmony between the North and the South in Korea.

Anti-communism also left South Korea undeveloped in terms of social welfare. Lee Jung-seop (*Hankyoreh Sinmun*, 17 December 2002) argues that in Western societies democracy allows freedom of speech and thought, and it includes ideologically differentiated parties spread across the ideological spectrum from the left to the right. The very concept of socialism is distorted in South Korea especially under the National Security Law and the Anti-Communist Law. Anti-communism closed the door to the dynamics of political ideology in both politics and society. Lee raises questions as to whether South Korea is ready to develop social welfare and if Korean society is equipped with a truly democratic society. As Lee argues, the Kim Dae-jung administration was struggling with implementing the Sunshine Policy as well as social welfare because large segments of society were not ready to accept such reforms. The National Security Law and the Anti-Communist Law 'caged' parties and people towards the right or centre of the ideological spectrum. This meant that those who held dissenting views – promoting social and economic equality – constituted easy targets as they could be dismissed as leftist by the opposition parties.

The ruling party's attempt to abolish the so-called 'evil law'

The National Security Law was crucial to ensure the support and legitimacy not just of the authoritarian governments, but of post-authoritarian ones, too. Questioning it, as Kim Dae-jung did, placed severe strains on the government and its governability. Many scholars, writers and social activists were accused under the National Security Law and Anti-Communist Law, and during the Sunshine Policy many visitors to North Korea were also accused by members of the opposition parties and later arrested by the police.

Park Sang-cheon, from the Ministry of Justice, emphasized the need to amend the National Security Laws on 26 March 1999. The report suggested that Act 7 and 10 of the National Security Law needed to be either abolished or amended, as already mentioned. Act 7 bans public displays of praise and support of communism in general or the North Korean systems in particular; whereas Act 10 punishes individuals who do not report any suspicious people ('suspicious' here refers to anything ranging from bearing a leftist ideology to spying for North

Korea). Acts 6 and 8, which do not allow smuggling goods into or accessing North Korea, or contacting spies, were also seen to be in need of amendment (*Donga Ilbo*; *Jungang Ilbo*, 27 March 1999). Since the proposal by the Ministry of Justice to amend the NSL, negotiations to abolish the Law and attempts to achieve a majority for that purpose have continued for years. At the Legislation and Judiciary Committee meeting in the National Assembly on 11 December 2000, nine members out of 15 finally agreed to support the amendment of the National Security Law (*Hankyoreh Sinmun*, 12 December 2000). On 29 December, civil society organizations, including well-known NGOs such as the People's Solidarity for Participatory Democracy, *Boanbeoppyeji Gugminyeondae* (Peoples' Society for Abolishing National Security Law), and wider members of civil society, visited the National Assembly to show their support for the abolition of the National Security Law on 9 January 2001. Parallel to this, three members of the University Students Associations (*Hanchongryeon*) and Nation Associations (*Bumminreon*) started a hunger strike at Chonnam National University for ten days, criticizing the legislators' apparent neglect of the people's desire for unification and hence the need to abolish the National Security Law (*Jungang Ilbo*, 1 February 2001). At the same time, the Liberal Citizen Association and the Veterans' Society of the Korean War also held demonstrations in front of the National Assembly opposing the amendment of the National Security Law (*Jungang Ilbo*, 5 February 2001). This shows the extent of the ideological cleavage in South Korea, but also suggests that the cleavage was about clearly defined issues (as opposed to broad ideological questions), such as the National Security Law and the policies towards North Korea. Furthermore, it also shows a clear generational divide between the younger generations pushing for the abolition of the National Security Law and older ones who vehemently defended the existing law.

President Kim Dae-jung confirmed his intention to pass reform laws such as a human rights law, and an anti-corruption law, and to abolish the National Security Law at the annual press meeting on 11 January 2001 (*Jungang Ilbo*). The latter issue yielded two internal conflicts within the ruling party and with the opposition party. What is noteworthy is that the attempt to abolish or at least amend the National Security Law and Anti-Communist Law was pursued not only by the members of the MDP but also by some members of the opposition party (GNP). The two parties therefore faced severe internal conflicts, the MDP with its coalition partner ULD, and the GNP with a relatively progressive faction within the party who mostly included young, newly elected deputies, with recent involvement with pro-democracy social movements.

A generational conflict within the GNP

The young progressive members of the National Assembly gathered to draw up a proposal to amend and eventually abolish the National Security Law. They created a political faction named Jeongchi Gaehyeogeulwihan Moim (Society for political reform), consisting of members belonging to both the MDP and

GNP. Twenty-one members of the Political Reform Lawmakers' Society passed a motion to abolish the National Security Law in the National Assembly on 28 November 2000. Among those 21 law-makers were four belonging to the GNP; the number grew to six in April the following year (*Segye Ilbo*, 5 June 2001). Eventually, about 13 GNP members supported the motion (*Maeil Kyungje*, 12 June 2001). The party leader, Lee Hoe-chang, expressed his disapproval at the behaviour of this small faction, arguing that party members should follow the party's directives rather than acting individually. In the end, 20 GNP law-makers signed up to abolish the National Security Law in April 2001 (*Hankook Ilbo*, 4 June 2001).

On the issue of abolishing the National Security Law the GNP suffered from severe internal conflicts. In early 2001, 52 members of the 'Society of Lawmakers for the Just Unification and Strong Security', another major conservative faction in the GNP, announced that it was not possible to amend the National Security Law unless North Korea renounced the goal of unification of Korea under the North (*Jungang Ilbo*, 18 January 2001). Kim Yong-gap, a conservative legislator, who was also the chairman of the conservative faction, accused the progressive young faction of being a group of 'pro-North Korean leftists' (*Hankook Weekly*, 14 June 2001). Progressive faction members also suggested that a cross-voting system should be introduced in the legislature so that the lawmakers could vote according to their own conscience and ideological beliefs rather than obeying party whips. In contrast, the conservative elements of the GNP accused the younger progressive members of undermining party unity and stability. In early June 2001, the progressive factions were actively preparing for the motion to be voted on in the National Assembly Session with a cross-voting system so that they could vote according to their own ideological preferences.

The GNP party elites persuaded the progressive faction to stick with party discipline. Some progressive members were persuaded that their action would cause fractures within the GNP. In most cases, however, the progressive faction continued to insist on cross-voting in the legislature on the issue of the National Security Law. While the progressive faction proceeded with their meeting on the issue, about 30 conservative members of the GNP also gathered on 8 June 2001 announcing that 'Abolishing the National Security Law would not be an issue to be discussed at that time. It is simply too early' (*Hankook Weekly*, 9 June 2001). The GNP law-makers were gathering over the issue separately to promote their opinion in the National Assembly Session. The conservative faction was responding to the demands of the conservative elements of society and the progressive faction acted in line with civil society movements that supported abolishing the National Security Law and the legislators of the MDP.

Munhwa Ilbo (12 June 2001) noted at the time that there should not be any meddling with the ideological orientations of law-makers, not even by their own party. Though the progressive faction within the GNP party did not achieve a majority, this should not lead to their voice being forcibly silenced. When the leaders of the GNP repressed the internal divisions after obtaining a majority vote, the progressive faction was left marginalized, and any hope for compromise with the ruling party shattered. This episode shows a lack of basic democratic rules in the Korean political culture and the hegemony of a top-down hierarchy, leaving little choice for the ruling party other than to seek to attract defectors from the opposition.

Jang Seong-min,[11] a former member of the National Assembly, recalls:

> I organized a society among young legislators of the MDP and named it *Saebyeok* [dawn] *21*, and we launched reform policies; however, it was very hard to persuade senior legislators especially when the reform policies were targeting those senior legislators to be changed. When young legislators tried to introduce reform policies they had to object to the views of senior legislators who preferred to maintain the existing rules and laws. We [young legislators mostly elected for the first time as a member of the National Assembly] objected to their opinion at the party meeting but we could not say a word when they accused us as young rude persons, saying, 'Don't you have grandparents at home? Where's your family education? You need to listen to your seniors [who have been elected more than twice at the general election].' It is hard to hold negotiations among legislators when a few senior legislators have most power in the decision-making processes. As party leaders hold most of the financial resources during electoral campaigns, they are free to appoint suitable and amenable candidates at the following election. Dissenters would have very few chances to stand again.

In the meantime, the party leader, Lee Hoe-chang, took an even harder line by expressing his respect for the former president, Park Chung-hee. By moving his party's stance further to the right, he designed his electoral strategy for the following year in order to attract conservative voters. By that time in June 2001, South Korea was suffering from the most severe droughts in over 100 years. As a result, most members decided to visit rural areas and the conservative members who finally agreed to have debates on the National Security Law issues, which were supposed to be held on 12 and 15 June, chose to delay the debates for an unlimited period, and the conflict was protracted further (*Hankyoreh Sinmun*, 12 June 2001). Debates over predictably controversial issues were thus delayed because of the drought crisis.

The ideological debate over the National Security Law did not simply manifest itself across parties but also within each party between relatively young progressives and the conservatives. As the internal struggle within the GNP showed, there was the possibility for the ruling MDP to gain support for abolishing or amending the NSL. Considering the support of the NGOs and the relatively progressive law-makers in the opposition party, there was a possibility that the ruling party could bring out some agreement from the opposition party. However, when the law-makers faced the strict top-down hierarchy within the party, and when it was directly related to their potential candidacy in the next election, the young politicians' voice could not be equal to those with seniority within the party. This shows a low level of institutionalization within the party and lack of internal democracy. The procedure of gathering opinion within the party was not institutionalized equally, but rather 'caged' in the Confucian[12] political culture where 'seniority matters' within the party organization. If, as law-makers had requested, cross-voting had been introduced by then, it would have been possible to gain support from the opposition party and the ruling minority party would not have had to struggle to attract numerous defectors that would harm the solidity of the organization from its early period of running government.

The ruling party's conflict with their coalition partner

The MDP also faced internal conflicts. The legislators were gathering to vote on the abolition of the National Security Law. It was about the time when the MDP was set to rebuild a coalition with the ULD, which had run its own electoral campaign during the 2000 elections. The ULD did not have a sufficient number of legislators to form a floor negotiation group, as discussed in Chapter 3, and at the same time the ruling party again tried to merge with the ULD as the MDP also could not survive in the legislature on its own number of legislators in terms of introducing new laws. As I have shown in Chapters 3 and 4, when a party could not negotiate with individual legislators and gain supporters from opposition parties to pass any reform policies, the party in question opted to build a coalition with other small parties or to attract defectors from the opposition party, offering better positions in return. When the mechanism of negotiation is lacking, the only way for the ruling party to survive in the legislature seems to be by enlarging the size of the ruling parties. Otherwise, due to the size of the opposition, any reform policies would not proceed but face stalemate.

So this suggests that defection is an option for politicians not willing to tow the party line. This time the ULD gained 17 seats in the legislature and it caused long-term conflicts over lowering the quorum from 20 to 15 so that the ULD could still be a member of a floor negotiation group. The MDP finally decided to allow three legislators to defect from the MDP and join the ULD so that the ULD could meet the minimum number (20 seats) to register as a floor negotiation group. Three MDP members in the National Assembly changed their party affiliation to the ULD. In this case, defectors left their party, the MDP, not because they wanted to for their own interests but because it was 'suggested from above' (probably by the chairman of the party) in order to maintain the coalition partner, ULD (see Chapter 3). The three[13] legislators joining the ULD were: Bae Gi-seon, a life-long supporter of Kim Dae-jung; Song Seock-chan, a member of the Society for Political Reform striving to abolish the National Security Law; and Song Young-jin, who wanted to support Lee In-je in the next presidential elections. Kang Chang-hee, a vice-chairman of the ULD, strongly rejected the offer of 'borrowing' legislators from the MDP. He insisted the three held different political views from the ULD and felt that renting legislators to be a floor negotiation group was unacceptable (*Jungang Ilbo*, 1 January 2001). The MDP built a coalition with the ULD again after a nine-month break-up; however, it was also the moment at which the Sunshine Policy was a hot issue. According to Hyun Jae-ho's (2002) research on party position from 1990–2000, JP (Kim Jong-pil, the leader of the ULD) and DJ (Kim Dae-jung, the leader of the former NCNP and the MDP) are on the far end, scoring 10 and –10 respectively, and the DJP coalition party remained on –5 (see Figure 5.4). The conservative HC (Lee Hoe-chang, the leader of the GNP) is located in the middle at 0. Considering the ULD's position over the decade, they merged together to the left of centre compared with the GNP; however, a radical change of policy position by the ULD shows the potential conflict over policy issues or a great deal of sacrifices to move towards the position of the MDP. This is obvious due to the coalition between the two parties, but this also leads to a question about what the ULD gained in return for 'sacrificing' their position. As a matter of fact, the ULD enjoyed large shares of power and, through the second coalition-building, they gained three more seats to be able to qualify as a floor group in the legislature. However, the two parties seemed to move apart from then-policy positions of 2001 as far as the JP is concerned.

Due to attracting many defectors from the opposition GNP in previous years, the MDP also faced opposition from within the party from those who did not support abolishing the NSL. Kim Jong-pil, the coalition party leader, announced his opposition to amending the National Security Law unless the Labour Party in North Korea changed its own Labour Party Law (*Jungang Ilbo*, 15 January 2001). During the Extraordinary Session starting in February, the progressive legislators in the MDP, the GNP and the ULD (in the ULD they were mostly 'rented' legislators from the MDP) insisted on adopting a cross-voting system at least on this issue and allowing a free vote of conscience according to the legislators' individual ideological preference. However, Park Sang-gyu, a general officer of the MDP, announced it would be difficult to deal with in the following Assembly session because the coalition partner did not bring forward any suggestion for this issue and there was no agreement between the parties (*Jungang Ilbo*, 2 February 2002). Lee Sang-su, a legislator in the MDP, argued that if they could reach agreement they should admit a cross-voting system as, then, whoever lost the vote would accept the result as fair. *Maeil Kyungje* (12 June 2001), a daily business newspaper, noted that if the parliament accepted a cross-voting system there would be fewer floor negotiation group meetings where party leaders decided the most important issues before they were handed down to the plenary session. The cross-voting system might bring internal democracy

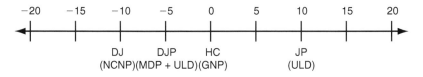

Figure 5.4 Party position on the policy space: 1990–2000 (source: modified from Hyun 2002: 159).

to the party. An anonymous legislator mentioned that he did not understand why people were afraid of adopting a cross-voting system. Considering the majority numbers of the GNP and the ULD, one can doubt whether the progressive legislators could actually abolish the law (*Jungang Ilbo*, 12 June 2001). The procedure to abolish the law could not even pass on to the Plenary Session but was interrupted at the party elites' level, for the GNP at the committee level, and for the MDP by the objection of the ULD. Questioning internal democracy, Lee Yang-hee,[14] a former legislator of the ULD and also a core member of those politicians seeking to build a coalition, stated:

> legislators who hold different views on the policy should leave the party. It is not a matter of having a cross-voting system or oppression by those above. I think each party which has a clear ideological difference is a positive fact. How can a party satisfy every person and group? A party should be able to represent certain groups' interest. The problem of parties in Korea lies in that they try to attract everybody. Can a nationwide party be possible? One policy would satisfy some people and groups and at the same time it would bring disadvantage to other people and groups.

His comments illustrate how by then the party struggled internally with people holding different views over the NSL and Sunshine Policy.

Kim Dae-jung made a call to solve the issue of the National Security Law during the Extraordinary Session in June 2001 and, in case the ULD opposed it, to try to amend at least Act 2 (organization of any societies or groups against the nation's security) and Act 10 (reporting suspicious individuals and activists as spies). Kim Jong-pil also requested the resolution of the National Security Law issue and also the National Assembly Law based on the quorum of the negotiation group during the session. He also sent a final note to the Blue House suggesting that if the National Assembly Law was passed, it would no longer be possible to continue the coalition between the two parties (*Maeil Kyungje*, 12 June 2001). The rupture within the coalition started within half-a-year of rebuilding it. The ULD also requested more seats in the Special Committee on Budget and Accounts from the MDP in return for its support. The committee consisted of 50 seats and it was divided by the ratio of the total seats each party gained in the legislature. The GNP had 24 legislators in the committee and the MDP 21 legislators, whilst the ULD had four and one for non-affiliated legislators. However, the ULD requested two more seats in the committee. Lee Sang-su, a member of the MDP, said it was possible to give one more seat if the floor negotiation groups agreed to do so. After that, the ULD required a change to the National Assembly Law for the quorum of the floor group. It was not only the issue of National Security Law the two coalition parties did not agree on but also issues over maternity leave for women, a paid-day off to take their babies for a hospital check-up, private school bills, and so on (*Kukmin Ilbo*, 18 June 2001).

The effort to change the National Security Law was continued by the progressive legislators for the following months and years, up until very recent times.

Over the endless dispute between the two coalition parties, the ULD announced that it was able to support the GNP on selective issues such as the National Security Law, media taxation and the issue related to developing tourism in the Mount Kumkang area in North Korea (*Maeil Kyungje*, 16 August 2001). By then the spokesman mentioned it did not mean that the party would leave the coalition with the MDP; however, a month later the ULD announced the break-up of the coalition over the issue of the dismissal of Im Dong-won, a minister of the Ministry of Unification. After the 8.15 Liberation Festival in Pyongyang in 2001, the legislators of the opposition GNP and the coalition partner ULD insisted on dismissing Im Dong-won, holding him responsible for the failure of the Sunshine Policy, as seen by North Korea's frequent provocation by ships around the border in the sea between South and North Korea. The legislators of the GNP and the ULD agreed to adopt the proposal of dismissing Im Dong-won from his position as a minister of the Ministry of Unification in the National Assembly meeting. On 3 September 2001, the motion was passed with 148 votes in favour and 119 votes against. Considering that 152 was the total potential vote from the GNP and the ULD, four seats were missing. They were the three members who were originally from the MDP and the then-prime minister, Lee Handong, who did not attend the National Assembly Ordinary Session meeting (*Munhwa Ilbo*, 4 September 2001). As shown here, identifying those who did not follow the party whip is relatively straightforward, and this also proves how well party members were disciplined within the organization. In this case, the only way of implementing reform policies was to attract defectors from the opposition parties. The ULD announced the coalition break-down right after the votes in the National Assembly meeting, and at the same time the four[15] legislators who joined the ULD to help it qualify as a floor group in the legislature in December 2000 and in January 2001 – Jang Jae-sik, Bae Gi-seon, Song Young-jin and Song Seok-chan – defected from the ULD and joined the MDP again (*Kyunghyang Sinmun*, 4 September 2001). Kim Dae-jung later mentioned that he failed to pass one of his reform laws, abolishing the National Security Law, because the majority of opposition parties in the legislature strongly opposed it (interview with *Wergens Tidende*, a daily newspaper, while he was visiting Norway on 5 December 2001, as reported in *Jungang Ilbo*, 6 December 2001).

The ULD did strive to increase its share of seats in the legislature and in the various committees. Therefore, a different policy stance was used as leverage to gain a greater interest in the government and in the legislature. To accommodate coalition partners to retain the size of the ruling parties, the MDP had to negotiate with the ULD on many different policy sectors. The coalition government, suffering from internal conflict over different policy issues and seats, eventually harmed the internal cohesiveness between the coalition parties, and the break-up of the coalition for the second time weakened both parties. The cost of building the coalition did not seem to be high as they shared more seats and secured agreement over different policy preferences; however, the conflict of interest and the final break-up created turbulence in the government and led to the failure to introduce and implement reform policies. The question that arises here is

150 *The debate over the National Security Law*

whether it was politically wise to break up the coalition over the controversy related to the dismissal of a minister of the Ministry of Unification. In the debates about the Sunshine Policy and the National Security Law, Kim Jong-pil failed to mobilize support in Chungcheong province. One reason was no doubt that, in the coming local elections and the presidential elections in the following year (2002), Kim Jong-pil had to listen to his supporters who held traditionally conservative views over the National Security Law and the Sunshine Policy. For Kim Jong-pil, securing victory in the following year's elections was more important than saving the coalition between the ULD and the MDP.

When the Sunshine Policy was adopted, the opposition reacted furiously. One of the biggest incidents saw ten visitors to the North Korean 8.15[16] Pyongyang festival accused of violating the National Security Law and taken to court (*Chosun Ilbo*, 7 September 2001). In total, 16 South Korean representatives attended the Pyongyang Festival in 2001. During their visit there was an unexpected trip to Mankyongdae[17] where a memorial tower is located with three unification quotes enshrined. Kang Jeon-gu, a professor at Dongkuk University, wrote in the visitors' notebook: 'Let's achieve unification with the Mankyongdae spirit', which could be interpreted as violating the National Security Law. More than ten members who joined this unexpected visit were immediately arrested under the National Security Law (*Jungang Ilbo*, 22 August 2001).

The committee of the GNP dismissed Im Dong-won from his ministerial position as he was deemed responsible for picking those who would travel to the North. The ULD also agreed with the GNP in insisting that those who violated the National Security Law should be punished and the government 'should stop wasting people's hard earned [tax] money on North Korea' (ibid.: 18 August 2001). After the vote in the National Assembly meeting on 3 September 2001, Im Dong-won had to leave his position. In December 2001, Kim Dae-jung resigned from his position as chairman of the MDP. The continuous disputes over ideology even among candidates within the MDP – for example, between Roh Moo-hyun and Lee In-je on the issue of reform policies – were disappearing, and President Kim Dae-jung entered the 'lame-duck period' (the second half of his tenure) in the following year (2002). Namgung Jin,[18] a former minister of culture and tourism during the Kim Dae-jung administration and a close aide of Kim Dae-jung during his political life, said, 'it was due to his son's involvement with fundraising corruption. However, that kind of event was fairly common by then.' It seems that when fund-raising was not highly institutionalized, the only way to raise funds was through entrepreneurs.

Summary

Anti-communism dominates the ideological debate in South Korea. The Kim Dae-jung administration faced strong opposition from both the opposition party and its coalition partner over an ideologically charged issue such as the abolition of the NSL. This chapter has shown that the cleavage in Korea was not between left and right, but concerned the attitude towards the Sunshine Policy and the abolition of the National Security Law. However, although the Kim Dae-jung administration brought significant changes in relations with North Korea compared to previous administrations, it did not succeed in abolishing or even amending the National Security Law because of the deep ideological divide within and across political parties holding different ideological positions. One is left wondering whether the MDP would have in fact performed better without a coalition partner which had actually been a hindrance – rather than an actual partner – in abolishing the so-called evil law. What emerges clearly is that persisting ideological differences ultimately hindered the performance of the government or governability. In addition, why the government preferred to rule with a partner in such conditions rather than governing alone demands questioning. However, looking at intra-party politics, there was no opt-out as the ruling party could not gain any agreement from individual progressive law-makers from the opposition party (GNP) and the coalition partner (ULD) in the legislature.

The chapter has shown that conflicts were more than 'just' about ideology. A rigid and strict political culture dominates the National Assembly and Korean politics as a whole. The ideological divide could have been bridged through an alliance between the MDP and the more progressive elements of the opposition party. Negotiation and compromise could have occurred had the parties shown some signs of internal democracy rather than being mere top-down organizations. Setting internal rules or introducing a cross-voting system could be another option, as many young, progressive politicians from both the ruling and opposition parties requested in the process of negotiation. When the legislators are only allowed to raise their hands in the National Assembly meeting, it is obvious that young legislators would not dare to vote against the dominant view within the party. They fear not being appointed by party leaders as a candidate in the following election, and also receiving less financial support from the centre of the party. Financial resources are mainly concentrated in the hands of party leaders, as is the right to appoint candidates for the following general election.

To summarize, it is possible to conclude that ideological differences combined with a strict Confucian political culture embedded in the political actors' mindsets shaped a government that relied on the support of defectors from other parties without much regard to the ideological coherence of the ruling coalition itself. In examining the attempt to abolish the NSL, I looked at intra-party politics to elucidate what actually happened in the legislature and within the party, and how the political actors behaved when they faced a rigid top-down hierarchy in the party. This shows that there was no margin for attracting law-makers belonging to the opposition party and coalition partner party when the individual actor was not allowed to vote on his or her own conscience but instead had to follow the party line. Elite interviews show that policy-makers thought it was possible to gain support from the opposition party if a cross-voting system were in place in the legislature but, without such rules, it would have been difficult to gain any support from the opposition unless individual members defected from the party.

Finally, the chapter has shown that the level of institutionalization matters more than political culture. Had a cross-voting system been introduced earlier, legislators could vote according to their views rather than being hand-raisers in the Assembly session following the mainstream of the party. If candidate-selection procedure is not in the hands of party elites but based on the grass roots, individual legislators can be free to vote for their policy preference. Abolishing the NSL or amending it was not impossible considering the wide support for change from the public and the progressive members within the opposition party. Survey data show that the population is not deeply divided along ideological and regional lines, contrary to widespread common belief. Since the ideological preferences of people have been nurtured under authoritarian rule towards the right by the National Security Law and the Anti-Communist Law, ideological preferences cannot be neatly divided along a left–right scale, but rather they show a combination of left and right. The so-called South–South conflict was primarily about political matters or political conflicts among parties over the NSL and Sunshine Policy rather than any fundamental cleavage of the people in the country. Regionalism also shows only a strong division in the electoral preference of votes since there is no clear division between parties but elites, who are fundamentally interested in winning office. When party platforms converge, without any clear differences, ordinary voters can simply identify with leaders and their regional background (see Chapter 4). Ideological and regional conflicts are not a result of social divisions or deeper intra-Korean cleavages, but more the consequence of a low level of party institutionalization that allows political elites to mobilize support by exploiting policy differences. This leaves margins for improving mechanisms of compromise and negotiation – and by extension, nurturing political culture – through the introduction of measures to increase the level of institutionalization of the parties and the party system.

6 When the majority does not rule
The Roh Moo-hyun and the Lee Myung-bak administrations

Introduction

The previous chapters have shown that when voters did not grant political parties a majority in the parliament, the elites by-passed the obstacle by means of party mergers or coalition-building. All of this was aimed at enlarging the base of support of the government in the parliament. However artificially attained majority rule proved to be short-lived, and under the converging pressures of intra-party factionalism and regionalism in the electoral process, the government returned to its minority status.

Since 2004, the situation has seemingly changed. The Uri Party and the Grand National Party not only won the 2004 and 2008 parliamentary elections, but finally achieved the long-craved-for prize: a clear majority. Under the Lee administration, the ruling Grand National Party started off with a surplus majority of 172 seats and later in the Eighteenth General Election in 2008, the GNP gained 153 seats out of 299. What one would have expected was that without any pressure to strike deals with other actors, the ruling party would finally be able to legislate and implement policies. Instead, the majority ruling parties could not consolidate their position; government action was impeded by a combination of internal and external opposition. This seems to contradict the most basic argument within coalition research, according to which a bare majority would secure governing stability and allow the government to remain in power. Understanding why this was not the case, and what this shows about the argument presented throughout this book constitutes the aim of this chapter.

The focus here is on the two most recent presidential administrations. The Roh Moo-hyun administration is examined first: its attempts at introducing reform policies and the late president's call for a grand coalition are given special consideration. The remainder of the chapter examines the current Lee Myung-bak administration; the protests following the signing of the Free Trade Agreement with the US, the scandals that led to the death of former-president Roh Moo-hyun, and the local elections and reform policies in 2010 are specifically discussed.

The Roh Moo-hyun administration

Roh Moo-hyun was a presidential candidate for the New Millennium Democratic Party (MDP). His candidacy for the MDP was only made possible by the introduction of primaries before the presidential elections. On that occasion youth groups and especially politically active citizens operating on the Internet (the so-called 'netizens') played a determinant role in the making of Roh's victory. This, however, made Roh Moo-hyun's stance uncomfortable within the MDP as he could not rely on strong support within the party. Reformists within the MDP tried to differentiate themselves from the old politics and especially the 'three Kims' personalized party politics, and requested reform and changes within the party. Roh Moo-hyun and his followers defected from the MDP and attracted numbers of reformists from the Grand National Party and founded the Uri Party in November 2003 (*Donga Ilbo*, 11 November 2003). When Roh showed his support for the Uri Party during the campaign for the up-coming general election in April 2004, the MDP and the GNP initiated the procedure to impeach him on the grounds that he was openly campaigning for a specific party. Within only a year of his election, the Roh Moo-hyun administration was plunged into drama when the opposition initiated presidential impeachment. The proposal was passed in the National Assembly on 12 March 2004 with 193 votes out of a possible 195.

In the general election that followed, voters expressed their clear disapproval of the move by granting the Uri Party a clear majority in the house (152 seats out of 299). The 'coalition' behind the impeachment suffered a heavy defeat: the GNP gained only 121 seats, the MDP nine seats and the ULD four seats (see Table 6.1). The election also saw the emergence of the Democratic Labour Party (DLP) as the third-largest party (ten seats).[1] This is due to the new voting system with 'two votes' system[2] (one vote for the candidate and the other for a favourite party). The new electoral laws allowed a small minority party to emerge in the National Assembly with visible numbers of seats as well as mitigating regional cleavage.

The following section shows how, despite a majority status in the legislature, the UP struggled to pass four key reform policies and became embroiled in the very same type of politicking and factionalism that had characterized about two decades of democratic politics in Korea. Emboldened by the majority secured in the general election, the Uri Party embarked on bringing some structural changes to Korean politics and society. The proposed landmark reforms would be in the areas of National Security Law, media, education (private schools), and human rights with the introduction of the Truth and Reconciliation Law.

The National Security Law

Reforming the National Security Law has been an extremely controversial issue since the Kim Dae-jung administration, as shown in Chapter 5. Confident of strong public support, the Uri Party set out to amend the law, but eventually failed to do so.

Table 6.1 Seat numbers (by party) in the National Assembly from 2004 to 2010

	2004	2005	Dec. 2006	June 2007	Sept. 2007	March 2008	July 2008	Aug. 2008	Dec. 2008	Feb. 2009	July 2009	Dec. 2009	March 2010
UP	152	144	139	73	143	136	81	81	83	83	84	87	84
MDP/UNDP/DP	9	11	11	34		111	153	172	172	170	168	169	169
GNP	121	127	127	128	129								
PPA/FHA						3	13	8	8	8	5	8	8
LFP						9	18	18	20	20	20	17	16
CKP						1	3	3	1	1	1	2	2
DLP	10	9	9	9	9	6	5	5	5	5	5	5	5
ULD	4	3											
PFP/PFU			5	5	5								
NPP											1	1	1
NPA	3	5	5	50	4	25	26	12	10	7	8	9	5
Total seats	299	299	296	299	290	291	299	299	299	294	292	298	291

Source: Author. Data from National Assembly Progress Reports

In the aftermath of the general election, *Research Plus*, a public opinion research centre, and the *Hankyoreh* newspaper conducted a survey on the topic of support for abolishing the NSL among the legislators and the public. According to the survey, 87.7 per cent of legislators (236 out of 269) supported either amending or abolishing the law.[3] Among the 101 legislators of the opposition GNP, 74.3 per cent of respondents (75 legislators) supported amending the NSL. Ordinary voters also strongly supported amending or abolishing the NSL (61.7 per cent) (*Hankyoreh Sinmun*, 18 April 2004). Roh commented:

> we need to see how the law influenced our history and how it functioned. The NSL has been mainly misused to oppress the people in opposition [...]. If we are aiming for a society where people have sovereignty and human rights are respected isn't it better to put the old law in the sword sheath and send it to a museum? [...] We should abolish the NSL so that we can say Korea is finally walking toward a civilized state.
>
> (*Oh my news*, 5 September 2004)

For the conservatives, the NSL is a fundamental law that defines the Republic of Korea in its current form and ideology (anti-communism). The UP's mission to abolish the NSL was met with a fierce opposition by the GNP, which considered the move to be jeopardizing the country's security. The progressives see the NSL as an instrument of abuse and human rights violation. For the conservatives, the NSL is the main tool to protect South Korea from its main threat, the North. In the end, the amendments to the NSL were not passed and the UP lost its competence in the eyes of public.

The Truth and Reconciliation Law

The introduction of the Truth and Reconciliation Law was another controversial reform policy. This was the only reform law the UP actually managed to pass, in May 2005. The law was aimed at revisiting the cases of human rights violations during the Japanese colonial period, the Korean War and the authoritarian period. Despite the monumental achievement in terms of achieving social justice, even this law managed to be controversial in Korea. Reassessing the authoritarian era, especially the Park Chung-hee and Chun Doo-hwan regimes, has been extremely divisive in Korea. Hyung-a Kim (2004a) sees the *Yushin* system and state-led development under the Park Chung-hee administration as a coin, whose two faces should be considered together. For the conservatives, the authoritarian governments were at the core of the country's successful economic development, despite the high social and political costs. For the progressives, such massacres as in Gwangju in 1980 had nothing to do with economic development.

In his memoir, Roh Moo-hyun (2009: 123–125) notes that the economic achievement and the wrongdoing of the Park Chung-hee administration should be evaluated separately, despite the understandable memories full of agony people have about the past. In his high school days, Roh was a recipient of scholarship from *Buil Janghakhoe* (*Buil* foundation); after the 5.16 Coup, Kim Ji-tae, the founder of *Buil Janghakhoe*, *Busan Ilbo* and *MBC*, was arrested for refusing to support the coup government. *Buil Jangjakhoe* was renamed later as *Chung-soo Janghakhoe*, named after the first letter of Park Chung-hee's first name and the last letter of his wife's first name, Yook Young-soo. *Chung-soo Janghakhoe* has been run by the family members of Park Chung-hee, and the then-opposition GNP leader Park Geun-hye, daughter of Park Chung-hee, was a head of the board of *Chung-soo Janghakhoe* from 1995 to 2005. The committee of the Truth and Reconciliation asked *Chung-soo Janghakhoe* to return the property to the previous owner, the family of Kim Ji-tae. Park Geun-hye then claimed that *Chung-soo Janghakhoe* be returned to society, pointing out that the foundation is public, not private. To Park's complaint that this was all the UP's plot to discredit the opposition, the committee of the Truth and Reconciliation and civil society organizations replied underlining how *Chung-soo Janghakhoe*[4] was de facto run by Park Chung-hee's family members (*Media Today*, 31 May 2007).

Hyung-a Kim maintains that 'those foundations are indeed run in a kind of privatized way by the Park family but Roh Moo-hyun's position was largely discredited by the fact that it was perceived as moved by an anti-capitalist agenda'.[5] Typically for Korean politics, the administration's position was defined by a sentiment of revenge, a desire to 'make history right'. Passing the law was a noticeable achievement for the Roh administration, and more so given the fierce resistance from the opposition.

The Media Reform Law

The Roh administration sought to introduce a Media Reform Law in order to prevent the conservative media conglomerates from achieving a monopoly in the market. In Korea, so-called *Cho-Chung-Dong* newspapers (*Chonsun Ilbo*, *Chungang Ilbo* and *Donga Ilbo*) control more than 70 per cent of the market sales. According to the proposed law, when a newspaper company occupies more than 30 per cent of the market and if three newspaper companies occupy more than 60 per cent, those newspaper companies are categorized as market dominating business actors and they can be taxed up to 3 per cent of their profits. They would also be excluded from government funds for media development. The proposal would have also established a collaborative delivery system for all the newspapers so that any newspaper could be delivered even to remote rural areas, otherwise a 'privilege' of the wealthier and more organized ones. The proposal also envisaged funding for developing the newspaper industry. The media law once again sparked an ideological conflict between the progressives and the conservatives.

The Korean newspaper market has experienced some chronic structural problems (though these are not unique to the Korean context). Readers are attracted by various kinds of gifts (reduced fees/first-six-months-free subscriptions, bicycles, electric fans, house-fixing tools set, etc.). New media outlets would not have access to the required capital to compete on such a scale, leaving the market in the hands of the conservative newspapers' marketing strategies (*Hankyoreh Sinmun*, 5 May 2005). Although already in a dominant position under authoritarian rule, Choi Jang-jip (2002: 192) notes that even 'after democratization the role of the conservative media has been magnified. The media now is playing a major role to keep the hegemony of anti-communism'. Bang Jeong-bae notes:

> the reform media law is about correcting distorted opinion market where it has freedom to talk but their voice is not fairly distributed in an unfair market. The state needs to step in the unfair market to create a fair media market.
>
> (*Munhwa Ilbo*, 27 November 2004)

On the other hand, Im Sang-won noted that the media law would be against media freedom and that there should be a limit to principles of fairness in the media market (*Munhwa Ilbo*, 27 November 2004). The Media Reform Law was widely supported by the public. According to the *Hankyoreh* newspaper, 52.7 per cent of respondents supported the laws limiting the owners' stock share in the newspaper companies, and 23.1 per cent were opposed to the laws (*Hankyoreh Sinmun*, 22 April 2004). However, things did not go as planned in the National Assembly Meeting Sessions. Prime Minister Lee Hae-chan accused the GNP of being a *Chatteki* [truck] Party – a nickname the GNP earned due to illegal fund-raising with trucks full of cash (*Mediatoday*, 3 November 2004). This outraged the GNP, which urged the prime minister to apologize and resign. The GNP did not attend the National Assembly Session for 15 days. Lee Tae-ho (2006: 132) reports that, from the 223rd–231st National Assembly Session (1 June to 9 December 2004), the legislature had 38 days of stalemate out of 146 total days of meetings.

The bill on the media law was passed on 1 January 2005. The GNP appealed to the Supreme Court and many articles of the media law were overruled by the Supreme Court as unconstitutional in June 2006. The proposed media law ended in failure after three years of endless debates, continuous deadlocks within the National Assembly and demonstrations by the conservatives.

The Private School Law

The GNP opposed the Private School Law most vigorously. The law's aim was to ensure transparency in private school administration, curb corruption in the selection of teachers and students, and to prevent the involvement of students' parents in the school boards. Like other reform laws, the bid for the Private School Law also enjoyed high support from the public.

The Private School Law was passed on 9 December 2005 with support from the Uri Party, the Democratic Labour Party and the New Millennium Democratic Party, with 140 votes out of the 154 legislators in attendance (*Hankyoreh Sinmun*, 9 December 2005). This shows that, in principle, thanks to its majority status in the legislature, the ruling party was able to pass the bill; however, in practice, the opposition Grand National Party refused to bow to majority rule in the National Assembly and organized the usual picketing and blockade of the proceedings of the parliament. As mentioned before, *Chung-soo Janghakhoe*, Yeongnam University and the *Yookyoung* Foundation[6] are all heavily influenced by Park Chung-hee's family members, especially Park Geun-hye (*Shin Donga*, October 2004). The Grand National Party went on strike outside the National Assembly for 53 days, with its members not attending the National Assembly Session for 31 days (*Segye.com*, 7 March 2007). Vigorous strikes by the Grand National Party undermined the Uri Party's handling of the Private School Law. Moreover, many Uri Party legislators began having second thoughts and declared their openness to negotiate amendments of the Private School Law.

On 3 July 2007, the amended Private School Law was passed again, but this was after great divisions within the Uri Party had come out into the open. The Uri Party, a lame-duck President Roh Moo-hyun and a drop in the public support and confidence in the ruling administration left it with little choice. The new Private School Law allowed family members of the chairperson of the board to be presidents of private schools. The initial bill was aimed at curbing corruption in the school administration, but the amended version of the law left the problem basically unresolved.

The Uri Party enjoyed majority status in the legislature from April 2004 to April 2005. During this period it could have introduced some structural changes in the country, in principle even without dealing with the opposition. However, the Grand National Party did not hesitate to literally block the functioning of the assembly by refusing to attend its sessions, picketing outside and asking repeatedly for summit meetings between the party leaders. The strategy was effective. As a result, Park Geun-hye's leadership in the GNP was considerably strengthened.

Roh Moo-hyun's call for a 'grand coalition'

As the Uri Party became more and more embroiled in factional battles, conflict with the opposition and declining public support, Roh Moo-hyun officially called for a grand coalition with opposition parties in July 2005. After the April by-elections, the Uri Party was left with 146 seats and the Grand National Party increased its seats to 125 (from 120). The stalemate in the National Assembly put the Uri Party in a difficult situation where introducing reform laws became virtually impossible without the opposition's votes. The Uri Party lost its majority status within the legislature after the election, paving the way to the lame-duck period. Roh Moo-hyun expressed his concern that the Uri Party would lose again at the next by-elections in October 2005 and local elections in 2006. Roh Moo-hyun began voicing his support for building a coalition with the opposition in a meeting with high party officials at the Blue House on 24 June 2005.

On 5 July, Roh Moo-hyun published an open letter to the citizenry on the Blue House's homepage entitled, 'Korean Politics needs to return to normal.' In the letter, Roh Moo-hyun outlined the predicament in which the ruling party found itself, facing a big and uncooperative opposition in the legislature. The proposal's aim was two-fold: first to overcome the climate of secrecy that typically surrounds coalition-building and pacts in Korean politics, where all is done and agreed behind the scenes. Second, the call sought to overcome the institutional constraints which in semi-presidential systems often give rise to divided governments. By so doing, Roh also hoped to create a consensus to change electoral law with the goal of curbing the regionalism that so deeply pervades Korea's politics. President Roh had already proposed changing the electoral law in his early presidency in 2003. He also declared his openness to support a German-style mixed electoral system (a Mixed Member Proportional Representation System) as well. Both constituency and German-style electoral systems have multi-electorates in larger districts. Thus in those electoral systems a single party may not be able to monopolize a majority of votes in a district (Norris 1997).

Several scholars (Cheibub 2002; Cheibub *et al.* 2004; Mainwaring and Scully 1995; Strøm and Müller 2001) have argued that Cabinet stability or governability does not result from the size of the government but owes much to institutional constraints and internal mechanisms of bargaining and compromise. The opposition's reaction was fierce. The GNP spokesperson stated that 'abnormal politics' in Korea was due to the very persona of President Roh (*Hankyoreh Sinmun*, 6 July 2005). Unlike the GNP, the Democratic Labour Party expressed support for the plan. President Roh initially claimed that he would hand over half of the presidential powers to the coalition partner should they agree to support the introduction of electoral reform (*Breaknews*, 7 July 2005). However, his call for a grand coalition was perceived as an attempt to regain his lost political power and win elections by changing electoral laws to the benefit of the Uri Party (*Donga Ilbo*, 29 July 2005). A grand coalition would create surplus majority ruling parties that would take 90 per cent of the total seats in the legislature.

As examined in the previous chapters, among the main factors hindering governability in Korea is regionalism. The three main parties are strongly based in different regions. This means that, even if a party monopolizes votes in its respective region, this would not result in any majority being attained in the National Assembly, forcing it to enter a coalition with other parties. President Roh proposed a grand coalition after losing by-elections, concerned about forthcoming by-elections as well as local elections. This was also the very moment when the president normally entered the lame duck period. President Roh's call for a grand coalition was criticized as a desperate Uri Party plot to remain in power (*Munhwa Ilbo*, 11 July 2005).

Figure 6.1 and Table 6.1 show the seat number changes after the by-elections in October 2005. The Uri Party had 144 seats and the Grand National Party 127 seats. After the proposal for a grand coalition fell on deaf ears, and two by-elections had passed, the Roh Moo-hyun administration became embroiled in merely attempting to survive; by late 2006, fission and fusion of political factions and parties along with politicians' defections had started again in the run-up to the 2007 presidential elections. On 6 February 2007, 23 UP legislators

When majority does not rule 161

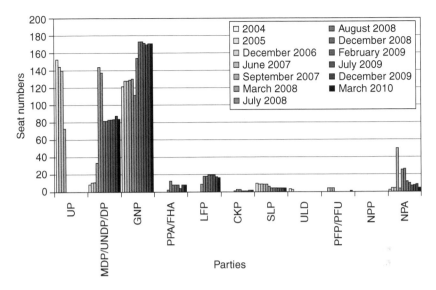

Figure 6.1 Party seat numbers from the 2004 general election to the 2010 local elections (Source: Author. Data from National Assembly Progress Reports).

defected; as a result of more defections in the following months, the UP had 73 seats left in the parliament. In August 2007, the Uri Party ceased to exist and merged with the defectors from the Democratic New Party and later built a coalition with the United New Democratic Party in February 2008. In July 2008, the remaining supporters of the Roh administration merged with some former members of the Kim Dae-jung administration and established the Democratic Party.

The conservatives come back into power: the Lee Myung-bak administration

The GNP's Lee Myung-bak won 48.7 per cent against his opponent Chung Dong-Young's 26.1 per cent in the Seventeenth Presidential Elections held on 19 December 2007. Despite a solid majority, the GNP faced continuous protests, from the opposition party and the public in the streets. This section examines three instances of deadlock the Lee administration faced in the early part of its tenure in office: the protests over the Free Trade Agreement with the US and the subsequent candlelight vigils in 2008, the death of former-president Roh Moo-hyun in 2009 and the loss in the local elections in 2010.

The candlelight vigils and the FTA deal

The Lee administration encountered political hurdles from the very beginning when it sought to introduce a key reform in the education system. The committee working on the reform announced that, by 2010, most high school education would be conducted in English. Promoting English-speaking skills among pupils would – the argument went – help solve the problems of parents spending a lot of money on private tuition education and even sending their children abroad (along with their mothers), an increasingly common situation in Korean families. This was indeed a huge social problem referred to as *Gireogi appa* [a wild goose daddy] phenomenon, where fathers would send their wives and children abroad while remaining at home working to support their family abroad. The Lee administration soon started to be referred to as the '*Ko So-yeong*' or '*Kang Bu-ja*' government.[7]

While protests over this policy initiative had not yet settled, a new wave of protests broke out. In early April 2008, the United States and South Korea signed a free-trade agreement after months of intense negotiation.[8] While this was heralded by the officials of the two parties as a way to take the already significant trade turnover between the two countries to a new level, reaction on the streets of South Korean cities suggested that many were unhappy with the deal. On the Korean side, concerns focused on a lack of competitiveness of South Korean business and the scrapping of tariffs would ensure that companies such as KIA, Hyundai, Samsung and others would benefit from easier access to the US market. The decision sparked a large wave of nationwide strikes, rallies and demonstrations. One of the issues at stake – and definitely the one that most captured the public's imagination and attention – concerned the implications that beef imports would have for the health of the Korean population (possibly affected by mad cow disease).

What was surprising in this case was that protests started out of online discussions among teenagers and were sparked by groundless rumours about mad cow disease. The major current affairs TV programme, the *PD Sucheop* [*Producer's Note*] on 29 April 2008 joined this dispute and even broadcast a number of reports with the aim of heightening political tensions. Later in 2008, the programme was criticized for its strongly anti-government agenda, which included erroneous reporting over the mad cow issue. The TV programme was later accused of being the main source of rumours by a Grand National Party member at the National Assembly hearings on the FTA-related incidents in Korea (*Donga Ilbo*, 5 September 2008). Online discussion boards were dominated by this one issue. The situation quickly spiralled out of control. A high school student suggested campaigning to impeach the president in a blog; within three days, the website received a million visitors (and supporters) who signed up online for presidential impeachment (*Sisa Journal*, 15 July 2008). The street vigils were initially peaceful and often resembled festivals with entertainers singing and dancing. This festival-like atmosphere came to an end when protests became more violent and were met with riot police and a sudden government crackdown. The real origins of the rumours and candlelight vigils are still disputed. MBC (Munhwa Broadcasting Corporation) and KBS (Korea Broadcasting System) are state-run companies and many of the high officials within the companies were appointed by the previous governments and held progressive views. Thus, many current affairs programmes seemed to promote a political (that is, anti-government) agenda.

The vigils, protests and endless rumours pushed the Lee Myong-bak administration into political paralysis. Support for the administration plummeted. The National Assembly appeared powerless in the face of the protests. Angry citizens marched to the Blue House requesting to talk with the president directly, while police officers piled up containers on the main road leading to the Blue House as a way to fence off protesters.[9]

The death of former-president Roh Moo-hyun

After the general election, the GNP gained a surplus majority (172 seats out of 299) by attracting five members of the Pro-Park Geun-hye Alliance (PPA) and some non-party-affiliated members. All this notwithstanding, the Lee administration faced the same predicament as its predecessors. This was due to the acrimonious factional conflict between the Lee and Park factions. The origins of the conflict lay in the pre-election period when supporters of Park Geun-hye's bid for the leadership of the GNP were not selected as candidates for the general election. Among those, some left the GNP and founded the Pro-Park Geun-hye Alliance and others ran as independent/non-party-affiliated candidates, whereas Park remained within the ranks of the GNP.

One of the main items on the GNP's agenda entailed recouping the lost ten years of the progressive governments and re-instated – among others – a business-friendly economic environment. Rejecting the predecessor's legacy has been the one defining and common feature of every single administration in the democratization era. In addition, common tactics of the incoming administration included emphasizing the wrong-doings of the previous government and revealing the corruption pervading it, hoping this would weaken and de-legitimize the opposition. When Kim Young-sam started his presidency, two previous presidents were put in jail; Kim Young-sam himself could not avoid his son, Kim Hyun-chul, becoming involved in a corruption scandal when Kim Dae-jung took power. When Roh Moo-hyun was elected, Kim Dae-jung's son, Kim Hong-up, was also arrested; the Roh administration also supported the prosecutors' special investigation over illegal financial aid to North Korea during the Kim Dae-jung administration. After his presidency, Roh Moo-hyun himself could not avoid the same fate. Roh Moo-hyun's elder brother and his close aides[10] Lee Kwang-jae, Lee Gang-cheol and Chung Sang-moon were arrested for taking bribes. The media revealed that Roh Moo-hyun's son and daughter were similarly involved in taking bribes from his long-time political supporter Park Yeon-cha. Roh Moo-hyun's wife, Kwon Yang-sook, was vocal and bitter about her husband's involvement in politics:

> Power is with people with money, media and the prosecutors. Politicians are just shells. Politicians without any means of daily living only have big voices. What do you have? Money? Power? Politicians are often invited to prison, such poor people.
>
> (Roh 2009: 75)

164 *When majority does not rule*

Roh's administration fell under the attacks of the opposition as well as its own internal divisions. The 'moral question' meant the end of his political life, also causing a dramatic drop in the image of the left in Korea, which looked no different from the conservatives. Roh committed suicide on 23 May 2009 by jumping off a cliff in his native home town Bongha.

There is a perverse irony in Roh Moo-hyun's death. His success owed much to online supporters. His humiliation was made even more devastating because of the power of the media and especially the Internet in Korea. Park Myung-rim noted the national chaos that followed Roh's death, where 'there are now two presidents to the people, one in the Blue House and the other in their heart, "paralysed president" and "deceased president." The people suddenly lost two presidents' (*Hankyoreh Sinmun*, 31 May 2009). Although the Lee administration enjoyed a surplus majority in the legislature, former-president Roh's suicide was a serious blow to its capacity to govern. After a tumultuous start in mid-2009 the Lee administration finally seemed to 'settle down' politically and regain enough strength to embark on a new reform drive. The administration enjoyed reasonably high support rates of 37.9 per cent (*Chosun Monthly*, August 2010). Another public opinion survey conducted by the Korea Society Opinion Institute compared support for the presidential performance before the local elections in 2006 and 2010. In general, the local elections are often considered as a signalling point for the presidents entering the lame-duck period, but the Lee Myung-bak administration enjoyed 40.4 per cent in April 2010, considerably higher than Roh Moo-hyun administration's 31 per cent in April 2006 (*Weekly Kyunghyang*, 13 May 2010) (see Figure 6.2).

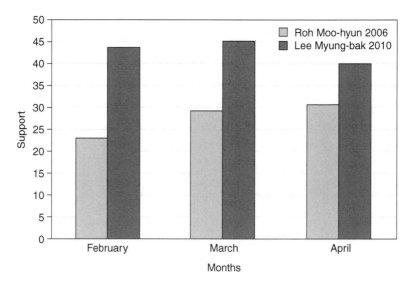

Figure 6.2 Support for presidential performance in 2006 and 2010 (Source: Author. Data from a survey conducted by Korea Society Opinion Institute, *Weekly Kyunghyang*, 13 May 2010).

The Four-River Reconstruction Project and the Sejong City plan

The Lee Myung-bak administration focused especially on the Four-River Reconstruction Project and the proposal to move key administrative offices from the capital Seoul to Sejong.

The proposal to move the administrative offices to Sejong City in the Chungcheong province was passed during the Roh Moo-hyun administration to decentralize resources from the capital to the regions. The original plan was to relocate 40 government ministries and offices to the Yeongi-Gongju areas in South Chungcheong province, creating an administrative hub there. The Lee Myong-bak administration pointed out a number of difficulties with this plan, which it considered costly and inefficient. Park Geun-hye, who has a strong electoral basis in the region, opposed Lee's proposal to amend the bill. Park supported the Roh administration on this question when she was the leader of the GNP. Amending the law over the Sejong City plan would ruin her political reputation. Relations between the two factions soured and the Sejong City plan became heavily politicized.

The political conflict between Lee and Park was not new. In the early days of the Lee administration, the Lee faction also sought to marginalize the Park faction by not selecting many members of Park's faction as candidates for the Eighteenth General Election. Those who could not be appointed as candidates for the general election defected from the GNP and established the Pro-Park Geun-hye Alliance Party, which later won 14 seats in the legislature.

As this book has shown, before as well as after the elections it has been common for parties to merge or build a coalition, and for legislators to defect from parties and switch allegiance. The LFP built a coalition with CKP in the National Assembly in 2009 but the two split in 2010. The Lee Myung-bak administration proposed to build a political alliance with the LFP and CKP coalition party and its leader, Shim Dae-pyung, was asked to take the position as prime minister. For the Lee administration, this would help secure success in the local elections and possibly rally support over the Sejong City plan. Lee Hoe-chang, the leader of LFP, vigorously opposed this and Shim and Lee broke-up their coalition between the LFP and the CKP.

In the run-up to the local elections, the former Pro-Park Geun-hye Alliance members (eight total seat), now known as the Future Hope Alliance, agreed to join the GNP at its party meeting on 2 April 2010, subject to approval by the GNP, which would then increase its seats in the parliament.[11] However, Lee Q-taek, the representative of the Future Hope Alliance, resigned from the party and announced that he would establish the Future Alliance Party in an attempt to keep the spirit of the Pro-Park Geun-hye Alliance alive. Given that Park Geun-hye has a strong vote base in the Gyeong-sang province and that the ruling party traditionally loses the local elections towards the late period of the presidency, the upcoming local elections represented the point where the president would enter the lame-duck period. For this reason, preventing a split among the conservatives was of paramount importance for the GNP.

166 *When majority does not rule*

The GNP would be then able to consolidate its position and increase its chances of securing a victory in the next presidential elections. A merger of the former Pro-Park Alliance (now the Future Hope Alliance) with the GNP would also help Park to consolidate her political status within the party, whereas the GNP would benefit from having fewer competitors in certain regions, especially in Chungcheong where support for Park is especially strong.

In the meantime, the opposition parties also moved swiftly to build an electoral coalition before the June local elections and the July by-election. Four opposition parties (the Democratic Party (88), the Democratic Labor Party (5), the Creative Korea Party (2), the People's Participation Party (mainly former Uri Party members of Roh Moo-hyun administration) and four NGOs gathered to discuss candidates for local elections. They aimed to gather support for common candidates against the GNP (see Figure 6.3).

The June 2010 local elections had the second-highest turnout (54.4 per cent) since the first local election in 1995 (68.4 per cent). The DP gained seven mayoral seats, the GNP six and the LFP one, and the non-party-affiliated candidates gained two mayoral positions (*Chosun Ilbo*, 4 June 2010). In the city councils, the GNP gained 82 seats and the DP gained 92, the LFP thirteen and the DLP gained three seats for members in the Local Assembly. This resulted in a major loss for the GNP, made even more significant by the fact that support from local mayors and councils was crucial for implementing the Four-River Project and the Sejong City plan. In the Seoul Metropolitan Council, the DP gained 79 members and the GNP only 27 seats. In the Gyeonggi province, the GNP had 115 seats out of 119 in the provincial council in 2006, but in 2010 its representation in the council dropped to a mere 42 seats, while the DP gained 76 seats (*Kyunghyang Daily*, 4 June 2010). Strong opposition in those two councils

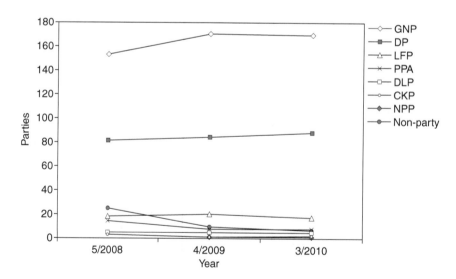

Figure 6.3 Seat numbers in the National Assembly (Source: Author).

meant that the government would face greater hurdles to implement its two projects.

The loss of local elections severely influenced the government's agenda. The bid to downscale the Sejong City plan was rejected with 164 votes against out of 275 total votes at the National Assembly Session on 29 June 2010. The opposition could rely on its own 120 votes and 44 votes from Park Geun-hye's faction within the GNP (*Presian*, 29 June 2010). The GNP's surplus majority in the National Assembly could not secure the government's success.

Summary

Despite a majority status in the legislature, the two administrations examined in this chapter were plagued by the same problems that had affected their predecessors.

Considerable effort has been put in institutionalizing political parties and the party system as a whole, and some success has to be acknowledged. Parties are better-working organizations and the effects of regionalism have been partly mitigated. At the same time, Korean politics continues to be defined by intra-party factionalism, continuous defections and party switches, and conflictual relations between government and opposition, eventually impeding the administration's functioning and jeopardizing governability (see Figure 6.4).

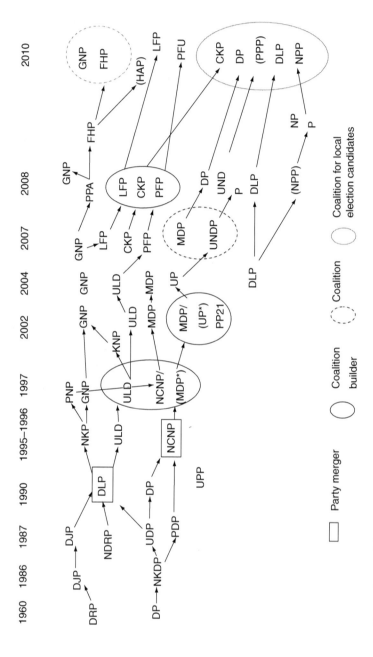

Figure 6.4 Coalition-building (Source: Author, revised from Kim 2008c: 373).

7 Conclusions

Introduction

The main question this book sought to answer concerned the causes of instability and the lack of governability in post-authoritarian South Korea. It has done so by looking at how political coalitions formed and broke apart during the various administrations. In particular, attention has been given to the more recent phase of democratic politics in Korea, namely the Kim Dae-jung (in greater length) and the Roh Moo-hyun and Lee Myung-bak administrations. Despite popular expectations that democratization would also bring effective governability and political stability to South Korea, the reality of politics in the country was characterized by continuous political crises and the government's failure to implement reform policies. As noted by Choi (2002) and Diamond and Kim (2000), Korea's 'crisis of success' even led some citizens to look back with nostalgia to the old authoritarian times as newly established democratic institutions became associated with constant political turmoil and in-fighting.

This was particularly the case with Kim Dae-jung's administration, which I identified as a typical case of how post-democratization governments in Korea struggled to implement any reform policies. In fact, Kim Dae-Jung's coalition minority government struggled with political crises and deadlocks in the legislature. Proposals to introduce reform policies that would consolidate not only electoral but also social and economic democracy were opposed by the opposition party and sometimes even by their coalition partner. As a result of conflicts in the legislature, many bills could not be passed in the National Assembly. To put an end to such chronic deadlock and achieve governability, Kim Dae-jung's administration tried to legitimate itself by calling for a 'political reorganization' (*Jeonggye-gyepyeon*) of the political system, which in essence consisted of attracting defectors from other parties and thus enlarging the size of the (main) ruling party. However, this strategy was unsuccessful. In order to understand why this was the case, I examined in detail three situations when Kim Dae-jung's attempts to carry out reforms stumbled in the face of fierce opposition and ultimately failed: the restructuring of the party organization, the introduction of new electoral laws and the attempt to abolish the National Security Law (examined in Chapters 3, 4 and 5, respectively).

The research focused on the level of institutionalization of the parties and party system as main explanatory variables, while also considering political culture as an intervening variable. To examine the level of institutionalization, I examined the level of factionalism, leadership, party linkage, regional cleavages, cohesiveness of organization and ideological cleavage. Instead of a parsimonious quantitative analysis, I proposed that a thick description of intra-party politics and political culture would provide a more in-depth understanding and explanation of the factors undermining governability and political stability in the legislature during the Kim Dae-jung years.

This enabled me to examine the dynamics of Korean politics at different levels, within the party, within the ruling coalition and in the political system as a whole (see Figure 6.4). I found that the level of institutionalization of the party and party system mattered a great deal in accounting for the instability and lack of governability under the Kim Dae-jung administration. I also showed that Confucian culture, which consists of a strict top-down hierarchical structure and father-figure-like leadership, is embedded among political actors and the voters. Confucian culture undermines the institutionalization of the individual party and the party system. That being said, I argued that inefficient governability is primarily the product of a weakly institutionalized party organization and party system, and that political culture can be cultivated by increasing the level of institutionalization within the party and the party system. Though a highly institutionalized party organization and party system are not necessarily a panacea for any polity, as Mainwaring (1998) and Randall and Svåsand (2002) note, low levels of institutionalization of party organizations and party systems certainly affect governability, as seen in South Korean politics. In this concluding chapter, I review this book's main findings; I then locate them within the broader literature on both coalition and regime studies and Korean politics; finally, I suggest some possible paths of enquiry that have emerged in light of the findings presented here.

Summary of the main arguments

In Chapter 2, I provided some essential background to contemporary Korean politics. Since its very foundation, South Korea has faced the challenge of threats to national security (North Korea and communism). During the almost four decades of authoritarian rule, political actors and voters had no other option but to converge to the right of the ideological spectrum. The National Security Law was used to marginalize and repress dissent, including leftist parties and politicians. Despite continuous repression, anti-authoritarian movements emerged and the two Kims (Kim Young-sam and Kim Dae-jung) emerged as popular and charismatic leaders. For decades, the two were in competition against each other in the same party at the same time as they cooperated in order to attain the same goal (democratic reforms). After South Korea finally achieved electoral democracy, the two Kims were freed from house arrest by the government, but decided to part ways in fighting the presidential elections. A review of Korea's post-war history highlighted the two main dynamics that had emerged in the political system. First, anti-communism was the only viable (or, in fact, allowed) ideology, and this was sanctioned and legitimized via the National Security Law. Second was the strong loyalty of the regions towards the two leaders of the anti-authoritarian movement, as the strong regional cleavage in the presidential and general elections showed. The third political leader, Kim Jong-pil, previously the main advisor to the Park Chung-hee administration (1961–1979), played a pivotal role in the coalition-building process in both 1990 and 1997, and also built on support in his regional support (his native Chungchong province) to achieve electoral success.

I then turned to the Korean party system during the era of democratic consolidation (1988–1997) and emphasized the under-development of the whole party system. There I could identify three main characteristics of the Korean party system. First, each party is very much personalized. One person, a charismatic leader, virtually controls the party. This includes appointing candidates, raising funds and making key policy decisions. Second, these charismatic leaders nurtured the regional cleavage by relying on the 'loyal votes' of their respective home provinces. Finally, due to anti-communism and the National Security Law, the only ideological platform allowed was anti-communism. When parties do not have differentiated party platforms, voters have voted for local leaders. The fact that Confucianism is deeply embedded in Korean society and politics made regionalism a politically salient issue. Voters followed father-like figures in the person of their political leaders. They would vote for them and, by extension, their party. Voting for their regional leaders was seen as rational by the local population as they believed that these regional leaders would work for the development of their own regions. The following chapters (3, 4 and 5) discussed three specific instances of how the Kim Dae-jung administration, my main case study, sought and failed to introduce key reforms of the country's political system.

The level of institutionalization of the party organization

I began my analysis by examining the dynamics of intra-party politics and the politics of the ruling coalition (Chapter 3). To measure the level of institutionalization within the party, I looked at the role of factionalism, leadership, the funding system, and the linkage between parties and citizens. First, I examined the conflict between the ruling and the opposition party over the parliament's vote to approve the prime minister at the very beginning of the Kim Dae-jung administration. That was also the first condition of the coalition agreement, alongside changing the constitution in order to replace the presidential regime with a parliamentary system. The chapter further examined the ensuing political deadlock in the legislature when the National Assembly became paralysed. For this very reason, it later became known as the 'Vegetable Assembly' or the 'Bullet-Proof Assembly'. The opposition Grand National Party was either protesting outside the Assembly instead of attending parliamentary sessions or held National Assembly Extraordinary Session meetings without the participation of

172 *Conclusions*

the other parties. Therefore the National Assembly meetings were either attended exclusively by the ruling parties or by only the opposition. During the stalemate, a series of proposed laws piled up as the political turmoil continued.

I then moved on to discuss the conflict between the coalition partners over the approval of the National Assembly Law. One of the deadlocks in the legislature occurred due to lowering the quorum of the floor negotiation group from twenty to ten seats in the legislature. With strong opposition from the GNP, 'the lightning bill', passed over the lowering of the quorum, was nullified. Had the quorum of the floor negotiation group been lowered, South Korea could have turned into a multi-party system. Given that many factions would have had a chance to become a floor negotiation group, this would have provided enough subventions to help them survive as small parties. As a result, multi-partism could have brought stable governability, as many scholars in political science, such as Sartori (1976), Mainwaring (1993), Cheibub (2002) and Tsebelis (2002), contend.

Next I discussed the issue of party funding. Korean parties crucially rely on subventions and political donations. Fund-raising is yet again mainly in the hands of party leaders at the legislative level and controlled by the individual legislators at local level, and is not based on raising individual party dues from the ordinary members. Strong leaders within the parties actually lack popular legitimacy as they fail in linking the party with citizens. Failure in the linkage role also allowed individual legislators to switch party affiliation without the voters' mandate to do so; fission and fusion of the parties ultimately undermined the party's internal cohesion.

The cases of conflict with the big opposition party (GNP) and the coalition partner (ULD) showed how the political conflicts in the legislature affected governability, especially in terms of implementing reform policies at the initial stage of passing the laws. Again, it appeared necessary to look at the *internal* mechanisms of the political parties to see how these organize and operate in Korea. Thus I concentrated on the question of party organization. An analysis of how Korean parties organize brought to light how the low cohesiveness of the organization, the funding system and the structure of leadership are deeply intertwined. Strongly hierarchical parties undermine internal democracy within the party, but also mechanisms of compromise and negotiation across parties, which explain the early difficulties of the Kim Dae-Jung administration. A strict top-down hierarchy hinders compromise and negotiation with the opposition party and also with internal party legislators. Once party leaders make their own decision, legislators do not have many options other than to follow the party line, typically shaped by the party leaders. This political culture leaves individual legislators with two options: to stick with the party's decision or to leave the party itself. This also means that legislators sticking with party leaders would secure their future seats as candidates for the following general election. Parties seeking to attract defectors would be willing to make similar offers. As politicians in South Korea are well-known office-seekers, legislators who want to be appointed as candidates in the following general election have little choice but to follow the party leader. In this sense, I argued that, in South Korea, party leaders, not the party members, create the party.

In this chapter, I argued that scholarship focusing on democratic institutions often overlooks the reality of party organization in Korea and also neglects the history and the culture of political actors and voters. When the party fails in achieving cohesiveness of the organization, it boosts factionalism within the party, and without cohesiveness of the ruling party's organization it is highly unlikely to be able to implement reform policies. As a result, the administration rapidly plunged into the lame-duck period. The study shows conclusively that institutionalization matters because a weakly institutionalized party organization brings inefficient governability.

The level of institutionalization of the party system: strong regionalism

It is not just the political parties that were weakly institutionalized in Korea, but the whole political system itself. In Chapter 4, I discussed the attempt to reform the electoral law in order to overcome regionalism. As shown in the previous chapters, regionalism had been boosted after democratization and during the Kim Dae-jung administration the regional cleavage deepened even further.

Here I examine how the regional cleavage and the cohesiveness of party organization affected governability. In this regard, the case first showed that a larger government (in terms of number of legislators) could not secure governability as it still failed to introduce reform policies. To reduce the regional cleavage and its electoral impact, the Kim Dae-jung administration proposed the reform of the electoral law. The case study showed how the ruling party struggled to gain approval for introducing reform policies first from within the party and then later from the coalition partner and the opposition party. It also showed that each party's rational choices caused severe conflicts of interest among the parties and legislators and influenced the outcome of the vote on electoral reform. When the ruling parties embarked on reforming the electoral law, the question of passing the law did not pose a problem in itself as the ruling parties had secured majority status by then. However, laws passed by the ruling parties in the legislature would not give any legitimacy to the reform of the electoral law as, for this to happen, the support of the opposition was deemed to be necessary.

Second, another reason the government failed to pass the reform laws was that it failed to consolidate the internal cohesiveness of the party organization. When the parties finally agreed on the electoral law, public opinion criticized them for gerrymandering. The new law showed that each party secured their potential vote base and interests required to win elections rather than changing the electoral districts in such a way as to institutionally mitigate strong region-based voting. The opposition party leader officially apologized in public and President Kim Dae-jung ordered the resumption of the process of reforming the laws. When the new electoral law was finally passed two months before the general election, the ruling party could not make much progress on its reform plan but remained in more or less the same position as before, except the total seat numbers of the legislators fell from 299 to 273 and the Electoral Law Act 87 was changed to a minor extent in order to allow civil society groups and movements to be involved in a very limited way. The attempt to carry out reforms in order to mitigate strong regionalism in this way was abandoned.

I argued here that strong regionalism undermines fair competition in the region as each party has its own regional base and monopolizes the votes in the area. As Randall and Svåsand (2002) argue, party identification with certain groups undermines the level of institutionalization of the party-system because it hinders fair competition among parties in the regions. Strong regionalism allowed a monopoly of votes for each party in their own region and the effort of the ruling party to bring about reform of such regionalist tendencies vanished in the midst of pure office-seekers' rational behaviour. However, I should note that the government itself did not escape the accusation of being a pure office–seeker, as the new reform law was designed to benefit the ruling party the most.

The level of institutionalization of the party system: ideological conflicts

Chapter 5 examined the significance of the ideological cleavage in Korea's political system. In this chapter I posited that a deep ideological cleavage is likely to undermine the stability of the government as well as its efficacy in implementing new laws. It is worth recalling that all the parties are located on the right of the ideological spectrum. This is a legacy of the Korean War and the division of the Korean peninsula into two ideologically opposed states. This ideological confrontation has provided both regimes, in the North and the South, with much-craved legitimacy. In addition, the presence of a threat coming from the North enabled the authoritarian governments to marginalize and repress dissent and opposition. This led to the adoption of the National Security Law. While an alternative to official anti-communism was never an option, in practice there were differences in how each party decided to deal with North Korea. These differences and their impact on governability emerged dramatically when the Kim Dae-jung administration decided to adopt the so-called 'Sunshine Policy' (or engagement policy) towards the North. Again, the ruling party suffered from conflicts not only with the large opposition party, but also with their coalition partner and within the party itself. The root cause lay in that those defectors that the ruling party had attracted from other parties were not ideological soul mates with those in the coalition.

First, the chapter analysed the ideological differences among the parties and showed that a conventional left–right scale cannot account for the parties' distinct ideological preferences. The core distinction, in fact, lies in the policy preferences towards North Korea. Next, I explained how the National Security Law played a key role in shaping the ideology of political actors and voters. The National Security Law was notoriously misused to protect the authoritarian governments from challengers and allowed them to arrest or oppress many political opponents as well as people allegedly holding a socialist view or ideology. The final section focused on the attempt by the ruling party and the young progressive legislators from the opposition party to abolish the so-called 'evil law' (the National Security Law). On paper, it would have been possible to amend or even abolish the National Security Law counting on the progressive legislators in the opposition party; however, the ruling party did not gain any support from the opposition party because of strict party discipline.

The chapter also elucidated the internal conflicts within the opposition Grand National Party and the ruling party's conflict with coalition partners and over the Sunshine Policy. Such conflict in the end led to the coalition breakdown in September 2001. While the ruling party was seeking to abolish the NSL, a space for compromise and negotiation between the ruling party and the progressive and younger legislators within the coalition partner (ULD) and the opposition party (GNP) seemed to emerge. By providing insights into how the meetings and discussions among progressive legislators across the parties developed and also how the relatively progressive legislators' opinions were silenced within their respective (opposition) parties, I showed how and why the government's attempt to abolish the 'evil law' eventually failed, and ended up as 'a storm in a tea cup'. Key to this was a lack of internal democracy within the party where a strict top-down hierarchy within the organization hindered the mechanisms of compromise across parties and the possibility of introducing new rules in the legislature, such as a cross-voting system so that individual legislators could vote for their own policy preference. Korean political culture leaves legislators with only a very small margin for autonomous political action: thus, they either obey the party's main opinion or leave it. This is also related to the level of institutionalization of the party and the party system. The frequent defectors from other parties undermine the internal cohesiveness of the party organization as they would have different ideological preferences. However, when the party is highly institutionalized, it is strongly rooted within society; therefore, in this situation, the party is not created by charismatic leaders and the party's platform cannot be manipulated by a few key figures. Legislators also cannot defect from their party easily when they are strongly linked to the local districts and the voters rather than mainly relying on the party leaders' decisions.

Chapter 6 switched attention to the two more recent administrations (Roh Moo-hyun and Lee Myung-bak) as these represented a crucial testing ground for the argument developed throughout the book. If claims about the importance of majority rule and size held, this would be where we would find evidence. Conversely, if even under those circumstances ungovernability persisted and fission and fusion of political actors continued, then the claim that the cause is to be found in the low level of institutionalization of parties and party system would then be confirmed.

Broader implications and conclusion

This one-country in-depth study cannot, by its own nature, make any claim to generalizability. At the same time, the findings highlighted in these pages allow four broader points to be made. First, the book contributes to our understanding of factors affecting governability after coalition-building across regime types (Cheibub 2002; Cheibub and Chernykh 2008; Cheibub *et al.* 2004; Elgie 2001; Elgie and McMenamin 2008; Figueredo and Limongi 2000; Kim 2008a, b, c; Randall and Svåsand 2002; Yap and Kim 2008). Because coalition-building within (semi-)presidential systems (e.g. Taiwan, Portugal, Poland and Slovakia)[1] has occurred in other post-authoritarian contexts, explaining coalition-building in Korea has implications that go beyond the specificity of the case study. This book contributes to the building of a bridge between the two main streams of scholarship on coalition studies in the parliamentary systems in West Europe and democratic governability in the presidential regimes in Latin America.

Second, the study develops an original framework that integrates a rationalist approach with one that acknowledges the role of political culture. I showed that the weakly institutionalized party organization and party system undermine efficient governability, and the culture of the rigid top-down hierarchy and father-figure role of elites and local legislators also prevent the institutionalization of mechanisms of negotiation and compromise. I showed how political culture shaped the choices and behaviour of legislators and voters, and argued that this was not irrational in the social context in which they operate. Rational-choice theories and thin analyses do not explain the whys and hows of the individual political actor's fission and fusion in the party systems, while the quantitative large-N data miss many explanatory factors in social and historical contexts. By looking at the history and culture embedded in a given society – among political actors and the voters – the book is able to provide in-depth understanding of the political actors and the voters in South Korea. However, I do not argue that the specificity of a country's political culture (here a Confucian legacy of strong personalism and deference to authority) pre-determines the outcome (factionalism, fission and fusion, and eventually instability). Quite the contrary, I argued that culture can be cultivated by increasing the level of institutionalization of the party organization and the party system.

Third, empirically, the book provides a new data set that fills a gap in a field where Western cases constitute the main focus of research. Coalition theories have mainly paid attention to European countries in parliamentary systems. Instead of parsimonious thin analysis, a thick description of political actors' behaviour under the Kim Dae-jung administration as an example of minority coalition government in South Korea provides a new non-West European data set, with an in-depth explanation of intra-party politics. It elucidates the fission and fusion of the legislators across parties in the party system on the basis of their rational choice. The apparently irrational behaviour of political actors and voters seemed rational in the context of the history and culture of Korean society.

Finally, the study has implications for scholars of Korean politics. Research on South Korea has thus far concentrated on the presidency and on the broader issue of democratic consolidation. Overlooking the contribution of coalition theories has meant understanding how political actors behave, and why and how their behaviour actually influences the process of compromise and negotiation, has been neglected. Understanding the intra-party politics and the mechanisms of negotiation and compromise within the party and the party system in South Korea significantly enhanced our understanding of why coalitions form and especially break down in Korea, and how that affects governability.

In conclusion, the case of minority coalition governments in a semi-presidential system can open the way for dealing with the puzzle of (the causes of) inefficient governability by examining intra- and inter-party politics. Thick description of a single case study always risks facing the charge of a lack of generalizability and of not providing 'the leverage necessary to test counterfactual hypotheses' (Coppedge 1999: 472). However, Coppedge (ibid.: 473) recalls Eckstein's argument (1975) that 'some generalization could be based on a single case'. Additional single case studies could bring valuable insights to our understanding of intra- and inter-party politics and therefore make the findings more robust. Research could also develop comparatively, albeit within small-N designs, as that allows an in-depth analysis of the cases considered. Because coalition and regime studies bring distinct but valuable insights on coalition politics, it is suggested that comparisons are (also) conducted across regime types. Here attention to semi-presidential systems in particular is required because, as Elgie (2004: 320) notes, studies of governability or governance in semi-presidential systems have been neglected in the literature. Finally, since coalition-building among political actors has been common and pervasive in other recently democratized countries as well, comparisons could be extended in this direction. Making sense of the internal mechanisms of intra- and inter-party politics fundamentally enhances our understanding of *how institutions matter*.

Notes

1 Introduction

1 'Governability' is here understood as the government's ability to pass and to implement policies decisively (Coppedge 2001).
2 I return to this in Chapter 2. Suffice it here to say that one of the consequences of the rapid economic development promoted by the authoritarian governments from 1960 to 1987 (under presidents Park Chung-hee and Chun Doo-hwan's rule) was an increase in demands for democracy from civil rights movements. This brought authoritarianism to an end. President Roh Tae-woo announced the '6.29 declaration' on 29 June 1987, basically accepting fair presidential elections. This signalled the start of the democratization era in Korea.
3 It was only after the general elections in 2004 and 2008 that the voters started to support majority ruling parties.
4 By 'Korean scholarship' here I refer not only to Korean scholars, but in general to all those working on the country.
5 Voters cast two votes for a candidate and a party. One vote is to select a candidate in the Single Member District (SMD) and the other vote is for a party whereby the party gains seats in the National Assembly on the basis of Proportional Representation (PR).
6 Available from: www.kinds.or.kr (accessed from 1 September 2003 to 31 August 2010).

2 Historical background and the formation of the Korean party system

1 The National Security Law was established on 1 December 1948 for the purpose of eliminating opposition members, alleged leftists, who were by then members of the South Joseon Labour Party. When South Korea established the single government without the North, many leftists and the nationalists who were concerned about the division of the peninsular rebelled in Yeosu and Jeju Island. The law was passed at first to arrest those leftists protesting against the government. Gi Gwang-seo (2004) *Story of North Korean History* (*Bukhan Yeoksa Iyagi*) Korean History Association website. Available from: www.yangsimsu.or.kr/boanbub/byun_chun.htm (accessed 4 October 2004).
2 In February 1946, North *Joseon* People's Provisional Committee (BukJoseon Imsi Inminwiwonhoe) supported by the USSR carried out land reform in North Korea by utilizing the most brutal ways on the principle of forfeiture without compensation and distributing the land to others free of charge (*Musang Molsu Musang Bunbae* 無償沒收無償分配). Available from: www.koreanhistory.org/webzine/read.php?pid=6&id=46 (accessed 20 August 2006).
3 The demonstration caused 183 deaths in Seoul and more than 6,000 casualties. Avail-

Notes 179

able from: http://ko.wikipedia.org/wiki/4.19_%ED%98%81%EB%AA%85 (accessed 20 September 2004).
4 Founded by Rhee Syng-man.
5 The Democratic Party was founded in September 1955 to mobilize opposition against the electoral corruption of the Liberal Party. The main members of the Democratic Party were from the biggest opposition party, the Democratic People's Party. The Democratic Party gained the largest number of seats in the National Assembly in the Second General Election in 1950 and once suggested changing the party system from a presidential to a parliamentary system (Kim 2000: 257–301).
6 The miracle lies in the fact that, despite strong initial structural disadvantages (legacy of colonial rule, economic underdevelopment, destruction following the Korean war), in about 30 years South Korea emerged as one of the most dynamic systems in the world economy (in fact, one of the so-called 'Asian dragons'). The reference to the Han River derives from the fact that this is the river on whose banks lies Korea's capital, Seoul, the heart of the country's economy.
7 This has been a very sensitive issue between the countries until now as many Japanese believe Korea has benefited under the colonial period in terms of modernization of the nation, while on the other hand, most Koreans believe the nation suffered deprivation during the colonial period and hence request an apology. 'Comfort women' and war victims especially are still demanding reparations and apologies from Japan.
8 The Roh Moo-hyun government released to the public the background papers of the 1965 South Korea–Japan Treaty, a document normalizing bilateral relations between the two governments. This has led to serious attacks on the opposition party as Park Geun-hye, the leader of opposition Grand National Party, is the daughter of former-president Park Chung-hee. Many Koreans conceived the normalization with Japan as representing shameful or humiliating diplomacy (*Donga Ilbo*, 17 January 2005).
9 Park Chung-hee later invested the money to build a steel mill in Pohang, close to his hometown. The Pohang steel mill is widely regarded as one of the largest and most efficient steel mills in the world. It is now known as POSCO. Park Tae-jun was the founder of POSCO.
10 Cumings (1997: 385) states that [Yusin] is borrowed from the Japanese concept *isshin* [or *issin*] that the Meiji leaders used in 1868. However, according to Gari Keith Ledyard (2000) (available from: http://koreaweb.ws/pipermail/ksopen_koreaweb.ws/2000-December/000011.html (accessed 26 August 2006)), the word 'Yusin' is rather influenced by a seventh-century Chinese expression. The term 'Yusin' is also found in the Daewongun era (from 1886 to1895 when the Daewongun ruled the country on behalf of his young son Gojong, who is the last king of the Joseon Dynasty) and also found in the 1860s from the time of the Tongzhi reforms. It seems the word was used in the three countries at a similar time in the 1860s and the word was originally derived from China.
11 The Jeolla and Gyeongsang provinces are also known as Honam and Yeongnam, respectively.
12 I am not implying that there was no regionalism before, as some scholars note regionalism dates back to Joseon Dynasty or Three Kimgdoms' era (see Chapter 4).
13 UIM was founded by George Ogle who was a Methodist missionary in Korea in 1954. George Ogle worked for the labour union until he was deported by the Park's administration in 1974 (Cumings 1997: 387).
14 The National Security Law was established in 1948 under the Rhee Syng-man administration, and the Anti-Communist Law was introduced in 1961 after the military coup intensifying the crackdown against the opposition. Since 1980 under the Chun Doo-hwan administration, the Anti-Communist Law was merged with the National Security Law (*Hankook Ilbo*, 21 June 2004).
15 The Bu-ma democratization movement (October 1979) followed by the YH incident (August 1979). After the death of the female labourer at the headquarters of the New

180 *Notes*

      Democratic Party in 1979, vigorous protests against the government arose in Busan and Masan, both in Gyeongsang province. President Park Chung-hee was murdered by his aide Kim Jae-gyu over discussions about how to deal with these demonstrations. The incident was later followed by another civilian demonstration, the Gwangju 5.16 demonstration in May 1980.

16 The figure is reported on the May Memorial Foundation website. Available from: www.518.org/main.html?TM18MF=A030106 (accessed 2 June 2006).

17 He was sentenced to death on a charge of 'conspiracy to start a rebellion' after the 5.16 Gwangju Uprising in September 1980, although he was still in prison during the Gwangju democratization movement.

18 TK factions stand for factions from the Taegu and Kyoungsang regions. They are now spelled as Daegu and Gyeongsang.

19 The crisis of success occurred not only in Korea, but also in Spain and Taiwan (Huntington 1991; Im 1997; Kim 2001).

20 When three parties merged in 1990, Choi Jang-jip (1996) saw the merger as an application of 'transformism'. The concept of 'transformism' or 'trasformismo' derives from the behaviour of political elites in late-nineteenth-century Italy. The legislature was dominated by elites and the minority party members strived to gain power by reaching a stable majority. In so doing, the minority party actors were engaged in an informal patron–client system and were not ideologically stratified lacking strong social support, and the competition between highly organized parties was absent (Choi 2002: 110).

21 Here, it is better to be called a faction because this is after three parties merged into one, the Democratic Liberal Party.

22 Now spelled Daegue and Gyeongsang.

23 Hana is the former-president Chun Doo-hwan's *Ho* (號 written name), which means 'one', and Hanahoe means 'club or society of one mind'. In the old times, elites, including scholars, used to have *Ho* apart from their own names as an easy way to be referred to without any other title. Therefore Chun Doo-hwan was called *Hana*. *Hanahoe* was originally started as *Chilseonghoe* (Seven Star Society), founded in 1961 and supported by former-president Park Chung-hee. *Chilseonghoe* mainly consisted of very bright students (within the top 5 per cent of third- and fourth-year students) of the Eleventh Military Academy. Before the Eleventh Military Academy, the previous Academy had a short-term training programme from 24 days to six months. Park Chung-hee was a graduate of the Second Military Academy and the former-prime-minister, Kim Jong-pil, the Eighth Military Academy. The Steel King and former-prime-minister, Park Tae-jun, was a graduate of the Sixth Military Academy. The Eleventh Military Academy was actually the first Military Academy with a four-year programme and Chun Doo-hwan and the former-president, Roh Tae-woo, are both graduates of the Eleventh Military Academy. *Chilseonghoe* later changed its name in line with Chun Doo-hwan's written name, *Hana*. As mentioned earlier, *Hanahoe* was supported by Park Chung-hee and members of the *Hanahoe* could enjoy highly successful careers in the government or as military officers. The society has not existed officially since 1973 when Yun Pil-yong, a general who worked for Capital Security (Sudosaryeonggwan), suggested that Park Chung-hee retire and select the next potential leader of the nation from the members of *Hanahoe*. However, the society continued to meet informally and played a crucial role in the so-called 12.12 Sate (incident), when Chun Doo-hwan took part in a military rebellion or coup on 12 December 1979 (*Hankook Ilbo*, 1 May 2006; *Segye Ilbo*, 24 January 2006).

24 Interview held in Seoul on 9 March 2006.

25 This is a traditional underwear that a man used to wear under the outer clothing. Here *hatbagi* was often used as metaphor meaning that the main stream of politics isolated interest of the regions or elites such as Kim Jong-pil from Chungcheong province.

3 Internal factors: party politics and organization

1 The floor negotiation group is also called 'floor group' or 'negotiation group' (Wonnegyoseopdanche).
2 The opposition, however, could not win office without building a coalition with the former government's coalition partner, the ULD.
3 The National Congress for New Politics (NCNP) was the ruling party led by Kim Dae-jung. In January 2000, it changed its name to the New Millennium Democratic Party (MDP).
4 This is a term O'Donnell (1994) used to explain that a popularly elected president with the wide support of the people can harm democracy.
5 Ordinary legislators were often called hand-raisers (*Geosugi* 擧手機) at the National Assembly Meeting and most important issues are decided among party leaders.
6 When Kim Young-sam merged his party, the New Democratic Party, with two other parties, the Democratic Liberal Party and the United Liberal Democrats in 1990, some party members, including Lee Gi-taek and Roh Moo-hyun, left the party and founded the Democratic Party but, after failing in the general election, they all scattered; some such as Roh Moo-hyun joined with the New Millennium Democratic Party, and some the Grand Nation Party. Since that time, the Democratic Party is often called the 'little' Democratic Party (see Chapter 4, Figure 4.1).
7 Interview held in Seoul on 2 March 2006.
8 Choi Yeon-hee was a member of the Seventeenth National Assembly for the Grand National Party, but he was accused of harassing a female newspaper (*Donga Ilbo*) reporter at a restaurant on 24 February 2006. When the female reporter sued him for sexual harassment, he had to leave the GNP, resigning his position in the party organization. The committee of the Grand National Party also decided to expel him from the party organization. By then he was the Secretary General (*Samuchongjang*) of the GNP (*Seoul Kyeongje Sinmun*, 27 February 2006).
9 See Chapter 2 for more on this.
10 As a part of the National Assembly member privileges, legislators cannot be arrested during the period of attending the legislature. Two legislators (Seo Sang-mok and Lee Sin-haeng) of the GNP were under suspicion over the improper use of funds. It was called the *Sepung* incident. The National Tax Administration deducted tax from *Jaebeol* and the previous government, the Kim Young-sam administration, received illegal political funding in return (*Hankook Ilbo*, 10 August 1999).
11 It is a unit of Korean money and one billion *won* is about one million pounds sterling.
12 He used to work for *Kyunghyang Sinmun*, a daily newspaper, and has a brother who was a member of the Sixteenth National Assembly. Interview held in Seoul on 9 March 2006.
13 There are four kinds of plant called 'four virtuous men (四君子)', traditionally adored and respected by noble men in East Asia. They are hawthorn flower, orchid, chrysanthemum and bamboo, and have been used as drawing objects in oriental drawings since the twelfth century in China. Each represents the four seasons – spring, summer, autumn and winter, respectively – and the characteristic of each plant is often used as a metaphor to teach perseverance, strong will, faith, constancy and (political) fidelity in Confucianism. Available from: http://kr.oldarts.net/en/sub.php3?cell=A&dir=help&load=menu&lang=html&load2=sagunja&lang2=html (accessed 9 September 2004).
14 See Chapter 2 for more on this.
15 By-elections are held to replace the loss of seats in the National Assembly, when parties lose their seats due to resignation, illness or death of the legislators.
16 Honam represents Jeolla province and Yeongnam, Gyeongsang province.
17 When Kim Jong-pil was prime minister, he opposed the amendment of the electoral law that would make Park Chung-hee easily elected in the following presidential election. Park Chung-hee persuaded him, saying, 'Next time will be your turn [to be a president]'. However, two years later there was only the Yusin constitution

that secured the life-long presidency of Park Chung-hee (*Hankook Ilbo*, 6 April 1999).
18 In the primary election for a candidate in the presidential elections, Lee Hoe-chang, Lee In-je and Lee Han-dong were competing with each other. Once Lee Hoe-chang won the primary election, he became a candidate for the presidential elections in 1997 from the New Korea Party (a predecessor of the GNP) and Lee In-je left the party and founded his own party, the People's New Party, and also took part in the presidential elections as a candidate. Lee Han-dong remained in the party as vice-chairman but eventually left the party in 1999 (see Figure 3.1).
19 He was the Sixteenth National Assembly member for the ULD and played the main role in building the coalition with the NCNP. Interview held in Seoul on 9 March 2006.
20 Interview held in Seoul on 2 March 2006.
21 'Cronyism' is a term often used to make sense of the form of rapid economic development in East Asia – e.g. Japan, South Korea, Singapore and Taiwan – where Confucian culture is deeply embedded. In most cases, elite education is seen as the source of crony networks. David Kang (2002) argues, in fact, that the school background provides strong social networks that, once forged, continue life-long.
22 A similar case occurred in 2009. The LFP and the CKP built a coalition to meet the quorum of a floor group in the National Assembly (see Chapter 6).
23 Officially, the president would not attend the negotiation meeting in the legislature, but the chairman (Chongjae) of the MDP at the meeting is not free from the influence of the president's opinion. For the chairman of the party is often appointed by Kim Dae-jung, the practical leader of the MDP; the chairman of the MDP is rather a delegate for the original leader of the party, President Kim Dae-jung. Under this circumstance, if the chairman acts against Kim Dae-jung's opinion, he might risk his position as a chairman. This also hinders the process of negotiation among the party leaders in the legislature.
24 That is approximately 1.5 million pounds sterling.
25 The names of regions are now spelled as Daegu, Gyeongsang, Busan and Gyeongsang respectively.
26 In the case of Tsebelis (2002: 4), he is concerned about the numbers of veto players, rather than the number of political parties. He contends that the more veto players like Italy or the United States have, the higher policy stability.
27 The coalition between the MDP and the ULD broke in January 2000 and was rebuilt later in January 2001, although the coalition broke up again in September 2001 (see Chapter 5).
28 There were four members who defected from the MDP and joined the ULD to help the ULD become a floor group from October to December 2000: Bae Gi-sun, Song Seok-chan and Song Young-jin joined the ULD in October 2000, and Jang Jae-sik joined the ULD in December 2000. However, they all defected from the ULD and rejoined the MDP when the coalition broke down in September 2001 (see Figure 3.1 and Chapter 5).
29 See the cases of Lee In-je and Lee Han-dong in this chapter, and Sohn Hak-kyu in Chapter 6. They all left the party when they could not win internal elections (primary).
30 Kim Young-ho notes that it is modified from Korea, based on the Central Electoral Committee report (2000) *99 Party Activities and Revenue Report*, p. 16 and pp. 33–34, and EU countries based on Mair and van Biezen (2001) *Party Membership in Twenty European Democracies, 1980–2000*, p. 9.
31 Concentration of power on the party leader was relaxed during the next Roh Moo-hyun administration.
32 Gunther and Diamond (2003: 170) argue that classical party typology does not accommodate real-world parties, especially not West-European parties. According to Gunther

and Diamond (ibid.: 171), their recent work on party typology includes 15 species on the basis of 'the nature of party organization, the party's programmatic commitments and the strategy and behavioural norms of the party'. Among the 15 species of party Gunther and Diamond divide by five into elite based parties, mass-based parties, ethnicity-based parties, electoralist parties and movement parties. From their typology, parties in South Korea, especially during the Kim Dae-jung administration, can be characterized as a hybrid type of elite-based, clientelistic parties, that is, the first party type. They are organizationally thin and similar to Panebianco's 'electoral professional party'. For electoralist parties, personal charisma or attractiveness is more important than organizational functions or ideology. Gunther and Diamond add that parties in South Korea are catch-all parties but, given the strong regional base for elections parties in South Korea, can also be said to be similar to ethnic parties that are based on ethnicity, particularly in terms of lacking a mass-based organization.

33 In most of the time before the democratization, money politics had been at the core of the electoral campaign and the campaign was rather a competition in spending rather than over issues or policies among the parties. Paid party staff simply brought potential voters to the rally to listen to the candidates' speeches before the elections and voters used to receive gifts or envelopes of money in return for supporting certain candidates. This will be discussed more in a later section.

34 Interview held in Seoul on 27 February 2006. He was elected as a member of the National Assembly by the Thirteenth, Fourteenth and Fifteenth General Election, and during the Kim Dae-jung administration he was president of the Korea Tourism Organization from 2000–2003 after he failed in the Sixteenth General Election. His failure was due to the civil society movement, as he was one of the candidates on the list of 'anti-electoral candidates'.

35 Approximately 50 pounds sterling.

36 If the donation is made by a party member, it seems to be classified as membership dues. However, the average amount of donation is far too large to call it party dues.

37 They invite well-known singers or traditional music singers to hold concerts and candidates invite supporters to the concert.

38 Some general election candidates write autobiographies before the election.

39 Interview held in Seoul on 8 March 2006.

40 The Roh Moo-hyun administration faced opposition over the new reform policies on Private School Law that include introducing an open process of selecting board members. That is, by the new law, a few members of the school board would have to be outsiders of the school who are recommended by parents and teachers associations of the school to prevent corruption by the owners or founders at the private schools and universities. However, this issue brought deadlock and overnight strikes in the legislature. The GNP led by Park Geun-hye did not attend the National Assembly meetings but went on protesting outside the legislature, appealing to the people directly (*Oh My News*, 9 December 2005). See also Chapter 6. Available from: www.ohmynews.com/articleview/article_view.asp?no=263007&rel_no=1 (accessed 5 October 2006).

41 People in South Korea gather for family events but these not only involve the family but also friends and acquaintances. This occurs for weddings, sixtieth or seventieth birthdays, a child's first birthday, funerals and so on. For these kinds of family events, guests bring mostly money or in some cases flowers or a gold ring for a baby's first birthday. Therefore this kind of gathering shows the person's social status: that is, the higher position or wealthier he or she is, the more money is given, the more flowers to decorate an event (e.g. either restaurants or hotel banquet rooms).

42 Interview held in Seoul on 9 March 2006.

43 Interview held in Seoul on 10 March 2006.

44 For a more recent figure, see Chapter 6.

45 Interview held in Seoul on 8 March 2006.

46 Interview held in Seoul on 9 March 2006.

184 *Notes*

47 Interview held in Seoul on 9 March 2006.
48 However, during the Roh Moo-hyun administration, the gap between the rich and the poor became wider and class divisions have been developing since then. Many blame this is on the Asian Crisis. During the economic crisis, many ordinary people lost jobs and many in the middle-class fell to the lower level.
49 The Democratic Labour Party gained ten seats in the legislature in the Seventeenth General Election in April 2004.
50 As observed in a private meeting of politicians in Seoul on 27 February 2006.
51 Donggyo-dong is a name of the area in Seoul where Kim Dae-jung's former house was located. As his former secretaries or colleagues, the members of his faction spent their political life with Kim Dae-jung, literally decades from the Park Chung-hee administration.
52 Kim Dae-jung is a graduate of Mokpo high school, Roh Tae-woo from Gyeongbook high school and Kim Young-sam from Gyeongnam high school. Therefore, the portion of high school factions taking up important official positions is related to the ups and downs of the presidency.
53 This trend continues until the present government, the Lee Myung-bak administration, as it was criticized as 'Ko So-yeong' or 'Kang Bu-ja' administration selecting high officials among Korea University graduates, *Somang* church-goers and people from Yeongnam province, or pursuing policies oriented towards the rich (see Chapter 6 for more on this).
54 In the early Kim Dae-jung administration in 1999, the wife of the president of *Sindonga*, one of *Jaebeols*, who was by then in prison due to the *Jaebeol* restructuring policy, accused the wife of Kim Tae-jung of receiving very expensive clothes as a bribe from the wife of the president of *Sindonga* (this is not the monthly journal, *Sin Donga*) and this led to national hearings for over a month and finally Kim Tae-jung had to resign as a minister.
55 Kim Dae-jung was also oppressed as a leftist during the Park Chung-hee administration and Chun Doo-hwan administration. He was even sentenced to death on the basis of the National Security Law (see Chapters 2 and 5).

4 Regionalism and the reform of the electoral law

1 The NCNP changed its name to the New Millennium Democratic Party (hereafter, MDP) in January 2000 (see Chapter 2).
2 In Korea, there are six provinces. Two provinces, Gangwon and Jeju island, are isolated geographically by the mountains and sea, and are mainly famous for tourism with small populations; the other four provinces (Gyeonggi, Chungcheong, Jeolla, Gyeongsang) have a bigger population and Gyeonggi, where Seoul the capital city is located, has the biggest population, about ten million out of a total population of 50 million (recent data expects the population to be about 50 million by the end of 2010) (*Hankyoreh Sinmun*, 16 March 2009).
3 He is a son of Chung Ju-young, a former president of Hyundai, the biggest conglomerate in South Korea.
4 Available from: www.nec.go.kr/sinfo/index.html (accessed 17 September 2005).
5 Percentages are taken from the National Election Commission data.
6 Although, as mentioned earlier, the remaining four legislators are non-party-affiliated and they insisted that they would join the MDP if they were elected.
7 I translated 'Seongeogu' as an electoral district.
8 PK faction means factions from Pusan and Southern Kyoungsang province. Pusan is now spelled as 'Busan' and Kyoungsang as 'Gyeongsang'.
9 It is most likely to be combined in Chungcheong province as the voting population is relatively small in the rural areas.
10 TK faction members in the ULD are as follows: Park Tae-jun, Park Cheol-eon, Kim Dong-ju, Park Gu-il, Park Jun-kyu (*Hankook Ilbo*, 10 December 1999).

11 In South Korea a well-known or respected man such as a legislator (elected in the region), a teacher or a professor, instead of ministers or priests, runs a wedding and officiates at a wedding ceremony.
12 Interview held in Seoul on 7 March 2006.
13 Lee Je-jung, a policy committee member and Kim Seong-jae, policy secretary in the Blue House were some of them from civil society.

5 Ideological cleavages and the debate over the National Security Law

1 While parties accused each other of being 'leftist' or 'reactionary', in reality the conflict was not between North and South Korea, but within the South and therefore was named the 'South–South conflict'.
2 Identifying criteria that divide parties along a left–right axis inevitably entails some degree of arbitrariness. In their study of party manifestoes, Budge *et al.* (2001: 22) have provided one of the most comprehensive attempts at categorization. Though differences in reality are more blurred than on paper, a left–right scale can be identified as follows. Right-wing parties typically emphasize: military-positive, freedom, human rights, constitutionalism-positive, effective authority, free enterprise, economic incentives, protectionism-negative, economic orthodoxy, social service limitation, national way of life-positive, traditional morality-positive, law and order, social harmony. Left-wing parties, instead, emphasize: decolonization, military-negative, peace, internationalism-positive, democracy, regulate capitalism, economic planning, protectionism-positive, controlled economy, nationalization, social service-expansion, labour groups-positive.
3 See Chapter 2.
4 The survey was conducted by the Korea Social Science Data Center asking questions over the phone to 1,000 respondents aged 20 and over from 14 to 20 May 2002.
5 To measure association for nominal variables, we need to look at two particular coefficients: Phi or Cramer's V. When the table contains more than two rows and two columns, we need to look at Cramer's V especially as Phi may produce values greater than 1. Phi is suitable for only 2 × 2 tables. Considering Cramer's V is 0.131, the relationship between the province and preference towards aid to North Korea showed relatively weak association. The values of Cramer's V range between 0 and 1. If the figure appears as 0, it means no association and 1 means a perfect association (Miller *et al.* 2002).
6 On the historical dispute over why Korea was colonized by Japan Confucian scholars, literati including the Joseon Dynasty were largely blamed for their stubbornness. Many believed Japan had opened its country to the West earlier and modernized early; on the other hand, Korea was much more closed to Western influence.
7 South Korea has achieved rapid economic growth since the Korean War; however, labour unions and human rights have been oppressed, especially under the authoritarian regimes. With the pressure of social movement and agreement among the political elites, electoral democracy was achieved in 1987; however, as scholars note, social and economic democracy is still to be achieved in terms of social welfare.
8 The figure is reported on the May Memorial Foundation website. Available from: www.518.org/main.html?TM18MF=A030106 (see Chapter 2) (accessed 9 September 2004).
9 Yeongnam was home to most of the military leaders and presidents under authoritarian rule.
10 'Jaeya' means group of social elites who are not practically involved in administrative politics but are more or less influential in politics.
11 Interview was held in Seoul on 8 March 2006.
12 One of the Confucian tenets teaching attitude of virtue says seniority is the best in the

186 *Notes*

government, and for the village age is the best, and to govern the country virtue is the best. 曾子-日朝廷 莫如爵 鄉黨 莫如齒 輔世長民 莫如德 明心寶鑑 遵禮篇 Myeongsimbogam Junryepyeon. Kim Sung-suk and Kim Jip (1999) *Saimdang Hanmun Seodang* (Chinese Letter Class). Available from: http://user.chollian.net/~k71421/myung1.htm (accessed 16 April 2006).

13 The total number of legislators from the MDP who joined the ULD is four (see Chapter 3).
14 Interview was held in Seoul on 9 March 2006.
15 There was one more legislator, Jang Jae-sik, who was a member of the MDP who defected from it and joined the ULD in December 2000 to promote a coalition between the MDP and the ULD.
16 Liberation Day in South Korea is 15 August. This is when the end of Japanese colonization is commemorated.
17 Mankyongdae is also Kim Il-sung's birth place.
18 The interview was held in Seoul on 28 February 2006.

6 When majority does not rule: the Roh Moo-hyun and the Lee Myung-bak administrations

1 The DLP won two legislator seats in the elections and gained eight seats of proportional representation allocated by 13 per cent of votes for the party (*Donga Ilbo*, 26 April 2004).
2 This is different from the Mixed Member Proportional System. The new voting system in Korea is a mixture of Single Winner Voting system and Proportional Representation with a Closed Party List.
3 58.7 per cent of legislators supported for partial amending of the NSL and 29 per cent of legislators voted for abolishing the laws.
4 *Chung-soo Janghakhoe* has a 30 per cent share of MBC (Munhwa Broadcasting Corporation) and 100 per cent of stock share of *Busan Ilbo* (*Busan* daily newspaper) (*Hankyoreh Sinmun*, 11 June 2007).
5 Phone interview with Professor Hyung-a Kim (Australian National University), on 15 July 2010.
6 *Yookyoung* Foundation and *Yeungnam Hakwon* (academy), which includes Yeungnam University, Yeungnam College of Science and Technology, and Yeungnam University Medical Center were all established during the Yusin system and many entrepreneurs were forced to donate their property to build the foundations. For example, Yeongnam University was established in 1968 by merging two colleges: Cheonggu College established by Choi Hae-cheong in 1950 and Daegu College established in 1947 by the Choi Jun family (a family line that stretched back over 400 years in Gyeongju) and later run by Lee Byung-chul, the founder of Samsung. By then, Cheonggu College was plagued with corruption scandals. To solve the problem, the board decided to donate the college to the military regime in 1967, and Lee Byeong-chul donated Hankook Biryo Jusikhoesa (Korea Fertilizers Company) and Daegu College to the state. Although they are all public establishments, Park Chung-hee's family members and their close aides were all involved in their administration. At the National Assembly's audit of state affairs, a legislator, Paek Won-woo, said that Chungsoo Foundation, *Yookyoung* Foundation and Yeongnam Academy should all be returned to society (*Oh my news*, 24 September 2005). Park Geun-hye was chair of the board of Chung-soo Janghakhoe from 1995 to 2005. Her sister, Park Geun-young, was chair of the board of the *Yookyoung* Foundation from 1990 to 2009 (*Yonhap News*, 5 March 2009).
7 Both terms are the names of famous TV celebrities, but the initial stands for 'Ko' as Korea University graduate alumni, 'So' as a Somang Church goer (Lee Myung-bak is a treasurer of Somang Church, which is one of the biggest churches on the south part

of river, the most expensive area) and 'Yeong' stands for those who are from Yeongnam region. 'Kang' stands for Kangnam, the southern part of Han River, and 'Bu-ja' means 'the rich' in Korean.
 8 The FTA agreement was in fact 'inherited' by Lee from the previous administration.
 9 These street blockades gained the popular nickname of 'Myong-bak sanseong [walls]' or 'Castle MB' (*Hankyoreh Sinmun*, 22 June 2008).
10 All the close aides were involved in corruption investigations. Lee Kwang-jae, a legislator of the Democratic Party was arrested on charges of receiving bribes. He later became a mayor of Gangwon province in the 2010 local elections, but because of the investigation he was eventually forced to step down for a couple of months. He was back in office by September 2010 but the investigation is still ongoing. Two of the main fund-raisers behind Roh Moo-hyun's presidential election, Kang Geum-won and Park Yeon-cha, were also arrested in connection with a corruption investigation. Kang Geum-won, a president of Changshin Textile, was also detained for embezzlement and tax-evasion.
11 Whether the FHA would join the GNP or not is still in question in September 2010.

7 Conclusions

1 After the collapse of authoritarian rule, they all adopted a semi-presidential system.

Bibliography

Ahn, Byoungman (2003). *Elite and Political Power in South Korea*. Cheltenham, Edward Elgar.
Ahn, Cheongsi and Hoon Jang (1999). *South Korea*. New York, United Nations University Press.
Altman, David (2000). 'The Politics of Coalition Formation and Survival in Multiparty Presidential Democracies. The Case of Uruguay, 1989–1999.' *Party Politics* 6: 259–283.
Axelrod, Robert (1967). 'Conflict of Interest: An Axiomatic Approach.' *The Journal of Conflict Resolution* 11: 87–99.
Axelrod, Robert (1970). *Conflicts of Interest*. Chicago, Markham.
Axelrod, Robert (1972). 'Where the Votes Come From: An Analysis of Electoral Coalitions, 1952–1968.' *American Political Science Review* 66: 11–20.
Bäck, Hanna (2001). 'Explaining Coalition Formation: The Case of Swedish Local Government.' *Strathclyde Papers on Government and Politics* 117: 138.
Bäck, Hanna (2003). 'Explaining and Predicting Coalition Outcomes: Conclusions from Studying Data on Local Coalitions.' *European Journal of Political Research* 42(4): 441–472.
Baek, Yeongcheol (1996). *Je 2 Gonghwaguggwa Hangug Minjuju-ui (The Second Republic and Korean Democracy)*. Seoul, Nanam Publisher.
Baron, David (1991). 'A Strategic Bargaining: Theory of Government Formation in Parliamentary Systems.' *American Political Science Review* 85: 137–164.
Blaikie, Norman (2000). *Designing Social Research*. Cambridge, Polity Press.
Bogdanor, Vernon, ed. (1983). *Coalition Government in Western Europe*. London, Heinemann Education Books.
Browne, Eric C. (1973). *Coalition Theories: A Logical and Empirical Technique*. London, Sage.
Browne, Eric C., Dennis W. Gleiber and Carolyn S. Mashoba (1984). 'Evaluating Conflict of Interest Theory: Western European Cabinet Coalitions, 1945–80.' *British Journal of Political Science* 14(1): 1–32.
Bryman, Alan (2001). *Social Research Methods*. Oxford, Oxford University Press.
Budge, Ian and Hans Keman (1990). *Parties and Democracy: Coalition Formation and Government Function in Twenty States*. Oxford, Oxford University Press.
Budge, Ian, Ivor Crewe, David McKay and Ken Newton (2004). *The New British Politics*. London, Pearson Longman.
Budge, Ian, Hans-Dieter Klingemann, Andrea Volkens, Judith Bara and Eric Tanenbaum (2001). *Mapping Policy Preferences: Estimates for Parties, Electors, and Governments 1945–1998*. Oxford, Oxford University Press.

Chae, Jangsu (2004). 'Hanguk Jwapajipdanui Insikgwa Jihyang' ('Cognition and Prospectus of the Leftist Groups in South Korea'). *Hanguk Jeongchi Hakhoe (Journal of the Korean Political Association)* 3(38): 93–112.
Cheibub, Jose Antonio (2002). 'Minority Governments, Deadlock Situations, and the Survival of Presidential Democracies.' *Comparative Political Studies* 35(3): 284–312.
Cheibub, Jose Antonio and Svitlana Chernykh (2008). 'Constitutions and Democratic Performance in Semi-Presidential Democracies.' *Japanese Journal of Political Science* 9(3): 263–303.
Cheibub, Jose Antonio and Fernando Limongi (2002). 'Democratic Institutions and Regime Survival: Parliamentary and Presidential Democracies Reconsidered.' *Annual Review of Political Science* 5: 151–179.
Cheibub, Jose Antonio, Adam Przeworski and Sebastian M. Saiegh (2004). 'Government Coalitions and Legislative Success Under Presidentialism and Parliamentarism.' *British Journal of Political Science* 34: 565–587.
Choi, Jang-jip (1996). 'Je 2 Gonghwagugha-eseo-ui Minjuju-ui-ui Deungjanggwa Silpae' ('The Emergence and Failure of Democracy Under the Second Republic'). *Je 2 Gonghwagugha-eseo-ui Minjuju-ui-ui Deungjanggwa Silpae (The Emergence and Failure of Democracy under the Second Republic)*, Yeongcheol Baek, ed. Seoul, Nanam Publisher.
Choi, Jang-jip (2002). *Minjuhwa Ihuui Minjujuui: Hanguk Minjujuuiui Bosujeok Giwongwa Wigi (Democracy After Democratization: The Crisis and Origin of Conservative Democracy in South Korea)*. Seoul, Humanitas.
Choi, Jang-jip and Hyunjin Im (1997). *Hanguk Sahoewa Minjujuui: Hanguk Minjuhwa 10 Nyeonui Pyeonggawa Banseong (Korean Society and Democracy: Democratization and its Evaluation)*. Seoul, Nanam Publisher.
Choi, Junyeong and Soonheung Kim (2000). 'Jiyeokgan Georigameul Tonghaeseo Bon Jiyeokjuuiui Silsanggwa Munjejeom' ('The Problem and Fact of Regionalism Through the Lenses of the Regional Divide'). *Sahoe Yeongu* 1: 65–95.
Chong, Dennis (1996). 'Rational Choice Theory's Mysterious Rivals.' *The Rational Choice Controversy: Economic Models of Politics Reconsidered*, Jeffrey Friedman, ed. New Haven, Yale University.
Colomer, Josep M. and Gabriel L. Negretto (2005). 'Can Presidentialism Work Like Parliamentarism?' *Government and Opposition* 40(1): 60–89.
Coppedge, Michael (1995). 'Instituciones y Gobernabilidad democrática en América Latina' ('Institutions and Democratic Governability in Latin America'). *Síntesis* 22 (July–December).
Coppedge, Michael (1999). 'Thickening Thin Concepts and Theories: Combining Large N and Small in Comparative Politics.' *Comparative Politics* 31(4): 465–476.
Coppedge, Michael (2001). *Party Systems, Governability and the Quality of Democracy in Latin America*. Representation and Democratic Politics in Latin America, Buenos Aires.
Croissant, Aurel (2003). 'Legislative Powers, Veto Players, and the Emergence of Delegative Democracy: A Comparison of Presidentialism in the Philippines and South Korea.' *Democratization* 10(3): 68–98.
Cumings, Bruce (1997). *Korea's Place in the Sun: A Modern History*. New York, London, W.W. Norton & Company.
Denzin, Norman (1970). *The Research Act in Sociology*. London, Butterworth.
De Swaan, Abram (1973). *Coalition Theories and Cabinet Formations*. Amsterdam, Elsevier.

De Vaus, David A. (2001). *Research Design in Social Research*. London, Sage Publications.

De Winter, Lieven, Rudy B. Andeweg and Patrick Dumon (2002). *The State of Art in Coalition Research: Critical Appraisals and Alternative Avenues*. European Consortium for Political Research, Torino.

Diamond, Larry and Byungkook Kim, eds. (2000). *Consolidating Democracy in South Korea*. Boulder, Lynne Rienner.

Diamond, Larry., J. Hartlyn, *et al.*, eds. (1989). *Democracy in Developing Countries: Latin America*. Boulder: Lynne Rienner.

Diermeier, Daniel (1996). 'Rational Choice and the Role of Theory in Political Science.' *The Rational Choice Controversy: Economic Models of Politics Reconsidered*, Jeffrey Friedman, ed. New Haven, Yale University Press.

Dodd, Rorence (1976). *Coalitions in Parliamentary Government*. Princeton, Princeton University Press.

Duverger, Maurice (1990). 'Caucus and Branch, Cadre Parties and Mass Parties.' *The West European Party System*, Peter Mair, ed. Oxford, Oxford University Press: 37–45.

Eckstein, Harry (1975). 'Case Study and Theory in Political Science.' *Strategies of Inquiry*, Fred Greenstein and Nelson Polsby, eds. Reading: Addison-Wesley: 79–138.

Elgie, Robert (2001). *Divided Government in Comparative Perspective*. Oxford, Oxford University Press.

Elgie, Robert (2004). 'Semi-Presidentialism: Concepts, Consequences and Contesting Explanations.' *Political Studies Review* 2: 314–330.

Elgie, Robert and Iain McMenamin (2008). 'Semi-Presidentialism and Democratic Performance.' *Japanese Journal of Political Science* 9(3): 323–340.

Esterberg, Kristin G. (2002). *Qualitative Methods in Social Research*. London, McGraw Hill.

Figueiredo, Angelina Cheibub and Fernando Limongi (2000). 'Presidential Power, Legislative Organisation, and Party Behavior in Brazil.' *Comparative Politics* 32(2): 151–170.

Fukuyama, Francis (1995). *Trust: The Social Virtue and the Creation of Prosperity*. London, Penguin Books.

Giannetti, Daniela and Michael Laver (2001). 'Party System Dynamics and the Making and Breaking of Italian Governments.' *Electoral Studies* 20(4): 529–553.

Gramsci, Antonio (1971). *Selections from the Prison Notebooks*. New York, International Publishers.

Gunther, Richard and Larry Diamond (2003). 'Species of Political Parties: A New Typology.' *Party Politics* 9(2): 167–199.

Hahm, Chaebong (1999). 'Hangukui Bosujuuiwa Yugyo' ('Conservatism in South Korea and Confucianism'). *Hangukui Bosujuui (Conservatism in South Korea)*, Byung-kook Kim, Yongmin Kim, Hyojong Park, Byunghoon Seo and Chaebong Hahm, eds. Seoul, Ingansarang: 199–240.

Hahm, Chaibong (2004). 'Irony of Confucianism.' *Journal of Democracy* 15: 93–107.

Han, Honggu (2001). 'Hanguk Hyeondaesaui Jwaik Nonjaeng 1 Nyeon. Uik Dokju 55 Nyeon' ('Conflict Between the Left and the Right Over One Year in Modern Korean History. 55 Years of the Right's Single Running'). *Sin Donga* 9.

Harrison, Lisa (2001). *Political Research: An Introduction*. London, Routledge.

Helgesen, Geir (1998). *Democracy and Authority in Korea: The Cultural Dimension in Korean Politics*. Surrey, Curzon Press.

Henderson, Gregory (1968). *Korea: The Politics of the Vortex*. Cambridge, Harvard University Press.

Huber, John D. (1998). 'How Does Cabinet Instability Affect Political Performance? Portfolio Volatility and Health Care Cost Containment in Parliamentary Democracies.' *American Journal of Political Science* 92: 177–615.

Huber, John D. and Martinez-Gallardo Cecilia (2004). 'Cabinet Instability and the Accumulation of Experience: The French Fourth and the Fifth Republics in Comparative Perspective.' *British Journal of Political Science* 34: 27–48.

Huntington, Samuel (1968). *Political Order in Changing Societies*. New Haven, Yale University Press.

Huntington, Samuel (1991). *The Third Wave: Democratization in the Late Twentieth Century*. Norman, London, University of Oklahoma Press.

Huntington, Samuel P., ed. (2000). *Culture Matters: How Values Shape Human Progress*. New York, Basic Books.

Hyun, Jae-ho (2002). *Seongeo Gangryeong Bunseogeul Tonghan Hanguk Jeongdanggan Gyeongjaeng Yeongu: 1952–2000* (*Research on party competition in South Korea through party platforms: 1952–2000*). Seoul, Korea University.

Hyun, Jae-ho (2004). 'Jeongdanggan Gyeongjaeng Youngu: 1952–2000 – Seongeokangryenge Daehan Gongganjeok Bunseogeul Jungsimeuro' ('Research on party competitions: 1952–2000-analysis of ideological spectrum through party platforms'). *Hanguk Jeongchi Hakhoe* (*Journal of the Korean Political Science Association*) 38(2): 189–215.

Im, Hyugbaeg (1997). 'Jiyeondoego Issneun Minjujuui-ui Gonggohwa' ('Faltering Democratic Consolidation'). *Hanguk Sahoewa Minjujuu: Hanguk Minjuhwa 10 Nyeonui Pyeonggawa Banseong* (*Korean Society and Democracy: Democratization and its Evaluation*), Jang-jip. Choi and Hyugbaeg Im, eds. Seoul, Nanam Publisher.

Im, Hyugbaeg (2004). 'Faltering Democratic Consolidation in South Korea: Democracy at the End of the "Three Kims" Era.' *Democratization* 11(5): 179–198.

Jang, Gipyo (1991). 'Jeongdangchejil Gaeseon Banghyanggwa Hyundaejeok Jeongdangui Yogeon' ('The Direction of Political Party Reform and Conditions of Modern Political Party'). *Gyegan Sasang* (*Quarterly Thought*) Winter: 73–88.

Jang, Hoon (1997). *Jeongdang Jeongchiwa Jibangjachi; Hanguk Minjuhwa 10 Nyeonui Jeongdang Jeongchi; Yeonsokseonggwa Byeonhwa* (*Party Politics and Local Politics*). Hanguk Jeongchi Hakhoe Conference, Seoul, Hanguk Jeongchi Hakhoe.

Jang, Hoon (2003). 'Cartel Jeongdangchejeui Hyeongseonggwa Baljeon: Minjuhwa Ihuui Hangukui Gyeongu' ('The Rise of the Cartel Party System in Democratic Korea'). *Hangukgwa Gukjejeongchi* (*Korea and International Relations*) 19(4): 31–60.

Jeong, Geunsik (1997). 'Minjuhwa, Jiyeogjuuiwa Jibangjachi.' *Hanguk Sahoewa Minjujuui: Hanguk Minjuhwa 10 Nyeonui Pyeonggawa Banseong* (*Korean Society and Democracy: Democratisation and its Evaluation*), Jang-jip Choi and Hyukbaeg Im, eds. Seoul, Nanam Publisher.

Jeong, Youngguk (2000). 'Hangukjeongdangui Jigudang Jojiggwa Gineung' ('Organizational System and Functions of the District Party Chapters in Korean Politics: An Alternative Argument'). *Hangukgwa Gukjejeongchi* (*Korea and International Relations*) 6: 225–250.

Jo, Gi-suk (2000). *Hapnijeok Seontaekgwa Hangukjeongchi: Hangukui Jiyyeokjuui Seongeowa Minjuhwa* (*Rational Choice and Politics in South Korea: Democratization and Regionalism in Election in South Korea*). Hanguk Jeongchi Yeonguwonhoe (Korean Political Studies Researchers' Conference).

Kang, David (2002). *Crony Capitalism: Corruption and Development in South Korea and the Philippines*. Cambridge, Cambridge University Press.

Kang, David (2003). 'Regional Politics and Democratic Consolidation in Korea.' *Korea's Democratization*, Samuel S. Kim, ed. Cambridge, Cambridge University Press.

Kang, Wontaek (2005). 'Ideological Clash of Progressives and Conservatives in Korea.' *Korean Party Studies Review* 4(2): 1–13.

Kato, Junko and Yuto Kannon (2008). 'Coalition Governments, Party Switching, and the Rise and Decline of Parties: Changing Japanese Party Politics since 1993.' *Japanese Journal of Political Science* 9(3): 341–365.

Katz, Richard and Peter Mair (1995). 'Changing Models of Party Organization and Party Democracy: The Emergence of the Cartel Party.' *Party Politics* 1(1): 5–28.

Keat, Russell and John Urry (1975). *Social Theory as Science*. London, Routledge & Kegan Paul.

Kersbergen, Kees Van and France Van Waarden (2004). 'Governance as a Bridge Between Disciplines: Cross-Disciplinary Inspiration Regarding Shifts in Governance and Problems of Governability, Accountability and Legitimacy.' *European Journal of Political Research* 43(2): 143–171.

Key, V.O. (1964). *Public Opinion and Public Policy Models of Political Linkage*. New Haven, Yale University Press.

Kil, Soonghoom (1990). 'Hanguke Isseoseo Jeongdangjeongchiwa Jeongchimunhwa' ('Party Politics and Political Culture'). *Hanguk Nondan* 4: 46–53.

Kil, Soonghoom and Chungin Moon (2001). *Understanding Korean Politics: An Introduction*. New York, State University of New York Press.

Kim, Byung-kook (1999a). 'Hangukjeok Bosu: Jeontong Munhwaui Heowa Sil' ('Conservatism in South Korea: The Truth and Untruth of Traditional Culture'). *Hangukjeok Bosu* (*Conservatism in South Korea*), Byung-kook Kim, Yongmin Kim, Hyojong Park, Byunghoon Seo and Chaebong Hahm, eds. Seoul, Ingansarang: 241–307.

Kim, Byung-kook, Yong-min Kim, Hyojong Park, Byunghoon Seo and Chaebong Hahm, eds. (1999). *Hangukui Bosujuui* (*Conservatism in South Korea*). Seoul, Ingan Sarang.

Kim, Dojong and Hyeongjun Kim (2000). *Je 16dae Gukhoeuiwon Seongeogyeolgwae Daehan Bunseok: Jiphapjaryoreul Jungsimeuro* (*The Analysis of the Sixteenth General Election Result: From Collective Data*). 16dae Chongseon Pyeongga Haksulhoeui (Evaluation for the Sixteenth General Election), Seoul, Hanguk Jeongchihakhoe (Korean Political Science Association).

Kim, HeeMin (1994a). 'Hangug 3Dang Habdangui Woningwa Gyeolgwa' ('The Cause and Result of Three Party Merger in South Korea'). *Jeongdang Gudoron* (*Party System Realignment*), Jaehan Kim, ed. Seoul, Nanam Publisher: 45–83.

Kim, HeeMin (1997). 'Rational Choice Theory and Third World Politics: The 1990 Party Merger in Korea.' *Comparative Politics* 30(1): 83–100.

Kim, Hyeonu (2000). *Hangug Jeongdangtonghab Undongsa* (*History of Coalition Building in South Korea*). Seoul, Eulyoo Munhwasa.

Kim, Hyung-a (2004a). *Korea's Development Under Park Chung Hee: Rapid Industrialization 1961–79*. New York, Routledge Cruzon.

Kim, Jaehan, ed. (1994b). *Jeongdang Gudoron* (*Party System Realignment*). Seoul, Nanam Publisher.

Kim, Pan-seok (2004b). 'Daetongryeonggwa Insa: Jeongmu Gowijik Insahyeoksin' ('Presidential Personnel: Personnel Reform for Presidential Appointees'). *Hanguk Jeongchi Hakhoe* (*Journal of the Korean Political Science Association*) 37(2): 385–414.

Kim, Yong-ho (1998). '97nyeon Daeseone Daehan Jonghapjeogin Bunseok' ('Analysis of Presidential Election in 1997'). *Hangukeu Seongeo 2* (*Elections in South Korea*), K.E.S. Association, ed. Seoul, Pureungil.

Kim, Yong-ho (2001). *Hanguk Jeongdang Jeongchiui ihae* (*Understanding Party Politics in Korea*). Seoul, Nanam Publisher.

Kim, Yong-ho (2002). 'Gobiyong Jeongdanggujowa Jeongchijageumjedo Gaeseonbangan' ('A Proposal for Reforming the High-Cost Party Structure and Political Finance System in South Korea'). *Daehan Jeongchi Hakhoebo* (*Journal of Korean Political Society*) 10(2): 295–306.

Kim, Yongmin (1999b). 'Seogu Bosujuuiui Giwongwa Baljeon' ('The Origin of Conservatism in Western Society and Development'). *Hangukui Bosujuui* (*Conservatism in South Korea*), Byung-kook Kim, Yongmin Kim, Hyojong Park, Byunghoon Seo and Chaebong Hahm, eds. Seoul, Ingansarang.

Kim, Youngmi (2008a). 'Explaining Minority Coalition Government and Governability in South Korea: a Review Essay.' *Korea Observer* 39(1): 59–84.

Kim, Youngmi (2008b). 'Fission, Fusion, Reform and Failure: Roh Moo-hyun's Administration.' *Korea Yearbook 2008*, Rüdiger Frank, James E. Hoare, Patrick Köllner and Susan Pares, eds. Leiden, Brill: 73–94.

Kim, Youngmi (2008c). 'Intra-Party Politics and Minority Coalition Government in South Korea.' *Japanese Journal of Political Science* 9(3): 367–398.

Kim, Youngmi (2009). 'Digital Populism in South Korea? Internet Culture and the Trouble with Direct Participation.' *KEI Academic Paper Series 'On Korea 2009'* 2: 143–156.

Laver, Michael (1989). 'Party Competition and Party System Change: The Interaction of Electoral Bargaining and Party Competition.' *Journal of Theoretical Politics* 1: 301–325.

Laver, Michael (2001). 'Party System Dynamics in Japan and Italy: Introduction.' *Electoral Studies* 20(4): 505–507.

Laver, Michael and Daniela Giannetti (2001). 'Party System Dynamics and the Making and Breaking of the Italian Governments.' *Electoral Studies* 20(4): 529–553.

Laver, Michael and Junko Kato (2001). 'Dynamics Approaches to Government Formation and the Genetic Instability of Decisive Structures in Japan.' *Electoral Studies* 20(4): 509–527.

Laver, Michael and Norman Schofield (1990). *Multiparty Government: The Politics of Coalition in Europe*. Oxford, Oxford University Press.

Laver, Michael and John Underhill (1982). 'The Bargaining Advantages of Combining with Others.' *British Journal of Political Science* 12: 75–90.

Lawson, Kay (1988). 'When Linkage Fails.' *When Parties Fail: Emerging Alternative Organizations*, Kay Lawson and Peter H. Merkl, eds. Princeton, Princeton University Press: 13–38.

Lawson, Kay and Peter H. Merkl (1988). *When Parties Fail: Emerging Alternative Organizations*. Princeton, Princeton University Press.

Lee, Byung-hyu (1991). *Jiyeok Galdeungui Yeoksa* (*History of Regional Conflicts*). Seoul, Hakminsa.

Lee, Gap-yun (1998). *Hangukui Sungeowa Jiyeokjuui* (*Regionalism and Elections in Korea*). Seoul, Oreum Publisher.

Lee, Sunhwa and Mary C. Brinton (1996). 'Elite Education and Social Capital: The Case of South Korea.' *Sociology of Education* 69: 177–192.

Lee, Tae-ho (2006). 'Kukhoeui uiwon hwaldong pyeongga' ('Assessment of Legislators' Activity'). *Eujeong Yeongu* (*Parliamentary Politics Review*) 21: 131–158.

Lees, Charles (2000). *The Red–Green Coalition in Germany: Politics, Personalities and Power*. Manchester, Manchester University Press.

Leiserson, Michael (1968). 'Factions and Coalitions in One-Party Japan: An Interpretation Based on the Theory of Games.' *American Political Science Review* 62: 770–787.
Linz, Juan J. (1990). 'The Perils of Presidentialism.' *Journal of Democracy* 1(1): 51–69.
Linz, Juan J. and Arturo Valenzuela (1994). *The Failure of Presidential Democracy: The Case of Latin America*. Baltimore, Johns Hopkins University Press.
Lipset, Seymour M. (1959). 'Some Social Requisites of Democracy: Economic Development and Political Legitimacy.' *American Political Science Review* 53: 69–105.
Lipset, Seymour M. and Stein Rokkan (1967). 'Cleavage Structure, Party Systems, and Voter Alignment: An Introduction.' *Party Systems and Voter Alignment: Cross-National Perspectives*, Seymour M. Lipset and Stein Rokkan, eds. New York, Free Press.
Little, Daniel (1991). *Varieties of Social Explanation: An Introduction to the Philosophy of Social Science*. Boulder, Westview Press.
Mainwaring, Scott (1993). 'Presidentialism, Multipartism, and Democracy: The Difficult Combination.' *Comparative Political Studies* 26: 198–228.
Mainwaring, Scott (1997). 'Multipartism, Robust Federalism and Presidentialism.' *Presidentialism and Democracy in Latin America*, Scott Mainwaring and Matthew Shugart, eds. Cambridge, Cambridge University Press.
Mainwaring, Scott (1998). 'Party Systems in the Third Wave.' *Journal of Democracy* 9(3): 67–81.
Mainwaring, Scott and Timothy R. Scully, eds (1995). *Building Democratic Institutions: Party Systems in Latin America*. Stanford, Stanford University Press.
Mainwaring, Scott and Matthew Soberg Shugart (1997). *Presidentialism and Democracy in Latin America*. Cambridge, Cambridge University Press.
Mair, Peter (1990). *The West European System*. Oxford, Oxford University Press.
Mair, Peter and Ingrid van Biezen (2001). 'Party Membership in Twenty European Democracies, 1980–2000.' *Party Politics* 7(1): 5–21.
Mannheim, Jarol B. and Richard C. Rich (1995). *Empirical Political Analysis: Research Methods in Political Science*. New York, Longman.
Martin, Lanny W. and Randolph T. Stevenson (2001). 'Government Formation in Parliamentary Democracies.' *American Journal of Political Science* 45(1): 33–50.
Martin, Lanny W. and George Vanderber (2003). 'Wasting Time? The Impact of Ideology and Size on Delay in Coalition Formation.' *British Journal of Political Science* 33(2): 323–332.
Mershon, Carol (2001). 'Party Factions and Coalition Government: Portfolio Allocation in Italian Governments.' *Electoral Studies* 20(4): 555–580.
Mershon, Carol (2002). *The Costs of Coalition*. Stanford, Stanford University Press.
Mershon, Carol (2008). 'Legislative Party Switching and Executive Coalitions.' *Japanese Journal of Political Science* 9(3): 391–414.
Meyhew, David R. (1991). *Divided We Govern: Party Control, Lawmaking, and Investigations 1946–1990*. New Haven, Yale University Press.
Miller, Robert L., Ciaran Acton, Deirdre A. Fullerton and John Maltby, eds (2002). *SPSS for Social Scientists*. New York, Palgrave.
Mo, Jong-ryn (2001). 'Strong Government and the Challenge of Democratic Governance.' *Korea Focus* 9(3): 1–10.
Moore, Barrington Jr (1966). *Social Origins of Dictatorship and Democracy*. Boston, Beacon Press.
Negretto, Gabriel L. (2003). *Minority Presidents and Types of Government in Latin America*. The 2003 Meeting of the Latin American Studies Association, Dallas.

Negretto, Gabriel L. (2004). 'Government Capacity and Policy Making by Decree in Latin America: The Cases of Brazil and Argentina.' *Comparative Political Studies* 37(5): 531–562.

Norris, Pippa (1997). 'Choosing Electoral Systems: Proportional, Majoritarian and Mixed Systems.' *International Political Science Review* 18(3): 297–312.

O'Donnell, Guillermo A. (1994). 'Delegative Democracy.' *Journal of Democracy* 5(1).

Panebianco, Angelo (1988). *Political Parties: Organization and Power*. Cambridge, Cambridge University Press.

Park, Chanpyo (2002). *Hangukeuhoejeongchiwa Minjujuui: Bigyouihoeronui Sigak* (*National Assembly and Democracy in Korea: In Comparative Perspective*). Seoul, Oreum.

Park, Chanpyo (2003). 'Hanguk Jeongdang Minjuhwaronui Banseongjeok Seongchal: Jeongdang Minjuhwainga taljeongdanginga?' ('Reflective Aspects on Party Democracy in South Korea: Is It Party Democracy or Defecting from Party?'). *Sahoe Gwahak Yeongu* (*Social Science Studies*) 11: 137–164.

Park, Chanwook (2000). *IMF Ihu Hanguk Jeongchigaehyeog-ui Gwaje-wa Gughoe-ui Yeoghal* (*Political Reform Task and the Role of the Legislature in South Korea After IMF Governance*). Post IMF Governance Hagye Hagsulhoeui (Summer conference on Post IMF Governance), Seoul, Hanguk Jeongchi Haghoe (Korean Political Science Association).

Pech, Gerald (2001). *Coalition Governments Versus Minority Governments: Re-Election Uncertainty, Cohesion and Budgeting Outcomes*. The 2001 Annual Meeting of the American Political Science Association, San Francisco.

Popper, Karl R. (1959). *The Logic of Scientific Discovery*. London, Hutchinson.

Pye, Lucian W. (1985). *Asian Power and Politics: The Cultural Dimensions of Authority*. Cambridge, MA, Harvard University Press.

Randall, Vicky and Lars Svåsand (2002). 'Party Institutionalization in New Democracies.' *Party Politics* 8(1): 5–29.

Riker, William (1962). *The Theory of Political Coalitions*. New Haven, London, Yale University Press.

Roh, Jeong-ho (2003). 'Crafting and Consolidating Constitutional Democracy.' *Korea's Democratization*, Samuel S. Kim, ed. Cambridge, Cambridge University Press.

Roh, Moo-hyun (2009). *Seonggonggwa Jwajeol* (*Success and Frustration*). Seoul, Hakgojae.

Roper, Steven D. (2002). 'Are All Semipresidential Regimes the Same? A Comparison of Premier Presidential Regimes.' *Comparative Politics* 34(3): 253–72.

Rosenberg, Alexander (1988, 1995). *Philosophy of Social Science*. Oxford, Westview Press.

Sartori, Giovanni (1976). *Parties and Party Systems: A Framework for Analysis, Vol. I*. Cambridge, Cambridge University Press.

Sartori, Giovanni (1994). 'Neither Presidentialism nor Parliamentarism.' *The Failure of Presidential Democracy: The Case of Latin America*, Juan J. Linz and Arturo Valenzuela, eds. Baltimore, Johns Hopkins University Press: 106–118.

Sartori, Giovanni (1997). *Comparative Constitutional Engineering: An Inquiry into Structures, Incentives and Outcomes*. London, Macmillan.

Schofield, Norman (1983). 'Genetic Instability of Majority Rule.' *Review of Economic Studies* 50: 695–705.

Schofield, Norman (1993). 'Political Competition and Multiparty Coalition Governments.' *European Journal of Political Research* 23: 1–33.

Bibliography

Seo, Byounghoon (1999). 'Hanguk Bosujuuiui Seonggyeokgwa Baljeon Banghyang' ('Characteristics of Conservatism in South Korea and its Development Direction'). *Hangukui Bosujuui* (*Conservatism in South Korea*), Byung-kook Kim, Yongmin Kim, Hyojong Park, Byunghoon Seo and Chaebong Hahm, eds. Seoul, Ingan Sarang: 53–109.

Shapiro, Ian (1998). 'Can the Rational Choice Framework Cope with Culture?' *Political Science and Politics* 31: 40–42.

Shapiro, Ian (2002). 'Problems, Methods, and Theories in the Study of Politics, or What's Wrong with Political Science and What to Do About It?' *Political Theory* 30: 588–611.

Shapiro, Ian and Donald P. Green (1994). *Pathology of Rational Choice Theory: A Critique of Applications in Political Science*. New Haven, Yale University Press.

Shin, Bok-ryong (1996). 'Hangukui Jiyeokgamjeongui Yeoksajeok Baegyeong' ('Historical Background of Regional Conflicts in Korea'). *Reflectives of Modern Korean Politics: Pre-Modernity, Modernity and Post-modernity*. K.P.S. Association.

Shin, Dohcheol (1999). *Mass Politics and Culture in Democratizing Korea*. Cambridge, Cambridge University Press.

Sim, Jiyeon and Minjeon Kim (2002). 'Hanguk Jeongdangui Suipgujo yeongu – 1997–2002 Nyeondo Jeongdang Hoegyebogo Jaryoreul jungsimeuro' ('Revenue Structure of Korean Political Parties'). *Hangukwa Gukjejeongchi* (*South Korea and International Relations*) 38(3): 151–186.

Son, Hyeokjae (1999). 'Gukmin Musihan Jeongchigwonui Saepanjjagi: Jeonggyegaepyeonui Hyeonhwanggwa Gwaje' ('Making New Political Frame Ignoring People: The Situation and Assignments of Political Reorganization'). *Donghyanggwa Jeonmang* (*Tendency and Prospect*) Summer: 1–14.

Son, Keyyoung (2006). *South Korean Engagement Policies and North Korea: Identities, Norms and the Sunshine Policy*. London, Routledge.

Stepan, Alfred and Cindy Skach (1993). 'Constitutional Frameworks and Democratic Consolidation: Parliamentarism Versus Presidentialism.' *World Politics* 46 (1): 1–22.

Strøm, Kaare (1990). *Minority Government and Majority Rule*. Cambridge, Cambridge University Press.

Strøm, Kaare and Woolfgang C. Müller, eds (2000). *Coalition Governments in Western Europe*. Oxford, Oxford University Press.

Strøm, Kaare and Woolfgang C. Müller (2001). *Coalition Agreement and Governance*. The Annual Meeting of the American Political Science Association, San Francisco.

Taylor, Michael and Michael Laver (1973). 'Government Coalitions in Western Europe.' *European Journal of Political Research* 1: 205–248.

Tsebelis, George (2002). *Veto Players: How Political Institutions Work*. New York, Russell Sage Foundation.

Von Beyme, Klaus (1984). *Political Parties in Western Democracies*. Aldershot, Gower.

Von Newmann, John and Oskar Morgenstern (1953). *Theory of Games and Economic Behaviour*. Princeton, Princeton University Press.

Woldendrop, Jaap, Hans Keman and Ian Budge, eds (2001). *Party Government in 48 Democracies: Composition–Duration–Personnel*. Dordrecht, Kluwer.

Yap, Fiona. O. (2008). 'Executive–Legislature Divide and Party Volatility in Emergent Democracies: Lessons for Democratic Performance from Taiwan.' *Japanese Journal of Political Science* 9(3): 305–322.

Yap, Fiona and Youngmi Kim (2008). 'Pathologies or Progress? Evaluating the Effects of Divided Government and Party Volatility.' *Japanese Journal of Political Science* 9(3): 261–268.

Yin, Robert K. (1989). *Case Study Research: Design and Method*. Newbury Park, Sage.
Yu, Seok-chun and Hye-suk Wang (2006). *Chamyeo Yeondae Bogoseo (Report on Civil Organizations)*. Seoul, Jayugieopwon.

Internet sources

Democratization Activists' Family Association (*Mingahyeoup*). *Boanbeob Byeoncheonsa (History of National Security Law)* Available from: www.yangsimsu.or.kr/boanbub/byun_chun.htm (accessed 4 October 2004).
Gi, Gwang-seo (2004). *Story of North Korean History (Bukhan Yeoksa Iyagi)*. Korean History Association Website. Available from: www.koreanhistory.org/webzine/read.php?pid=6&id=46 (accessed 20 August 2006).
Kim, Sung-suk and Jip Kim (1999). *Saimdang Hanmun Seodang (Chinese Letter Class)*. Available from: http://user.chollian.net/~k71421/myung1.htm (accessed 16 April 2006).
Ledyard, Gari Keith (2000). *Yusin*. Available from: http://koreaweb.ws/pipermail/ksopen_koreaweb.ws/2000-December/000011.html (accessed 26 August 2006).
Lightning Bill Passing. *Donga Ilbo*, *English Donga*, 24 July 2000. Available from: http://english.donga.com/srv/service.php3?biid=2000072534158 (accessed 24 October 2004).
May Memorial Foundation website: www.518.org/main.html?TM18MF=A030106 (accessed 2 June 2006).
Oh My News website, 9 December 2005. Available from: www.ohmynews.com/articleview/article_view.asp?no=263007&rel_no=1 (Accessed 5 October 2006).
Roh, Gyeong-sang (2001). *Korea Old Arts Network*. Available from: http://kr.oldarts.net/en/sub.php3?cell=A&dir=help&load=menu&lang=html&load2=sagunja&lang2=html (accessed 9 September 2004).
Samgang-rok 三綱錄 Chungsin-pyeon 忠臣編, a government record published every year under the Joseon Dynasty (in the seventeenth and eighteenth centuries). Available from: http://hometopia.com/cgi/bbs/bbs.cgi?db=provQnA&mode=read&num (accessed 3 January 2004).
4.19 Student Uprising. Available from: http://ko.wikipedia.org/wiki/4.19_%ED%98%81%EB%AA%85 (accessed 20 September 2004).

Government websites

Government Buildings Management Service. Available from: www.chungsa.go.kr/ (accessed from 1 September 2003 to 30 September 2010).
Korea.net: Gateway to Korea. Available from: www.allim.go.kr/warp/webapp/home/kr_home (accessed from 1 September 2003 to 30 September 2010).
Korea E-government. Available from: www.egov.go.kr/default.html (accessed from 1 September 2003 to 30 September 2010).
Korean Integrated News Database System. Available from: www.kinds.or.kr/ (accessed from 1 September 2003 to 30 September 2010).
Korean National Assembly. Available from: www.assembly.go.kr:8000/ifh/html/index.html (accessed from 1 September 2003 to 30 September 2010).
National Archives and Records Service. Available from: www.archives.go.kr/ (accessed from 1 September 2003 to 30 September 2010).

National Assembly. Available from: www.assembly.go.kr/ (accessed from 1 September 2003 to 30 September 2010).
National Assembly Progress Reports. Available from: www.assembly.go.kr:8000/oth/html/index_2.html (accessed from 1 September 2003 to 30 September 2010).
National Assembly Secretariat. Available from: http://nas.assembly.go.kr/ (accessed from 1 September 2003 to 30 September 2010).
National Election Commission. Available from: www.nec.go.kr/index.html (accessed from 1 September 2003 to 30 September 2010).
The R.O.K. Official Web Portal. Available from: www.gcc.go.kr/index.asp (accessed from 1 September 2003 to 30 September 2006).

Daily newspapers

Break News (www.breaknews.com)
Chosun Ilbo
Donga Ilbo
Hankook Ilbo
Hankook Kyungje
Hankyoreh Sinmun
Jungang Ilbo
Kukmin Ilbo
Kyunghyang Sinmun
Maeil Kyeongje
Munwha Ilbo
Oh My News (www.ohmynews.com)
Segyeo Ilbo
Seoul Economy
Seoul Kyeongje Sinmun
Seoul Sinmun
Yonhap News (www.yonhapnews.co.kr)

Weekly magazines

Hankook Weekly
Hankyoreh 21

Monthly magazines

Monthly Chosun
Sin Donga
Voice of People

Index

'4.19 movement' 20
'6.29 democratization declaration' (1987) 28–9, 97

administrative offices, relocation of 165–7
anti-candidate movement 62–4, 117–18, 119
anti-communism 19–20, 132, 133, 134, 139, 140–2, 158, 171
Anti-Communist Law (1961) 25–6, 141–2, 143
approval votes, prime minister 53–6
Asian financial crisis (1997) 3, 45, 46, 106
authoritarian governments 25, 28, 29, 30, 32–4, 43, 56, 131–2, 156
autonomy, parties 12–13
Axelrod, Robert 8, 9, 123

Bäck Hanna 6
Bae Gi-seon 60, 146
Baron, David 123
Barrington Moore 30
Bi-cameral parliamentary systems 20
Blue House 89
Bogdanor, Vernon 2, 5
book structure 15–17
Brazil, intra-party politics 9
bribery 57, 87, 163
British Labour Party 71, 129
Budge, Ian 123, 127
Buil Janghakhoe 157, 159

cadre parties 71–6
Caesarean presidents 56
candidates: appointment of 34, 40–1, 42, 74, 83, 86–7, 101–3; funding from 76, 78, 79; recruitment of 71; *see also* anti-candidate movement
candlelight vigils 161–3

cartel parties 74–6
Carter Jimmy 28
catch-all parties 37, 48, 49, 74, 124
censorship 140
centre-right parties 129–42
Chae Jangsu 132
charismatic leadership 14, 31, 32, 43, 82, 83, 95, 98, 171
Cheibub, Jose Antonio 2, 5, 6, 8, 9, 10, 51, 52, 67, 68, 113, 160, 172, 176
Chernykh, Svitlana 2, 8, 51, 176
Chile, parliamentarianism 21
Cho Sun 55, 61
Choi Jang-jip 19, 21, 25, 26, 29, 30, 32, 34, 43, 44, 56, 100, 103, 122, 124, 131, 132, 134, 158, 169
Choi Junyeong and Soonheung Kim 107
Choi Kyu-ha 26
Chun Doo-hwan 25–6, 27–8, 38, 43
Chun Yong-aek 55
Chung Dong-Young 161
Chung Ju-young 42, 43
Chung Mong-joon 2, 98
Chung-soo Janghakhoe 157, 159
Chungcheong province: administrative offices in 165–7; economic development 27; officials from 89–90; regionalism 54, 83, 95–108, 118–19; voting patterns 62, 64, 113–14
Citizens' Coalition for Economic Justice 117, 118
civil organizations: anti-candidate movement 62–4, 117–18; involvement in politics 63, 119
Civil Rule Party 22
civilian government, emergence of 42–3
closed party lists 109, 110–13
coalition politics 2–3: after democratization 34–9; conflicts of interest within 39–41; study of 7–8

Index

coalitions, explaining 5–8
Cold War 19, 85, 124, 129, 132
Colomer, Josep M. 2
communism *see* anti-Communism
compromise process, electoral law reform 108–20
conflicts of interest: coalition party/opposition (1990) 39–41; electoral system 116–20; fission and fusion of political actors 58–61
Confucian culture 34, 54, 58, 77, 79, 101, 107, 129, 146, 171
conservative ideology 127–42
constitutional court 111
constitutional reform 31, 39–40, 41, 42, 52–3, 59, 98–9
Coppedge, Michael 2, 7, 177
corruption 91, 163; campaign against 62–4
Creative Korea Party 166
Croissant, Aurel 8
cross-voting system 144, 146, 147–8, 151–2, 175
Cumings, Bruce 19, 20, 21, 22, 24, 25, 28, 42

De Swaan, Abram 123
De Winter, Lieven 2, 5, 6
decision making powers 83–4
democratic consolidation period, party system during 29–48, 171
Democratic Justice Party 2, 27, 28, 36, 37, 39, 40, 60, 97, 98
Democratic Korea Party 38
Democratic Labour Party (DLP) 85, 154, 158, 160; election performance 166
Democratic Liberal Party 2, 39, 42–3, 97
Democratic Party (DP) 20–1, 22, 45, 80, 112; election performance 42, 43, 166
Democratic Republican Party 21–2, 54, 80, 97
democratization movement 26, 27, 28, 38, 43, 134
democratization: coalition politics after 34–9; eve of 30–4; process of 101–3
Diamond, Larry 13, 28, 29, 97, 169
district size, electoral system 115–16
divided governments 6–7
Donggyo-dong faction 67, 87–8
Duverger, Maurice 72

EAI Political and Social Survey 125
East Asia Institute 14, 15, 135
Eckstein, Harry 177

economic reform 24, 44, 52–3, 106–7, 109, 129, 131, 156
economy 20
educational reform: Lee Myung-bak administration 161–3; Roo Moo-hyun administration 158–9
Electoral Campaign Law Act 87 117–18, 119, 174
electoral campaigning 76–7
electoral districts, changes to 109–20
electoral law reform 12, 173–4; chronology of process of 120; conflicts of interests and outcome of new laws 116–20; gerrymandering agreement/criticism of 117–20; parties' stances 109–16; partial law amendment and aftermath 116–17
electoral success 3–5
Elgie, Robert 2, 5, 6, 8, 9, 51, 176, 177
elites 29–30, 37, 38, 44, 63, 80, 83, 96–8, 107
engagement policy 124; *see also* Sunshine Policy
English language teaching 162
European Consortium for Political Research (ECPR) 132

factionalism 34, 40–1, 43, 45, 52–3, 163; internal conflict between ULD/NCNP 86–7; opposition party leaders 32; within NCNP,/MDP 87–91
Fifth Republic (1980–1987) 25–8
Figueiredo Angelina C. 5, 9, 176
finance, parties 71, 72–4, 76–82, 172
First Republic (1948–1960) 19–20
floor leaders meetings 83–4
floor negotiation groups, importance of 64–9
Four-River Reconstruction Project 165–7
Fourth Republic (1972–1979) 24–5
free trade agreement (FTA), US 161–3
freedom of speech 140–2
Future Hope Alliance 165–6

Gangwon province: candidate nomination 86–7; economic development 27; regionalism 95–108, 124; voting patterns 83, 111, 112
'gate scandals' 69
general election results 104–6
generational conflict, GBP 143–6
German-style electoral system 109–20, 160
gerrymandering agreement 117–20

Giannetti, Daniela 4
governability: impact of 70–91; lack of 3–5, 52–3; and party size 6–7, 9–10, 69–70
government size: and approval votes for prime minister 53–6; and coalition break-up 62–4; and conflicts of interest 58–61; and 'floor negotiation groups' 64–9; and stability 6–7; and voting on legislation 57–8; unimportance of 69–70
Gramsci, Antonio 30
grand conservative coalition (1990) 34–9; demise of 45–6
Grand National Party (GNP): coalition with Uri Party 159–61; conflicts 172–3, 175; defections to 69, 165; and electoral law reform 109, 112, 115–16, 118–19; electoral performance 46, 47, 64, 83, 104–5, 159, 160, 161, 163, 166; factionalism 60–1, 90; funding 77–8; and floor groups 66–7; generational shift within 143–6; ideology 129, 133; and National Security Law 143–6; in opposition 59, 64, 68; 171–2; and PM approval vote 54–5, 57; and Private School Law 158–9
Gwangju high school 89
Gwangju uprising 26, 27, 28, 38, 43, 134, 142
Gyeonggi high school 89
Gyenoggi province: officials from 89; regionalism 101, 107; voting patterns 33–4, 54, 166–7
Gyeong-nam high school 89
Gyeongsang province (Yeongnam region): economic development 27; and electoral law changes 117; officials from 89–90; regionalism 95–108, 123–5, 134–5, 142; voting patterns 23–4, 33–4, 54, 64, 83, 116

Ham Seok-heon 139
Han Honggu 132
Hanahoe faction 43
Hankook Ilbo 134
Hannara Party *see* Grand National Party (GNP)
Helgesen, Geir 80
Henderson, Gregory 27
high school alumni networks 88–9
historical perspective, coalition politics 2–3, 171
Hong Ik-pyo 22
Huber, John D. 7

human rights violations 156–7
Huntington, Samuel 7, 61
hybrid ideology 129
hypotheses 11
Hyun Jae-ho 147
Hyung-a Kim 156

ideological distance 132–9
ideology: conflicts and institutionalization 174–5; differences among voters and parties 123–39; influence of National Security Law 140–2
Im Dong-won 69, 149
Im Hyugbaeg 28, 95, 97
impeachment 154, 162
Independent Central Committee 19
institutional restructuring 110–20
institutionalization: parties/party systems 9–14, 108, 173–5; party organization 171–3
inter-party conflicts: explaining 52–70; ULD/NCNP coalition 86–7
inter-party politics 10–11
International Monetary Fund (IMF) 109, 129
intra-party conflicts: explaining 52–70; NCNP 87–91
intra-party politics 10–11, 171–2

Jaebeols 28, 43–4, 129, 134
Jaeya 139
Jang Hoon 74–5
Jang Jun-ha 139
Jang Myeon 20
Jang Seong-min 145
Japan, relations with 22–3
Jeolla province (Honan region): economic development 27; and electoral law changes 110–13, 117; officials from 88–90; regionalism 23–4, 64, 95–108, 134–5; voting patterns 23–4, 26–7, 36, 46, 82–3
Jeong Geunsik 28
Jeong, Youngguk 72
Jeongchi Gaehyeogeulwihan Miom 143–4
'*Jeonggye-Gaepyeon*' 36–8
Jeonju high school 89
Jo Bong-am 140–1
Jo Yong-su 140
Joseon Communist Party 19
Joseon Dynasty 18, 27, 129, 131
Ju Yang-ja 91

Kang Chang-hee 69, 146

Kang, David 107
Kang Wontaek 122, 132–3, 134
Kannon, Yuto 4
Kato, Junko 4, 8
Katz, Richard 74, 75
KBS (Korea Broadcasting System) 162
Kennedy, John F. 22–3
Kersbergen, Kees Van 6
Key, V.O. 85
Kil Soonghoom 72, 85, 131, 132, 169, 176
Kim Byung-kook 29, 45, 97, 122, 124, 131, 132
Kim Dae-Jung 32, 38, 42, 45, 46, 82, 110, 112–13, 135, 143, 148, 149, 150, 163, 170; administration of 3, 4, 5, 10–11, 15, 46–8, 51–93; death of 24; electoral performance 23–4, 33–4, 36, 43, 46; founding of National Congress for New Politics Party 45; founding of Peace Democratic Party 31; and Gwangju massacre 26; imprisonment of 30; origins and challenges of administration of 46–8; and regionalism 95–108; re-entry into political life 30–1; as victim of oppression 26–7
Kim Dojong 105
Kim Go-seong 118
Kim HeeMin 31, 36–7
Kim Hyeonu 21, 28, 169
Kim Ji-tae 157
Kim Jong-pil 21–2, 36, 38, 40, 41, 45–6, 53–4, 55, 58, 59, 61, 62, 65, 66, 68, 86, 114, 119, 147, 171; electoral performance 33–4, 150; founding of NDRP; founding of UDP 45; and regionalism 95–108
Kim Pan-seok 90, 91
Kim Soonheung 107
Kim Su-young 139
Kim Tae-jeong 91
Kim Yong-ho 32, 37, 58, 72, 73, 76, 97, 98
Kim Yong-hwan 61, 64, 69, 114
Kim Young-Sam 24–5, 31, 32, 38, 39–41, 44, 45, 62, 90, 163, 170; electoral performance 33–4, 36, 43; and first civilian government 42–3; founding of NKDP 28; founding of Unification Democratic Party 31; political reform under 43–4; and regionalism 95–108
Kim Youngmi 2, 4, 5, 6, 8, 51, 176
Korea Democratic Party 19, 20, 80
Korea New Party 59, 64, 69
Korea People's Party 38
Korea Society Opinion Institute 14, 164

Korea, study of coalition politics 7–8
Korean Central Intelligence Agency (KCIA) 21, 24, 27
Korean Integrated News Database System (KINDS) 14
Korean Social Science Data Centre 129–31
Korean War 19, 85, 129, 134, 142, 143; and Truth and Reconciliation Law (2005) 156–7

labour movement 24–5
'lame duck' presidents 44, 46, 56, 86, 159, 160
large-N research data 8, 9
Latin America: data sets 9, 10; presidential regime 6, 8
Laver, Michael 2, 4, 5, 6, 8, 9
Lawson, Kay 75–6, 85
Lawyers Society for Democracy 141
Lee Byung-hyu 95
Lee Cheol-seung 30–1
Lee Gap-yun 24, 26, 27, 32, 33, 34, 35, 45, 100, 101, 102
Lee Gi-taek 42, 45, 55, 61
Lee Hae-han 158
Lee Han-dong 60–1, 62, 64
Lee Hoe-chang 45, 46, 55, 60, 61, 64, 66, 82–3, 144, 145, 165; electoral performance 103–4
Lee In-je 45
Lee Myung-bak 4, 10, 15, 161–7; presidential performance 164
Lee Q-taek 165
Lee Sang-ryong 86
Lee Su-in 55
Lee Tae-ho 158
Lee Yang-hee 62
Lee Young-hee 139
Lees, Charles 6
left-wing ideology 129–42
legislation, inability to pass 57–8, 65–9, 83
legislators: effect of electoral reform 113; expenses 79–80; funding from 76, 78, 79; reductions in number of 110–20
legitimacy 83, 85
Leiserson, Michael 8, 9
Liberal Citizen Association 143
Liberal Democratic Party 21, 22, 76
Liberal Party 20
liberalism 132–3
Limongi, Fernando 5, 9, 51, 113, 176
Linz, Juan J. 2, 5, 6, 8, 54, 83
Lipset, Seymour M. 21

local councillors, reduction in number of 110–20
Local Election Law (1990) 41

McMenamin, Iain 2, 8, 51, 176
mad cow disease 162
Mainwaring, Scott 2, 5, 6, 7, 8, 9, 10, 13, 14, 21, 51, 67, 83, 113, 160, 170, 172
Mair, Peter 74, 75
major parties, effect of electoral reform 112
majority governments 39, 46–8, 153–68
martial law 21, 24, 26
Martin, Lanny W. 8
Martinez-Gallardo 7
mass media 44
mass parties 71–6, 84–5
Mayhew, David R. 6
MBC (Munhwa Broadcasting Corporation) 162
media power 164
Media Reform Law (2005) 157–8
membership fees 76, 77–8
Mershon, Carol 4, 6
military coup 21, 25–6, 38
minority governments 6–7, 8, 9
'miracle on the Han River' 22
mixed electoral system 12, 109–20, 160
Mixed Member Proportional Representation System 12, 109, 112, 160
Mo Jong-ryn 56
moderate pluralism 67–8
modern values 132–3
Müller, Woolfgang C. 2, 4, 5, 160
multi-member electoral districts 113–15
multi-party systems: effective number of parties 67–8; and governability 113

Nation Associations 143
National Assembly: Central Personnel Committee 91; Constitution Judge Committee 68; Legislation and Judiciary Committee 143; selection of legislators 59; Special Committee on Budget and Accounts 148; Structural Reform Special Committee 116–17, 118, 119
National Assembly Law 148
National Congress for New Politics Party (NCNP): electoral performance 46, 47, 105–6, 118; founding of 45; funding 77–8; and electoral law reform 109, 110, 111, 112, 115–16; internal conflict 86–7
National Election Commission, political donations to 77–82
National Security Law: adoption of 174–5; attempts to abolish 124–5, 126–7, 142–50, 172; candidates list 59; defections from 59; influence on party ideology 140–2; name change 61; and regionalism 108; reform of 154–6; role of 131–2; surveys on 125–7, 131, 133, 134–5, 139; use of 19, 25, 26, 170, 171
National Young Society 139
negotiation process, electoral law reform 108–20
Negretto, Gabriel L. 2, 5
New Congress for New Politics 45
New Democratic Party 20, 22, 23, 24–5, 31, 32, 40, 45, 98, 99, 100; electoral performance 38
New Democratic Republican Party 2, 28, 31, 39, 200
New Korea Democratic Party (NKDP) 98, 99, 100
New Korea Party (NKP) 23, 52, 108, 110, 111–12; electoral performance 45, 76, 105
New Millennium Democratic Party (MDP): and anti-candidate movement 62; conflict with ULD 65, 146–50; and electoral law reform 115–16; electoral performance 64, 104–5; factional conflict 87–91; and floor negotiation groups 66–7, 68, 69; ideology 129, 133; leadership 84; name change 61; and National Security Law 142–50; and Private School Law 158; protests against ruling party 70
newspaper market 157–8
Nixon, Richard 23
Norris, Pipa 160
North Korea: aid 124–7, 133, 163; migrants from 37; reunification issue 20, 135, 144; spies from 43, 140; threat from 37, 134–5, 140–2; *see also* Sunshine Policy
North Korean Labour Party 147

O'Donnell, Guillermo A. 29, 43
'oil shock' 24
opposition parties: Roh Moo-hyun's call for coalition with 159–61; conflicts of interest with 39–41; creation of 27–8; hindering integration of 98–100

Panebianco, Angelo 10, 12, 14, 49, 51–2, 70, 71, 82, 85
Park Chan-pyo 8, 47–8, 72

Park Chung-hee 23, 32, 100, 157, 159; assassination of 24, 38; and Gyeongsang province 27; electoral success 23–4; in military coup 21–2
Park Geun-hye 157, 163, 165–6
Park No-cheol 56
Park Sun-cheon 22, 23
Park Tae-jun 58–9, 61, 64, 114
parliamentary election results 104–6
parliamentary system 6–7, 8, 9, 21, 38–41, 58
parties: creation of 84, 154; institutionalization of 9–14; stances on electoral law reform 108–20
party actors, fission and fusion of 58–61
party branches 79, 81
party chairmen 83–4
party characteristics 71–6
party conflicts: from success to ungovernability 52–3; importance of party size 53–70
party defections 46–8, 60–1, 67, 69, 70, 146, 147, 149, 160–1, 165
party finance 71, 72–4, 76–82, 116–17, 172
party identification 13–14
party ideology: differences in 123–39; influence of National Security Law 140–2
party leaders 82–5; appointment of candidates 101–3; as 'father figures' 80, 116; funding from 80–1; loyalty to 81–2
party membership 72–4
party mergers 37, 39–40, 61, 97, 161, 165–6
party organization: characteristics of 71–6; factionalism 85–91; leadership 82–5; level of institutionalization 171–3
party stances 74–6, 80–2, 85, 109–16
party systems 171; emergence of new 41–2; formation of 29–48; institutionalization of 9–14; level of institutionalisation 173–4; under-development of 29–30
patron–client relationships 63, 80, 97
PD Sucheop 162
Peace Democratic Party (PDP) 31, 36, 37, 39
Pech, Gerald 4
People's Nation 64, 76
People's New Party 45
People's Participation Party 166
People's Party 19, 23, 34
People's Power 21 (PP21) Party 2, 98

People's Society for Abolishing National Security Law 143
People's Solidarity for Participatory Democracy 63, 143
personal rivalry 98–100
personalized party politics 32, 34, 56, 88, 101–3, 154, 171
personnel, appointment of 89–91
PK faction 67, 113
policies, development of 88
political deadlock 52–70
political donations 77–82
political elites 29–30, 37, 38, 44, 80, 96–8; power of 83
political opponents, repression of 140–2
Political Reform Lawmakers' Society 144
political reform: Kim Dae-Jung administration 46–8; Kim Young-sam administration 43–4
post-modern values 132–3
'premature' democracy 34, 103
presidential election results 35, **99**, 102–4
presidential performance, support for 163–4
presidential power 83–4
presidential systems 6–7, 8, 9, 21–2, 38–9
presidential term 42, 99
presidents, loyalty to 88
prime minister, approval votes for 53–6
Private School Law (2005) 79, 158–9
Pro-Park Geun-hye Alliance Party (PPA) 163, 165–6
progressive ideology 129–42
Progressive Party 140–1
proportional representation system 109–20
public opinion polls 14–15, 124–7, 133–4, 135; Media Reform 158; National Security Law 124–5, 156; policy preferences 129–42; presidential performance 164; Sunshine Policy 124–5
Pye, Lucian W. 80
Pyongyang festival 141, 142, 149, 150

Randall, Vicky 9, 10, 12–14, 108, 170, 174, 176
rational voting behaviour 107
regime type 6–9, 21
regional policy preferences 124–7, 134–5
regionalism 26–7, 31–2, 33–4, 45, 59, 89–90; political elites 96–8; strength of 173–4; voters' behaviour 98–108
Republics (1948–1987) 18–28
research: hypotheses 11; implications of

176–7; methods/limitations 14–15; summary of main arguments 170–5
Rhee Syng-man 19–20, 23, 38
right-wing parties 129–42
Roh Jeong-ho 43–4
Roh Moo-hyun 42, 98, 115–16, 124–5, 156–7; administration of 10, 154–9; call for 'grand coalition' 159–61; death of 163–4; presidential performance 164
Roh Tae-woo 25–6, 30, 32, 33, 34–42
Rokkan, Stein 21

Sartori, Giovanni 6, 67, 71–2, 172
Schofield, Norman 2, 5, 8, 9, 123
Scully, Timothy R. 13, 160
Second Republic (1960–1) 20–1
secret ballots 55
Sejong City plan 165–7
semi-presidential systems 1, 4, 5, 8, 51, 86, 160, 177
Seo, Byounghoon 124, 132
Seoul 27, 83, 111
Seoul National University 89
Shanghai provisional government faction 19
Shim Dae-pyung 165
Shin Bokryong 95
Shugart, Matthew S. 2, 5, 6, 7, 8, 21, 51, 83
Sim Jiyeon 77, 78
Sin Hak-cheol 141
single member electoral districts 109–20
Sixth Republic (1988–1992) 30–4
Skach, Cindy 83
small parties, effect of electoral reform 112, 113
Social People's Party 21
social reform 52–3
social welfare 142
Society for Democratization Activists' Family Association 141
Society of Lawmakers for the Just Unification and Strong Security 144
Son Hyeok-jae 8
Son Keyyoung 122
Song Young-jin 146
South Joeson Labour Party 140
'South–South conflict' 124
'Special Act on the May 18 Democratization Movement' 43–4
Stepan, Alfred 83
Stevenson, Randolph T. 8
Strøm, Kaare 2, 3–4, 5, 8, 160
strong regionalism 173–4

subventions 65, 75, 77, 78
Sunshine Policy (or engagement policy) 124, 132, 133, 135, 139, 142, 147, 148, 149, 174–5
Supreme Court 36, 158
Svåsand, Lars 9, 10, 12–14, 108, 170, 174, 176

'T-K faction' 27, 43, 45, 67, 97, 113–14
Third Republic (1961–1972) 21–4
'three Kims era' 33, 34, 95–108, 154
top-down hierarchy 80, 84, 145–6, 151, 172, 175
Truth and Reconciliation Law (2005) 156–7
Tsebelis, G. 9–10, 67, 172

under-development, party system 29–30
ungovernability 3–5, 52–3
Unification Democratic Party (UDP) 2, 31, 36, 39, 40, 41, 42, 97, 98–9
Unification People's Party 42
United Liberal Democrats (ULD): and anti-candidate movement 62–4; conflict with coalition partner 123, 146–50, 175; defections 59, 60, 61; and electoral reform law 109, 110, 112, 114–15; electoral performance 45, 46, 47, 64–5, 104–6, 118; and floor negotiation groups 64–9; funding 78; ideology 129; internal conflict 86–7; and National Security Law 146–50; and PM approval vote 53–4; and regionalism 108; stance on electoral reform 113–15
United New Democratic Party 161
United People's Party 43
University Students Associations 143
Urban Industrial Mission (UIM) 25
urban–rural cleavage 100, 107
Uri Party 15, 154, 156, 158; coalition with GNP 159–61
US: economic support from 20; parties 72; troops in Korea 23, 28
US–Korea FTA 161–3

Valenzuela, Arturo 6, 8
Van Waarden, France 6
Veterans' Society of the Korean War 143
veto players 10, 41
vice-presidential systems 31, 99
voters: alienation of 82; behaviour of 48, 98–108; family events 80, 116; ideological differences 123–39
voting power, new legislation 57–8

Wang Hye-suk 63
West, ideological shifts 132–3
Western European data sets 9, 10
'Westminster' system 84

Yap, Fiona 2, 5, 176
Yeochonyado 31–2, 100

Yeongnam University 159
'YH incident' 24–5
Yookyoung Foundation 159
Yu Seok-chun 63
Yun Bo-seon 20, 23
Yusin Constitution 23, 24, 25